Stopping Spam

Stopping Spam

Alan Schwartz and Simson Garfinkel

O'REILLY™

Beijing · Cambridge · Köln · Paris · Sebastopol · Taipei · Tokyo

Stopping Spam
by Alan Schwartz and Simson Garfinkel

Copyright © 1998 O'Reilly & Associates, Inc. All rights reserved.
Printed in the United States of America.

Published by O'Reilly & Associates, Inc., 101 Morris Street, Sebastopol, CA 95472.

Editor: Deborah Russell

Production Editor: Nancy Wolfe Kotary

Printing History:

       October 1998:   First Edition.

This book is printed on acid-free paper with 85% recycled content, 15% post-consumer waste. O'Reilly & Associates is committed to using paper with the highest recycled content available consistent with high quality.

ISBN: 1-56592-388-X

Table of Contents

Preface

This is a book about unwanted email messages and inappropriate Usenet articles—what they are, who is sending them, how to stop them, and even how to outlaw them. It's a book about what has come to be called *Internet spam.**

This is a book for people who have seen their mailboxes fill up with useless messages and unsolicited advertisements. It's a book for people who are upset that they can't find the on-topic postings in their once-helpful Usenet newsgroups and fear that the community of newsgroup readers will dissolve in disgust. And it's a book for Internet service providers (ISPs) who are concerned about the growing toll that spam is taking on their systems—and are looking for ways to put an end to it once and for all.

What's in this Book

Our goal is to explain what spam is and tell you how to stop it. Some of the solutions in this book are technical. Others are political. Because different people prefer different approaches to spam fighting, and because some tactics are available only to system administrators, news administrators, or network administrators, some chapters may be more interesting to you than others. Here's an outline of the contents of each chapter so you can decide for yourself.

Chapter 1, *What's Spam and What's the Problem?*, introduces different types of spam and explains why spam is a problem. This chapter answers the question, "What's the big deal? Why don't you just click Delete?"

---

* SPAM® is also a registered trademark of Hormel Foods, which uses the word to describe a canned luncheon meat. In this book, the word "spam" is used exclusively to refer to Internet spam and not to the meat.

Chapter 2, *The History of Spam*, recounts the history of spam from the first junk mail messages sent over the Internet to the rise of spam news and spam email in the early 1990s.

Chapter 3, *Spamming Today*, examines the motives, methods, and justifications of spammers. It's a "know your enemy" approach to spam fighting.

Chapter 4, *Internet Basics*, explains how messages are sent across the Internet, showing how spammers have been able to exploit defects in the system and simultaneously shield their identity. We'll pay special attention to Internet email, Usenet news, and the Domain Name System (DNS).

Chapter 5, *A User's Guide to Email Spam*, looks at the ways you can minimize the amount of email spam you receive through a combination of filtering and active responses. We'll also explain how you can track a piece of spam mail back to its origin.

Chapter 6, *A User's Guide to Usenet Spam*, takes a look at spam on Usenet and the measures you can take to avoid seeing it or to track down the source of the spam and respond.

Chapter 7, *Spam Stopping for Administrators and ISPs*, focuses on issues faced by system administrators and ISPs. It covers how to develop anti-spam policies for customers, ways to block incoming spam, and ways to discourage or prevent customers from spamming.

Chapter 8, *Community Action*, explores the Internet community organizations that have assembled to fight the growing threat of spam email and newsgroups. It also considers legal and legislative solutions to the spam problem.

Appendix A, *Tools and Information*, collects the spam-fighting resources and tools mentioned throughout the book into a single appendix for easy reference.

Appendix B, *Cyber Promotions Timeline*, provides a chronology of the Cyber Promotions spam case.

Conventions Used in this Book

Italic is used for pathnames, filenames, program names, new terms where they are defined, newsgroup names, and Internet addresses, such as domain names, URLs, and email addresses.

`Constant width` is used in examples to show output from commands, the contents of files, or the text of email messages.

Constant bold is used in examples to show commands or other text that should be typed literally by the user; occasionally, it is also used to distinguish parts of an example.

Constant italic is used in code fragments and examples to show variables for which a context-specific substitution should be made. The variable *email address*, for example, would be replaced by an actual email address.

The **%** character is used to represent the Unix shell prompt in Unix command lines.

 This type of boxed paragraph with an owl indicates a tip, suggestion, general note, or caution.

Getting the Scripts

In a few places in this book, we provide scripts that may be useful in fighting spam. You can get a copy of these scripts from our web page at *http://www.oreilly. com/catalog/spam* or by FTP at *ftp://ftp.oreilly.com/published/oreilly/nutshell/spam.* We also mention many other scripts that are available on the World Wide Web, along with their URLs.

We'd Like to Hear from You

We have tested and verified all of the information in this book to the best of our ability, but you may find that features have changed (or even that we have made mistakes!). Please let us know about any errors you find, as well as your suggestions for future editions, by writing:

O'Reilly & Associates, Inc.
101 Morris Street
Sebastopol, CA 95472
800-998-9938 (in the U.S. or Canada)
707-829-0515 (international/local)
707-829-0104 (fax)

You can also send us messages electronically. To subscribe to the mailing list or request a catalog, send email to:

nuts@oreilly.com

To ask technical questions or comment on the book, send email to:

bookquestions@oreilly.com

For corrections and amplifications to the book, check out *http://www.oreilly.com/catalog/spam*. See the ads at the back of the book for information about all of O'Reilly & Associates' online services.

Acknowledgments

There are many people and organizations whose help and support have been invaluable in writing this book.

Sam Varshavchik kindly provided his collection of more than 1,200 junk mail and Usenet spam message examples for our edification.

The online archives at CNET's News.com and ZDNet proved extremely helpful in assembling the history of spam in Chapter 2, *The History of Spam*, and the timeline in Appendix B. Also helpful were the public relations teams at Bigfoot, America Online, and the Center for Democracy and Technology, which graciously set up interviews for the chapter.

Lorrie Faith Cranor, Brian LaMacchia, Chris Lewis, Patricia Paley, T. Alexander Popiel, Paul Vixie, and Lorrie Wood served as technical reviewers for this book. All of them provided comments that we found invaluable. Any remaining errors are ours.

At O'Reilly & Associates, we've had the pleasure of working with Debby Russell once again as the editor for the book and with Steven Abrams, her editorial assistant. The O'Reilly production crew for this book included: Nancy Kotary, production editor and proofreader; Edie Freedman, for the cover design; Debby English, copyeditor; Sheryl Avruch and Claire LeBlanc, quality control; Robert Romano, illustrator; Lenny Muellner, tools support; and Ruth Rautenberg, indexer.

This book is dedicated to spam fighters everywhere—too often they are unsung heroes in what seems like a never-ending war. Through your ingenuity and perseverence, we shall prevail.

This book is also dedicated by Alan Schwartz to his wife, M.G. (who has once again put up with weekends spent at the computer instead of by Lake Michigan, and who gave very helpful comments on an early draft of the book), and to his parents (who have been marvelously supportive in this, as in all his endeavors).

1

What's Spam and What's the Problem?

... or, *Why You Can't Just Click "Delete."*

Slapped in the Face

If you use email, it's likely that you've recently received a piece of spam—an unsolicited, unwanted message sent to you without your permission. Spam is the Internet's version of junk mail, telemarketing calls during dinner, crank phone calls, and leaflets pasted around town, all rolled up into a single annoying electronic bundle.

Spam is not democratic. If you are new to the Internet, you've probably seen only a few of these annoying messages. If you've been using the Internet for more than a few years, or if you participate in online discussion groups, you might receive a dozen or more of these messages each day. And if you administer a network for a business or university, you might be bombarded with hundreds.

Here's a typical message that we received while working on this book:

```
Received: (from mail@localhost)
        by apache.vineyard.net (8.8.5/8.8.5) id LAA01663
        for <simsong@vineyard.net>; Sat, 16 May 1998 11:57:57 -0400 (EDT)
From: charles7713@yahoo.com
Message-Id: <199805161557.LAA01663@apache.vineyard.net>
Received: from 209-142-2-72.stk.inreach.net(209.142.2.72)
        by apache.vineyard.net via smap/slg (V1.3)
        id sma001626; Sat May 16 11:57:27 1998
Date: Sat, 16 May 1998 05:18:34
To: <simsong@vineyard.net>
Subject: Search Engines, 400 for 5.75 (1)

   ***   LIMITED TIME SPECIAL OFFER   ***
```

```
For Only $5.75 (1) We Will Submit Your
Web Site To Over 400 Of The Net's Hottest
Search Engines, Directories & Indexes.

If you're site isn't listed in the Search
Engines, how can people find you to buy your
products or services?

* Your Competition Is Getting Noticed -
  Are You?  Get Noticed By Your Prospects.

Visit Our Web Site To Learn More:

http://www.tiffiny.com/sitesubmissions

Thank You

(1)
The price for this service is $69 prepaid which
covers the cost of submitting your site every
three months for an entire year.  We have shown
the price of $5.75 to show you how inexpensive
this program really is when the overall cost is
annualized. Minimum 12 month term and full
prepayment required.
======================================
Name removal requests.
Send to:
TO:    webmaster@tiffiny.com
SUB:   remove
======================================
```

This email from *tiffiny.com* has all the elements of a typical spam message:

- The message came from a business with which we had no prior relationship.

- It was sent from an email address (*charles7713@yahoo.com*) that either is ficti-tious or was created solely for the purpose of sending spam messages and has long since been discarded.

- The message advertises a service that is illegitimate, shady, or misleading at best. (The service being advertised is not $5.75, as the subject line says, but $5.75 *per month*, with a "minimum 12 month term and full prepayment required." Furthermore, there simply aren't 400 "hot" search engines, directo-ries, and indexes on the Internet.)

- The message does not clearly identify the person or group that has sent it.

- Removal requests sent to the address listed at the bottom, *webmaster@tiffiny. com*, were ignored.

- The company that's doing the advertising is not well known and typically isn't trying to establish a reputation or a loyal consumer following.

If you've ever gotten a piece of spam mail, you've probably experienced a wide range of emotions. At first you were probably confused. *What is this message?* you might have asked yourself. *Where did it come from? Where did these people get my name?*

Once your confusion passed and you received your second or third spam, you may have become angry. Perhaps you wrote letters of complaint to the spammer and were further angered when your complaints bounced back to you because the spammer had disguised his email address.

Finally, you may have passed through anger to helplessness once you began receiving spam on a daily basis. Reading your email, once a source of fun or information, was reduced to a time-consuming process of weeding out junk mail with no end in sight.

Don't give up hope. There are powerful tools for fighting back against spam. In this book, we'll show you how.

What's Wrong with Spam

Most spam messages on the Internet today are advertisements from individuals and the occasional small business looking for a way to make a fast buck. Spam messages are usually sent out using sophisticated techniques designed to mask the messages' true senders and points of origin. And as for your email address, spammers use a variety of techniques to find it, such as "harvesting" it from web pages and downloading it from directories of email addresses operated by Internet service providers (ISPs).

But spamming today could well be undergoing a revolution. Over the past year, AT&T, Amazon.com, and OnSale.com all have experimented with bulk email. Although the companies clearly identify themselves in the mail messages, these bulk mailings can cause many of the same problems as spam messages from less scrupulous individuals and companies. If these companies continue their experiments, and if they are joined by others, we'll surely see a dramatic increase in the amount of spam on the Net.

The people who send these messages say that the email is a form of electronic direct marketing—the cyberspace equivalent of radio advertisements and newspaper inserts. But there are important differences between electronic spam and conventional marketing techniques—differences that could ultimately destroy the usefulness of the Internet if spam is not stopped.

Spammers often say that spam isn't a problem. "Just hit Delete if you don't want to see it." And many spam messages carry the tagline "If you don't want to receive further mailings, reply and we'll remove you." But spam is a huge problem. In fact, junk email and junk postings to Usenet newsgroups are one of the most serious threats facing the Internet today.

Spam messages waste the Internet's two most precious resources: the bandwidth of long-distance communications links and the time of network administrators who keep the Internet working from day to day. Spam also wastes the time of countless computer users around the planet. Furthermore, in order to deliver their messages, the people who send spam mail are increasingly resorting to fraud and computer abuse.

How Much Spam Is There?

Just how much spam is out there? Although it's hard to come up with exact numbers, the initial reports from the field show that there's a lot and that the problem is getting worse:

- According to America Online, which testified about spam in front of the Federal Trade Commission in 1997, roughly a third of the email messages AOL receives on any given day from the Internet are unsolicited spam.

- According to the first academic study of spam, by Lorrie Faith Cranor at AT&T Labs-Research and Brian A. LaMacchia at Microsoft, between 5% and 15% of the email received by AT&T Research and Bell Labs Research between April 1997 and October 1997 was spam.[*]

- According to Spam Hippo (*http://www.spamhippo.com*), an automated Usenet anti-spam system written by Kachun Lee for PathLink Technology Corporation, roughly 575,000 articles were posted to Usenet in June 1998, of which roughly 200,000, or 35%, were spam. (That's down from a high of 60%, or 300,000 spam messages out of 500,000 postings, before Spam Hippo began operation.)

These numbers don't tell the whole story. Although they show that there is a lot of spam on the Internet today, they don't explain why it is a threat. Indeed, if the only problem with spam were the sheer volume, one could make equally urgent arguments about the number of advertisements in your daily newspaper, commercials on TV and radio, and even billboards in subways and on buses. Nobody is saying that advertising is about to bring newspaper journalism to an end. Indeed, most newspapers, broadcasters, and even public transit authorities rely on advertising to pay their bills. What's so different about spam?

The answer to this question lies not in technology, but in economics. The fundamental difference between spam and other forms of advertising has to do with cost and price.

---

[*] Lorrie Faith Cranor and Brian A. LaMacchia, "Spam!," *Communications of the ACM*, Vol. 41, No. 8 (Aug. 1998), pp. 74–83, *http://www.acm.org/pubs/citations/journals/cacm/1998-41-8/p74-cranor/*.

The Low Cost of Spam

With most forms of advertising, the cost of sending each message is significant—especially when compared to the cost of the item being sold and the size of the market. An advertisement in a newspaper can cost anywhere from $24 for a typical classified ad to $25,000 for a full-page advertisement in a major newspaper. Sending a catalog to 100,000 people can cost anywhere from $50,000 to $150,000, depending on the size of the catalog, the quality of the printing, and the type of postage used.

Compare these costs to the cost of sending an email message or posting an article on Usenet. A typical computer connected to the Internet over a 28.8 kbps dial-up modem can send more than 100 email messages a minute, which translates to 864,000 mail messages a day, or 26 million in a typical month. With ISPs offering "unlimited" dial-up access to the Internet for $20 per month or less, and a dedicated phone line costing another $15, a spammer can send roughly 10,000 email messages for a penny. Even if you add the cost of buying a computer (perhaps $1,000), electronic advertising is an incredibly cheap way to reach an audience.

This low cost encourages spammers to send huge numbers of messages. Businesses that advertise using traditional media normally make some kind of effort to target their messages. Common sense dictates that there's no reason to send an advertisement to somebody who can't buy the product being advertised—there's no reason to spend the money to advertise dog food to cat owners. But spammers have no motivation to target their messages, because the cost of sending out electronic messages is so low.

Merge/purge

The low cost of email encourages spammers to forsake another practice that's common among conventional direct marketers, a technique known as *merge/purge*. When a merge/purge is performed, a mailing list company merges several lists and then purges the duplicates. Because of the cost of sending messages, marketers normally try to avoid sending the same message again and again to the same consumer. Spammers, operating in a medium that's essentially without cost and frequently unconcerned about their reputation, don't care.

Because there is no merge/purge, it's common to log in to your email and see many copies of the same spam message awaiting your perusal—especially if you have several email addresses that all forward to the same location:

```
Id# From               To                           Subject
1   plan@earthlink.net simsong@apache.vineyard.net  Dental/Optical Plan
2   plan@earthlink.net simsong@vineyard.net         Dental/Optical Plan
3   plan@earthlink.net simsong@vineyard.net         Dental/Optical Plan
4   .@earthlink.net    simsong@acm.org              Dental/Optical Plan
```

```
5    .@earthlink.net    simsong@mit.edu             Dental/Optical Plan
6    .@earthlink.net    simsong@mail.vineyard.net   Dental/Optical Plan
```

The clever spammer

Spammers realize that it's pointless to send email that's not going to get read, so they're increasingly resorting to new, deceitful techniques to get you to read their mail before you delete it. Some tricks are designed to make it seem as if the message came from a new business partner:

```
From: Bob Brown <bob@gdi4.gdi.net>
Subject: RE:To selected new clients
```

Or the spammer might try to make it look as if he or she is an old friend:

```
From: Jane <jane234@yahoo.com>
Subject: What's up?
```

Or the spammer might even try to make it look as if the message came from you:

```
From: Jason Sears <jason@netcom.com>
To: Jason Sears        <jason@netcom.com>
```

As spammers get more clever, it's becoming harder to delete these messages without reading them first. Unfortunately for us, the more people there are who send spam, the more likely it is that *some* of them will be quite clever.

The High Price of Spam

Spam may be cheap to send, but bulk email and newsgroup postings come at a high price to recipients of the messages and to the Internet through which they travel. It's because of this price that "simply clicking Delete" isn't a good solution to the spam problem.

The price users pay

Under normal circumstances, computers can't tell the difference between spam messages and normal, important messages—the kind that we want. Each message, spam or otherwise, is treated with care and speedily carried to its appropriate destination (or destinations).

It may take a spammer just five or ten minutes to program his computer to send a million messages over the course of a weekend. Now it's true that each of these messages can be deleted with just a click of the mouse, which takes only three or four seconds: a few seconds to determine that the message is in fact spam plus a second to click Delete. But those seconds add up quickly: one million people clicking Delete corresponds to roughly a month of wasted human activity. Or put another way, if you get six spam messages a day, you're wasting two hours each year deleting spam.

The price users pay for spam increases if you include the cost to the business or organization that operates the computer that holds your mailbox. These computers, called *mail servers*, require full-time connections to the Internet that can cost anywhere from $250 to $2,000 per month or more. The cost of the connection is determined, in part, by the amount of data it can carry. If a company's Internet connection is filled with spam, that company will be forced to spend more money on a faster Internet connection in order to handle the rest of its email traffic. Likewise, the company will be forced to buy faster computers and more disk drives. These costs must eventually be passed on to end users.

This scenario is not theoretical. In July 1997, spam mail overwhelmed AT&T WorldNet's outgoing mail system, delaying legitimate email by many hours.

The price administrators pay

System administrators pay for spam with their time. The Internet's email system was designed to make it difficult to lose email messages: when a computer can't deliver a message to the intended recipient, it does its best to return that message to the sender. If it can't send the message to the sender, it sends it to the computer's postmaster—because something must be seriously wrong if the email addresses of both the sender and the recipient of a message are invalid.

The well-meaning nature of Internet mail software becomes a positive liability when spammers come into the picture. In a typical bulk mailing, anywhere from a few hundred to tens of thousands of email addresses might be invalid. Under normal circumstances these email messages would bounce back to the sender. But the spammer doesn't want their bounces! To avoid being overwhelmed by the deluge, spammers often send messages with invalid return addresses. The result: the email messages end up in the mailboxes of Internet postmasters, who are usually living, breathing system administrators.

System administrators at large sites are now receiving hundreds to thousands of bounced spam messages each day. Unfortunately, each of these messages needs to be carefully examined, because mixed in with these messages are the occasional bounced mail messages from misconfigured computers that actually need to be fixed. As a result, spam is creating a huge administrative load.

As the spam problem grows worse, system administrators are increasingly taking themselves off their computer's "postmaster" mailing lists. The result is predictable: they're deluged with less email, but problems they would normally discover by receiving postmaster email are being missed, as well. The whole Internet suffers as a result.

The price bystanders pay

In their attempts to distribute their ads and avoid complaints, spammers often engage in fraud or other kinds of system abuse.

For example, in 1996, America Online started blocking email from many domains associated with spammers. To bypass AOL's filters, some spammers started sending email with false "return addresses." Some of these return addresses were purely fictitious. Others were for existing businesses that had no connection with the spamming activities, but were nevertheless tarnished by them.

Another technique spammers have used to send email is to relay their messages through other computers on the Internet—often without the knowledge or the consent of those computers' owners. This practice constitutes a theft of service. It also can result in problems for the unsuspecting relay, as people mistakenly think that the relay is the spammer.

The price society pays

There are nonmonetary costs to spam as well. Unwanted postings destroy the community spirit on which Usenet is based. When newsgroups are inundated with spam, fewer people read the groups, and they are less effective as a resource for discussion, problem solving, and information dissemination. And when Usenet traffic becomes too high, ISPs are forced to cut back on the number of newsgroups they carry, damaging Usenet's usefulness in the process.

Some unwanted postings, like chain letter pyramid schemes, are illegal in themselves. Spam makes it easy for scam artists and hucksters to prey on some of the most vulnerable members of society.

Much spam is simply offensive to the recipients. On July 21, 1997, for example, a spammer appropriated CNN Interactive's CNN Plus mailing list and sent pornographic email to thousands of CNN customers. The incident was offensive to many of the subscribers and a terrible embarrassment to CNN.

Is it acceptable for a company representative—or a scam artist—to interrupt a productive discussion you're having with your colleagues, solicit business using a false name and address, and then leave you with the bill?

The price the Internet pays

The biggest problem with spam is that if it continues to grow unchecked, its electronic deluge threatens to crowd out all other legitimate messages, making the electronic commons of the 21st century an unusable cesspool of useless marketing

Attacked by a Spammer

The attack started at 2:30 a.m. on January 15, 1997. But I didn't know that something was amiss until 4:20 p.m. or so, when I tried to check my mail. Strangely, there were 25 mail bounces from MAILER-DAEMON. Somebody had tried to send a whole bunch of mail; the mail that bounced had ended up in my inbox.

Now, having weird mail show up in my inbox isn't an unusual occurrence for me. That's because I'm on *postmaster@vineyard.net*, the mailing list for my small ISP located on the island of Martha's Vineyard, Massachusetts. Over the past 18 months I'd seen quite a bit of bounced mail from folks who hadn't set up computers properly. In each case I would have sombody call up the customer so they could fix their system.

There was something different about these bounces. For starters, there were a lot of them. And they had all bounced from a computer called *empty.cabi. net*—a computer, I later learned, that had an invalid IP address. But the big giveaway was the content of the mail messages, hidden beneath more than 80 lines of bounced mail headers.

"Customers For You!" the message read. "CV Communications BULK EMAIL ADVERTISING SERVICE."

It didn't take me long to piece together what was happening. Somebody calling himself CV Communications had connected to the mail server on *vineyard.net*, and was using my computer to send his unsolicited bulk email. The nerve! This guy was using *my* Internet connection to further *his* commercial ends, and sticking me with his bounces. I had been spammed by a spammer advertising spamming services.

It got worse. Further on down in my mailbox I noticed the complaints. Across the Internet, people being hit by this fellow's spam were blaming me and *vineyard.net*. Most thought CV Communications was one of our customers.

I logged on to my computer and typed the *mailq* command to see how much mail this spammer had piled up on my machine. I was horrified: there were more than 2,000 messages waiting to go out. Nearly all of them were being shipped to AOL and CompuServe.

The good news, I thought wryly, was at least this guy hadn't broken into my system. He was slowing down mail for all my customers, giving me a bad name, and making lots of work for me, but at least he hadn't broken in. Nevertheless, he had still caused plenty of damage. It took us more than two weeks to clean up from the incident.

—Simson Garfinkel

The Dirty Dozen Spam Scams

In July 1998, the U.S. Federal Trade Commission (*http://www.ftc.gov*) issued a list of the 12 most common scams promulgated by spammers:

1. Pyramid schemes that promise a big return for a small investment.

2. Scams that suggest that money can be made by becoming a spammer, and offer to sell address lists or bulk mailing software. The lists are often of poor quality, and spamming usually violates the victim's contract with his ISP.

3. Chain letters.

4. Work-at-home schemes that offer money for stuffing envelopes or building handicrafts. Often the victims never receive payment for their work.

5. Health and diet scams—snake oil by email.

6. Currency exchange scams that aren't legitimate.

7. Scams promising free merchandise in return for a membership fee; victims discover (after paying the fee) that they don't qualify for the freebies until they sign up other members.

8. Bogus investment opportunities.

9. Offers of cable descrambler kits, which are illegal if they work—and most don't.

10. Bogus home-equity loans or unsecured credit cards that never materialize.

11. Credit repair scams in which the victim is promised a completely clean credit record upon payment. Establishing a new credit identity is illegal in the United States, and bad credit can't be magically removed.

12. Vacation prize promotions that offer luxury vacations at discount prices. Victims find that the vacation accommodations aren't deluxe—unless they're willing to pay to upgrade.

Nearly all these scams predate email, but spamming makes it easier than ever for con artists to recruit victims.

messages. This is a problem whether the spam messages are sent from shady operators or legitimate businesses. It is simply so cheap to send spam that every business can send it to all of us. And if this happens, there will be a deluge.

Remember what happened to CB radio in the 1970s? Although CB was designed as a low-power two-way communications medium, as radios became more popular, a few spoilsports started broadcasting music, political messages, and advertisements with 10 and 20 times more power than the law allowed. It didn't take long for the CB radio waves to become a vast wasteland. Today CB is useful only to very small, specialized groups of people. The same thing could happen to the Internet unless spam is stopped—and stopped soon.

A Taxonomy of Spam

Today people use the word "spam" to mean almost any kind of unwanted email message or news article they receive. In this book, however, we use the term to describe email or news articles that are sent in bulk without regard to the recipient's wishes. A *spammer* is someone who posts or sends spam, and *spamming* is the act of posting or sending spam. The word "spam" should not be capitalized unless it is at the beginning of a sentence, because to capitalize it would be to use it as a trademark.

Spam?

Obviously, in the context of the Internet, *spam* doesn't refer to the tasty canned meat produced by Hormel Foods. How did it come to mean bulk messages?

The genesis of this meaning can be found in a *Monty Python's Flying Circus* sketch in which a customer in a restaurant asks what's on the menu. The waitress tells him, "Well, there's egg and bacon; egg, sausage, and bacon; egg and spam; egg, bacon, and spam; egg, bacon, sausage, spam; spam, bacon, sausage, and spam; spam, egg, spam, spam, bacon, and spam; spam, sausage, spam, spam, spam, bacon, spam, tomato, and spam; spam, spam, spam, egg, and spam" (and so on). Then a chorus of Vikings begins chanting "Spam, spam, spam, spam; lovely spam, wonderful spam."

The first Internet use of the word originated in Internet chat rooms and on multiplayer Internet adventure games called MUDs (multiuser dungeons). According to Jennifer Smith, author of the Frequently Asked Questions (FAQ) list for the *rec.games.mud* newsgroup hierarchy, a few delinquents would "say" the same message again and again in a chat room, filling the screen in the process, and other people would call these messages "spam." It was just like the song in the Monty Python skit—senseless repetition.

From flooding someone's screen with repeated words to flooding someone's mailbox or a newsgroup with repeated messages seemed to be a natural extension of the concept.

Flavors of Spam

It's important to distinguish between the different kinds of unwanted messages on the Internet today. The following sections explain some terms you may see.

Email spam

- *Unsolicited commercial email* (UCE) is just what it sounds like: an email message that you receive without asking for it advertising a product or service. This is also called *junk email.*

- *Unsolicited bulk email* (UBE) refers to email messages that are sent in bulk to thousands (or millions) of recipients. UBE may be commercial in nature, in which case it is also UCE. But it may be sent for other purposes as well, such as political lobbying or harassment.

- *Make money fast* (MMF) messages, often in the form of chain letters or multi-level marketing schemes, are messages that suggest you can get rich by sending money to the top name on a list, removing that name, adding your name to the bottom of the list, and forwarding the message to other people. Some also advocate reposting the message to hundreds of newsgroups. MMF messages are considered lotteries in the United States and are illegal. They're also extremely common.

- *Reputation attacks* are messages that appear to be sent from one person or organization, but are actually sent from another. The purpose of the messages isn't to advertise a particular service or product, but to make the recipients of the message angry at the apparent sender. A typical reputation attack would be a spammer sending 10 million messages appearing to advertise this book. The most nasty reputation attacks include the actual email addresses, phone numbers, and street addresses of the victim or victims. Reputation attacks constitute wire fraud, since they use forged addresses, and are illegal.

Usenet spam

- *Excessive multi-posting* (EMP) refers to an identical news article posted individually to many newsgroups. Each copy of the article has a different Message-ID and typically appears in different newsgroups (forcing each message to be sent individually to every computer connected to the Usenet). This is the strict definition of spam; if you ever hear someone arguing that an unwanted message isn't "spam," they probably mean that it isn't an EMP.

- *Excessive cross-posting* (ECP) refers to news articles cross-posted to many newsgroups. A news article is cross-posted when multiple newsgroups are listed in its "Newsgroups:" header line. For example, an article containing this "Newsgroups:" header:

```
Newsgroups: rec.games.mud.admin,rec.games.mud.tiny,rec.games.mud.misc
```

has been cross-posted to three newsgroups, a number that isn't usually considered excessive. Cross-posting is better than posting individual copies to each newsgroup, because only a single copy is passed between news sites, and most newsreaders will show a crossposted article only once. Nevertheless, cross-posting an article to hundreds of newsgroups is clearly an abuse of the Usenet system. ECP is sometimes called *velveeta*.

- A *spew* occurs when a misconfigured news program posts the same article to the same newsgroup repeatedly.

- *Off-topic postings* are news articles with inappropriate content for the newsgroup in which they appear. For example, an article about model trains is off-topic in *rec.pets.dogs*. The appropriate topics for a newsgroup are decided when the newsgroup is created, in its charter. Many newsgroups regularly post either the charter or a list of Frequently Asked Questions about the newsgroup to help people learn what's on-topic and what's off-topic.

- *Binaries* are news articles containing encoded binary files: image files, programs, video, or music samples, for example. Binaries are inappropriate for any newsgroup that's not explicitly chartered to allow binaries, even if they're on-topic. The *alt.binaries* hierarchy is devoted entirely to binaries.

- *Commercial postings* are news articles advertising a product or service for sale. These postings are welcomed in some newsgroups, tolerated in others, and discouraged or forbidden in still others, even if they're on-topic.

In the next two sections, we'll look at MMF pyramid scams and reputation attacks.

(Can't) Make Money Fast

A substantial proportion of spam messages promise huge financial rewards if you simply send a few dollars to the name at the top of a list. Here is a typical message that you might have seen:

```
INSTRUCTIONS:  Follow these instructions EXACTLY and in 20 - 60 days
you will have received well over $50,000.00 cash in the mail. This
program has remained successful because of the HONESTY Integrity of the
participants. Welcome to the world of Mail Order! This little business
is somewhat different than most mail order houses. Your product is not
solid and tangible, but rather a service. You are in the business of
developing Mailing Lists.  Many large corporations are happy to pay big
bucks for quality lists. (The money made from the mailing lists is
secondary to the income which is made from people like yourself
requesting that they be included in that list.)
```

```
HERE IS THE LIST OF NAMES TO SEND TO:
1. N. Ames, PO Box 123, San Fransisco, CA
2. S. D. Nym, 456 Red Road, Mesquite, TX
3. Y. Shure, 7890 Alphabet Ave. #1, New York, NY
4. L. Bank, 222 Sky Terrace, Los Angeles, CA
5. L. Twain, 10 Montgomery Dr., Chicago, IL

Mail $1.00 to each of the 5 names listed above. SEND CASH ONLY (Total
investment: $5.00) Enclose a note with each letter stating: Please add
my name to your mailing list. Include your name and mailing
address. (This is a legitimate service that you are requesting and you
are paying $1.00 for this service.)

Remove the name that appears as number 1 on the list. Move the other 4
names up one position (Number 2 becomes number 1,number 3 becomes
number 2, and so on). Place your name, address, and zip code in the
number 5 position.

With your name in the number 5 position start posting this letter
everywhere. Post on your web page, email it, mail it, take it to work,
be creative give everyone you can think of a copy so they too can join
in on the cash! Remember, the more places people see the letter the
more people can respond and the more cash flows in for you! Tell them
to follow these directions also!
```

Despite the claim that this is a legitimate enterprise, these chain letters are *pyramid schemes* that are illegal in the United States and many other countries because they constitute gambling—you're sending money in hopes of an uncertain return. That's because it's mathematically impossible for everybody who receives the chain letter to be a winner—for everyone who makes a dollar with this scheme, somebody else must lose a dollar.

If somebody does get rich, it's usually the person who started the chain. He gets rich at the expense of all the others who pin their hopes on the pyramid. Indeed, a clever initiator will put his name on the letter several different times in different forms, so he will get all the money. You can find out more about chain letters on the U.S. Postal Inspection Service's web site, at *http://www.usps.gov/websites/depart/inspect/chainlet.htm.*

In a *Ponzi scheme*, a variant of the pyramid, "investors" are recruited; interest on the investment is to be paid by future investors. In 1996, the U.S. Federal Trade Commission filed suit against the Fortuna Alliance, a group advertising a Ponzi scheme over the Internet that had taken over $6 million from its victims. The following year, a U.S. District Court ruled that Fortuna must refund its membership fees and barred it from ever again engaging in any sort of pyramid or multilevel marketing business.

Do not be fooled if the chain letter is used to sell inexpensive reports on credit, mail-order sales, mailing lists, or other topics. The primary purpose is to take your money, not to sell information. "Selling" a product does not ensure legality. Be especially suspicious if there's a claim that the U.S. Postal Service or U.S. Postal Inspection Service has declared the letter legal. This is said only to mislead you. Neither the Postal Service nor Postal Inspectors give prior approval to any chain letter.

Remember that money doesn't come from thin air. For every $5 someone gets, someone else loses $5. By virtue of the pyramid structure, there are always many more losers than winners.

The Indefensible Reputation Attack

On April 20, 1998, a spammer placed a phone call to a dial-up modem located in Florida, connected to a computer in Nantucket, and proceeded to send tens of thousands of email messages to unsuspecting users at America Online.

"Hello once again," began the message. "I know you have heard of me. I am Jeanne Dixon, a well-known psychic, medium, healer, spiritualist, clairvoyant, and astrologer. My horoscopes and psychic predictions are found in all of the major newspapers and publications worldwide. I can predict your future."

At the bottom of the message were two phone numbers for The Psychic Connection—one phone number to call if you wished to pay by credit card, another if you wished to have your call to the telephone psychic billed at $3.99 per minute. But what made the advertisement truly noteworthy, aside from the fact that Jeanne Dixon died on January 25, 1997, was the fact that each email message was sent with a forged return address, *astrology@vineyard.net.*

Why pick *vineyard.net*? As near as we can figure, the spammer had used our email addresses because we had recently installed anti-spam software and made it freely available on the Internet to others who wished to defend their systems. The *vineyard.net* anti-spam software prevented email messages from being relayed through our mail server and blocked our customers from receiving email that came from nonexistent domains.

But there was no way that we could defend ourselves against this unauthorized use of our domain name. Over the next few days, thousands of people who received the astrology solicitation took a few moments out of their busy schedules to send *vineyard.net* complaints in return. Because of the nature of email, there is no way for people to defend themselves against this kind of attack. The astrology solicitation never passed through *vineyard.net*. It simply used our name, forcing us to deal with the consequences.

These so-called reputation attacks are becoming increasingly common on the Internet, as spammers realize that the same techniques they have developed for sending spam mail can be used with impunity to hurt or harass others.

One of the most public reputation attacks took place on October 20, 1996:

```
Hi! I sent you this letter because your email address was on a list
that fit this category. I am a fan of child pornography and for the
past 4 years, I have been able to gather quite a collection of it. I
have pictures, VHS tapes, posters, audio recordings, and games based
on child pornography. I am now selling my products (or trading for
other child pornography). I have a complete color catalog of all my
products now available.
```

The message concluded with a price list for a color catalog and videotapes, and an address in Jackson Heights, New York. It was spammed to millions.

Within hours, the FBI's switchboard in New York City was flooded with more than 50 complaints. Soon complaints were coming in from all over the world. Numerous investigators were dispatched to the address in Jackson Heights. On October 23, the FBI issued a statement: "Police departments and FBI offices around the country have received numerous reports relating to the email message. The message is a hoax and the matter is being investigated." No arrests in the case were ever made.

Reputation attacks continue to this day. Expect to see many of them in conjunction with the 1998 U.S. Congressional elections.

2

The History of Spam

Junk mail is a problem of the computer age. City dwellers earlier this century complained of door-to-door salesman brandishing encyclopedias and brushes, but the full frontal assault on our mailboxes that started in the 1960s wouldn't have been possible without computers to assemble mailing lists and then send them out.

Spam is a creature of the Internet age. No longer restrained by the physical limitations of paper and postage, spammers can send out thousands of messages for pennies. But while spamming may be a relatively new problem, it was not unanticipated.

Prehistory

Way back in November 1975, Internet pioneer Jon Postel realized that there was a fundamental flaw in electronic mail: as long as an email message was being sent to a valid address, there was no way for a mail server (then known as a Host) to refuse a message from the network (or IMP—Internet Message Processor—to use the 1975 terminology). In RFC 706, "On the Junk Mail Problem," Postel wrote that it would be possible to attack a computer simply by sending it more mail than it could handle (see the sidebar entitled "RFC 706").

Unfortunately, Postel didn't have a solution for the "Junk Mail Problem," other than to say, "It would be useful for a Host to be able to decline messages from sources it believes are misbehaving or are simply annoying."

Over the next 18 years, the inability of a network to refuse email messages caused occasional problems for users and administrators of the network—sometimes big problems. One famous case involved a graduate student who wrote a program called *vacation*, which sent an automatic email message saying, "I'm on vacation," to anybody who sent email to the program's author. Problems started one weekend when a second graduate student copied the program. The two programs got caught in a loop and proceeded to send each other message after message until the computer's disk filled up.

RFC 706

```
Network Working Group                    Jon Postel (SRI-ARC)
Request for Comments: 706                 Nov 1975
NIC #33861
                   On the Junk Mail Problem
```

In the ARPA Network Host/IMP interface protocol there is no mechanism for the Host to selectively refuse messages. This means that a Host which desires to receive some particular messages must read all messages addressed to it. Such a Host could be sent many messages by a malfunctioning Host. This would constitute a denial of service to the normal users of this Host. Both the local users and the network communication could suffer. The services denied are the processor time consumed in examining the undesired messages and rejecting them, and the loss of network thruput or increased delay due to the unnecessary busyness of the network.

It would be useful for a Host to be able to decline messages from sources it believes are misbehaving or are simply annoying. If the Host/IMP interface protocol allowed the Host to say to the IMP "refuse messages from Host X", the IMPs could discard the unwanted messages at their earliest opportunity returning a "refused" notice to the offending Host.

How the IMPs might do this is an open issue -- here are two possibilities:

The destination IMP would keep a list (per local Host) of sources to refuse (this has the disadvantage of keeping the network busy).

The destination IMP on receiving the "refuse messages from Host X" message forwards the message to the source IMP (the IMP local to Host X). That IMP keeps a list (per local Host) of destinations that are refusing messages from this source Host.

This restriction on messages might be removed by a destination Host either by sending a "accept messages from Host X" message to the IMP, or by resetting its Host/IMP interface.

A Host might make use of such a facility by measuring, per source, the number of undesired messages per unit time, if this measure exceeds a threshold then the Host could issue the "refuse messages from Host X" message to the IMP.

Chain Letters

```
This message has been sent to you for good luck. The original is in
New England. It has been sent around the world nine times. The luck
has now been sent to you. You will receive good luck within four days
of receiving this message - Provided you, in turn send it on. This is
no joke. You will receive good luck in the mail. But no money.

Send copies to people you think need good luck. Don't send money as
fate has no price. Do not keep this message. This message must leave
your hands in 96 hours.

A United States Air Force Officer received 470,000 Dollars. Another
Man received 40,000 Dollars and lost it because he broke the
chain. Whereas in the Philippines, Gene Welch lost his wife 51 days
after receiving the message. He failed to circulate the
message. However, before his death, he received 7,555,000 dollars.

Please send five copies and see what happen in four days.
```

Throughout the 1980s, a number of computer facilities were embattled by Internet chain letters. Like their paper cousins, these letters promised fame and riches if the recipient sent 5, 10, or more copies of the letter to his or her friends. Pain, suffering, and financial ruin would follow if the recipient did not take the letter seriously and "broke the chain."

Postal chain letters are self-limiting: it takes paper, postage, and time to send them out. But on the computer, sending 5—or 50—copies of a chain letter is easy. Just type a few commands, and off it goes.

System administrators soon learned that electronic chain letters were self-limiting as well. Each time a chain letter was forwarded to 5 more people, it consumed perhaps 10 times as much disk space (including the extra headers) and 5 times as much CPU power to deliver. After 4 generations, a simple 2 KB message would grow to consume 20 MB of storage. After 5 or 6 generations, it would shut down the computer on which it was replicating—there would be no more storage space available.

Many universities and businesses tried to educate their users about the dangers of sending chain letters. But the educational process proved to be nearly impossible: few users could see the harm in sending just 5 or 10 email messages.

"Virus programs and chain letters are not harmless pranks, as most of the comments I've read lately seem to imply," David G. Grubbs, a lead engineer at Cognition, posted to the RISKS Digest, a biweekly email newsletter about computer-related risks, on December 13, 1987. "They waste immense amounts of our two most precious resources: time and effort. And they are, to my mind, evidence of an anti-social behavior which deserves to be actively suppressed, even attacked. Persons caught sending a chain letter should have their mail privileges suspended for some period, as a first offense, then removed entirely if the idiocy continues." Many sites followed Grubbs's recommendation.

Christmas Virus

```
           X
          X X
         X X X
        X X X X
       X X X X X
      X X X X X X
     X X X X X X X
           X
           X
           X
```

```
A very happy Christmas and my best wishes for the next year.
          Let this run and enjoy yourself.
Browsing this file is no fun at all.   Just type Christmas.
```

While Grubbs was typing his message to RISKS, a computer virus that was sent as a chain letter was rampaging through IBM's VNET network. Called "Christmas," the program arrived as a file named *CHRISTMAS* in the user's directory. When run (by having the user type **CHRISTMAS**), the program scanned two files in the user's directory (*NAMES* and *NETLOG*) that contained the email addresses of individuals with whom the victim corresponded frequently. The program then sent itself to those individuals and deleted itself.

The chain letter/virus was seeded into the BITNET network on Wednesday, December 9, 1987. It spread like wildfire, shutting down systems and clogging email links. The virus was finally stamped out by Monday, December 14, but a few days later a copy jumped to IBM's VNET, where it was killed only by a massive network shutdown that Friday. (A detailed account of the virus can be found in RISKS 5.80.)

Early Bulk Email

Thanks to incidents like chain letters and the Christmas virus, the 1990s opened with most Internet users aware of the danger of automated programs sending junk mail to thousands or millions of addresses.

By 1991, the Internet's established user community found itself overwhelmed by a sudden onslaught of newcomers. A year later these people were outnumbered by still newer newcomers. New users were coming in so fast that much of the accumulated wisdom was soon lost: there were simply too many new people to educate.

Vixie's Warning

In August 1993, William Milheim (a professor at Penn State University and, at the time, a self-admitted "Internet novice") and a colleague bulk-mailed an electronic survey on the use of the Internet by academics to dozens of mailing lists. Milheim thought that even though his survey had nothing to do with the topic of most of the mailing lists, it was nevertheless a legitimate use of the Internet—which, at the time, was still largely a "research" network. Paul Vixie, an Internet pioneer, sent the researcher his "standard response" telling Milheim that he had acted inappropriately. But when Milheim defended his actions, saying that they had been approved by Penn State's resident "Internet expert" as well as the university's Human Subjects Approval committee, Vixie responded in public, arguing that there was such a potential for email abuse that even apparently well-intentioned efforts should be vigorously opposed:

```
To: WMILHEIM@PSUGV.PSU.EDU (William Milheim)
In-Reply-To: Your message of Mon, 30 Aug 93 14:08:42.
Date: Mon, 30 Aug 93 12:27:28 PDT
From: Paul A Vixie <paul>

William,

I'm afraid I may not have expressed myself in adequate detail. What
you did was wrong, and it is symptomatic of something hugely evil out
on the horizon.

The Internet is excruciatingly easy to use for mass mailing.
Collecting addresses is free; generating mass mailings from them is
close to free.  Can you fathom the effect these metrics will permit
once the Internet comes a little bit closer to the mass market?

All of the folks who now bombard you with junk mail based on your
magazine subscriptions; who now cause throwaway newspapers to be
deposited in your driveways; who now call you during dinnertime with a
voice-activated computers attempting to solicit your vote or your
willingness to test-market their products—all of those people are
going to _thrive_ when they discover the Internet. You, with your
mass-mailed survey, are paving the way for them and helping to
_establish_ the answers to the very same "etiquette questions" you are
trying to research.

I receive about one of these surveys per the average month, sometimes
more. You see your survey as an isolated instance and wonder why I
complain; I see it as one more student sociology experiment by one
more dippy professor who thinks the Internet is a "fertile ground for
socio-environmental research."

In spite of your intentions, which I knew in advance or at least
assumed in advance to be "good", the effect of your survey is to
hasten the Internet's downslide into common-market status.  We must
```

```
establish, here and every day thereafter, that unsolicited mass
mailings are _strongly_prohibited_ by the Internet code of ethics.

You can begin this process by posting an apology to the mailing lists
you targetted in your original post. I am still waiting to see this
done. I am not satisfied that you understand the problem or that the
steps you have taken so far mitigate in any substantial way the damage
you have caused. Act now.

Paul
```

Milheim was befuddled. "I was not aware of any specific code of ethics for the use of the Internet," he wrote back to Vixie. "From everyone we talked to (including our university 'Internet expert' and our campus computer director) the Internet was set up for research and other similar uses—we certainly fit within those guidelines."

What the school's "Internet expert" had failed to realize was the danger of the precedent that was being set. There are many worthwhile surveys to be conducted, Vixie argued. But if every worthwhile survey were sent to every Internet user, the Internet would become unusable.

Although Vixie's fears were dead on target, it's doubtful that any "Internet code of ethics" could have stopped the abuse that was to follow. Ethics matter only to people who wish to belong to civilized communities. But as Internet tools became easier to use and available to more and more individuals, there came into being the first generation of Internet spammers who saw the Net not as a community to join, but as a tool for getting rich at other people's expense.

The Green Card Lottery

Less than six months later, on April 12, 1994, Arizona lawyers Laurence Canter and Martha Siegel sent an advertisement to more than 6,000 Usenet newsgroups. The advertisement offered legal help to immigrants who were applying to the U.S. Government's "Green Card Lottery."

Canter and Siegel's action infuriated people for two reasons. The first was the extent and the audacity: nobody had ever posted a single message to every Usenet newsgroup before. The second was the message's content: the Green Card Lottery was free, yet Canter and Siegel's advertisement gave the impression that by paying $100 to their law firm, an illegal alien could somehow increase his or her chances of winning.

Tens of thousands of people on Usenet sent complaints to Canter and Siegel's ISP, causing the provider's news machine to crash. Within a few days, the ISP terminated Canter and Siegel's connection, rather than risk a repeat of the incident. After a few more spamming attempts with other ISPs, Canter and Siegel wrote a book, *How to Make a Fortune on the Information Superhighway*. In their book, the duo revealed how to gather email addresses from Usenet, how to send junk email, post commercials on Usenet, and even advertise on Internet Relay Chat.

The Spam King

One of the people who read Canter and Siegel's book was Jeff Slaton, a Yellow Pages sales representative at US West Direct in Albuquerque, New Mexico. Slaton decided to try email marketing to see whether it actually worked.

During the spring and early summer of 1995, Slaton started collecting email addresses, the addresses of mailing lists, and the names of Usenet newsgroups. Then in July 1995 he let out his first spam. Appropriately enough, the message advertised the plans for another weapon of destruction:

```
Fifty Years ago the first atomic test blast took place at the Trinity
test site in New Mexico.

I have a friend who just retired as the Associate Director of Los
Alamos Natl Labs in New Mexico.

We worked together to obtain the plans to the FAT MAN & LITTLE BOY
Atomic Bombs.  (Unique commemorative, declassified and "just"
released!)

This is a "must have" for anyone interested in Science or
History.... Please let me know if you want a set of these
blueprints. I will email you with more details.
```

Before he sent out the messages, Slaton asked the management at his ISP, Route 66, if they would mind if he spammed the world from his account. Bob Kelly, Route 66's webmaster, said they would mind very much. "We said: Listen, this is not the way to do it, why don't you go read a book about making money on the Internet instead of just being an asshole?"

What Kelly didn't realize was that Slaton *had* read such a book—it was simply the wrong book. Slaton informed Route 66 that he would terminate his account at the end of the month. Then, with just two days left on his account, Slaton sent out his advertisement hawking the plans for the first atomic bombs.

The advertisements went everywhere. They went to Usenet groups that might welcome the information, like *sci.energy* and *rec.pyrotechnics*. They went to groups that had nothing to do with the subject, like *comp.os.msdos.4dos* and *sci.math*. And they even went into groups where the message might be considered to be somewhat inappropriate, like a support group for people with brain tumors.

Slaton was unremorseful. The plans cost $18 plus shipping, he said, and "we sold thousands and thousands of them all over the world."

Being a former Yellow Pages salesman, Slaton realized that his skills lay not in marketing individual products, but in marketing advertising services. And with the concept proved, Slaton decided to advertise his service in the best way he knew—through spamming:

```
From: SpAmKiNg@505-821-1945-new.LOW.rates!! (YOU TO CAN SAVE$>>>)
Subject: Let Us Help You Spam the Net!
Organization: SpAmKiNg 505-821-1945 Spam King to the World!
Approved: spam-King

     SPAM KING HAS NEW LOW RATES! POST TO LIST SERVE MAILING
LISTS. DIRECT E-MAIL. AND NEWSGROUPS! REACH 6 MILLION+ INTERNET
SUBSCRIBERS! CALL 505-821-1945!!

     MASSIVE SPAMS! WE CAN SPAM AS MANY AS 7000 NEWSGROUPS AND
MAILING LISTS AT ONE TIME, SO THAT ALL SEE YOUR MESSAGE AT ONCE.

     CALL US TODAY AT 505-821-1945. WE WILL SEND YOUR FIRST SPAM
OUT FOR FREE TO SHOW YOU HOW WELL WE CAN DO THE JOB. ADDITIONAL SPAMS
AT OUR LOW, LOW RATES.  CALL US COLLECT FOR DETAILS AT 505-821-1945.

     SPAM KING! YOUR SOURCE FOR SPAMS NETWIDE.
```

Flamboyant and irrepressible, the self-proclaimed "Spam King" pioneered many techniques that are still used by spammers today:

- To limit the complaints he would receive by email, Slaton started sending his spam out from fictitious email addresses and domains (e.g., SpAm-KiNg@505-821-1945-new.LOW.rates.)

- To protect himself and his customers from harassment, Slaton made sure his spams contained the phone numbers of voicemail boxes, rather than the numbers of actual phone lines.

- Because ISPs would quickly kill his accounts and then hold him liable for the spams, Slaton would have his customers obtain throwaway Internet accounts and then phone him with the username, password, and phone number he was supposed to use.

- Slaton's bulk-email program would send batches of email messages to the mail servers of remote computers, which would then send individual messages. This allowed him to send many more messages over a conventional dial-up modem than would have been possible otherwise.

- In an attempt to minimize complaints, Slaton claimed he would maintain an "opt-out" mailing list of people who would not receive spam messages. However, since he sent spams to mailing lists and newsgroups, there was no mechanism for the opt-out list to be honored (if it even existed).

In the second half of 1995, Slaton sent out dozens—and possibly hundreds—of spams for different customers, charging up to $495 "per insertion" for each. At one point, Slaton said he was doing 15 spams *per week*. Among them, he sent out a political advertisement for Scott Glasrud, who was running for a local elected office in New Mexico; for the EUPHORIA TAPE, an allegedly mind-altering cassette; and for Compass International Telecom of Boston, a long-distance reseller. In many cases, Slaton's customers became victims as they experienced the wrath of the individuals on the Internet who received the unwanted messages.

As Slaton continued, and as others followed his lead, a growing number of Internet vigilantes sprang up to battle him in response. Soren Ragsdale, a student at the University of Arizona in Tucson, created an entire anti–Spam King web site with Slaton's photograph, his phone number and the number of his supervisor at US West Direct. Others posted his age, mailing address, and Social Security Number to the Usenet group *news.admin.net-abuse.misc*. The not-so-subtle message behind these postings was that netizens should harass Slaton with all the legal, and possibly illegal, means at their disposal.

Slaton said that all the publicizing attempts were really backfiring: whenever his phone number was published, he said, he actually got more people calling him and begging for his services.

Slaton even fueled the flames himself. Late in 1995, Slaton spammed an advertisement for himself, adding that people could have their email addresses removed from his database at a cost of $5. "That was actually a hoax," said Slaton. "It was designed to stir up the beehive, to create controversy. There were many, many threads going on that issue, which I enjoy, because all of a sudden there was a surge in business of people wanting to utilize my service."

As Slaton continued, some Internet mailing lists were closed so that only people who were actually members of the list could post. Others were set up to accept mail only from a moderator. But Slaton just scoffed at such technical solutions. "It's a band-aid approach," he said in a phone interview. "It makes it a little more challenging for somebody who is committed."

Sanford Wallace and Cyber Promotions

In the spring of 1996, a new spam master named Sanford Wallace appeared on the scene and dethroned Slaton, taking the "Spam King" crown for himself. Based in Philadelphia, Wallace's operation, called Cyber Promotions, Inc., differed from Slaton's in several key respects. Unlike Slaton, who spammed through dial-up accounts, Wallace obtained his own high-speed T1 connection to the Internet's backbone. Whereas Slaton sent out email that came from apparently fictitious domains, Wallace registered his own domain, *cyberpromo.com*. Saying that he wanted to legitimize spam mail, Wallace even offered direct bulk-mail services to other spammers. It was as if he had carefully analyzed Slaton's failure to gain legitimacy and drawn precisely the wrong conclusions.

Anti-Spam Vigilantes

Some people ignore spam. Others are simply annoyed by it. But some people see spam as an attack on their community and counterattack by any means necessary. Anti-spam vigilanteism is almost as old as spamming itself. Back in the day of the first Internet chain letters, many people devoted countless hours in selfless attempts to stamp them out. When Canter and Siegel spammed Usenet with their "Green Card Lottery" advertisement, tens of thousands of people sent complaints to them or their ISP, causing the ISP's news server to crash. But as spamming became more of a problem, anti-spammer attacks became personally directed at spammers themselves.

Patrick Townson, moderator of the Internet TELECOM Digest, began an aggressive campaign against Spam King Jeff Slaton after Slaton downloaded TELECOM's subscriber list and added it to his own list. Townson published Slaton's voicemail number and his Social Security Number and suggested that since Slaton saw no problem in sending irrelevant messages to TELECOM Digest, perhaps Slaton "would see no problem with irrelevant messages going to his voicemail." Townson said, "I took the logic and put it in reverse."

Alex Bolt, a graduate student of mathematics at the University of California, Santa Barbara, took a different approach. In 1994, Bolt started the "Blacklist of Internet Advertisers." Bolt's idea was to provide a single repository of information about spammers—including their names, phone numbers, and offensive behavior, so that "people who read it will punish the offenders in one way or another."

In recent years, vigilantes have resorted to a variety of techniques, many of them illegal, to fight spammers. They have made harassing calls to spammers' home phones and have broken into spammers' computers. They have even attacked ISPs seen as being "friendly" to spammers, disrupting service to both spammers and other, nonspamming customers.

Although spamming is probably not legal under U.S. law, neither are vigilante actions against spammers. Indeed, in some cases the vigilantes have actually broken more laws than the spammers whose actions angered them in the first place. If you are contemplating taking retaliatory action against a spammer, we urge you to speak with an attorney first.

From the beginning, Wallace's main target was America Online, the world's largest online service provider. Wallace harvested email addresses of AOL subscribers, quickly building a list of nearly a million email addresses, then opened the flood-gates, bombarding each person on his list with between two and five messages per day. The messages were a mix of "get rich quick" advertisements, diet plans, advertisements for spamming services, and "magazines" bundling several advertise-ments together.

Casual users who logged on once a week to read two or three email messages were finding their mailboxes flooded with spam. These customers complained loudly to the online service. "The number of complaints about junk mail is larger than we receive on any other issue. Over the course of a year, the junk mail issue has gone from being a low concern to the number-one concern," David Phillips, AOL's associate general counsel, told CNET that summer.

But by the fall of 1996, AOL had started to develop its own defenses for dealing with junk email. Since all of Cyber Promotions' emails came from a few domains, AOL developed a system that would block email messages claiming to be from those addresses. The system, called PreferredMail, went into operation on Tues-day, September 3. AOL users could choose to receive no email at all, no junk mail, or every email message that was sent them. The default was to block junk mail. To get it, the user had to check a box that said, "I want junk email!"

"We consider this a dirty trick on AOL's part," Wallace told CNET later that month. "People don't want them to play Big Brother. If a user doesn't want email from us, they can remove themselves from our list." But AOL said that it had no other choice: numerous customers who had tried to remove themselves from Cyber Pro-motions' lists found that the process didn't work.

On September 6, Wallace sued AOL, saying that the service, by blocking his email messages, violated the First Amendment of the U.S. Constitution by abridging his right to free speech. Cyber Promotions asked for a temporary restraining order that would prohibit AOL from blocking its email. The federal judge hearing Cyber Pro-motions agreed and ordered AOL to stop. But two weeks later, an appeals court reversed the lower court's injunction, reasoning that AOL, a private company, was not bound by the First Amendment.

A month and a half later, Cyber Promotions was back in court again—this time defending itself against lawsuits brought by CompuServe, Prodigy, and Concentric Network. CompuServe demanded that Cyber Promotions stop sending email mes-sages with CompuServe email addresses as the email's return address; Prodigy made similar demands. Wallace said that he needed to forge the email addresses to get past AOL's filtering software. But CompuServe argued that forging "From:" addresses was a form of fraud, since the email didn't really originate at Com-puServe, and that it was a form of trademark violation, since the domain name (*compuserve.com*) contains a registered trademark. A judge tentatively agreed and issued a restraining order against Cyber Promotions. Meanwhile, in the Concentric case, another federal judge ordered Cyber Promotions to stop using Concentric's facilities to either send or receive email. Then on October 18, 1996, Wallace's high-speed Internet connection, a T1, was terminated by Sprint, his upstream ISP.

In December 1996, Wallace simultaneously settled with Prodigy and issued a statement that he no longer needed to use CompuServe or Prodigy return addresses in his spam mail because he had discovered another way to bypass AOL's filters. Instead of buying its own T1, Cyber Promotions claimed that it had made arrangements with 50 different companies to "rent" their T1 lines for $1,000 a month and had sent them a computer that would send email over their Internet connections whenever necessary. To further bypass AOL's filters, Wallace said that he was constantly changing the domain names he used in his messages.

This pattern of lawsuits continued for a year. Wallace said that the lawsuits were a conspiracy designed to put him out of business. In May 1997, he told CNET Radio that the other Internet companies were angry at him because, while they were losing money, Cyber Promotions had made money every month of its existence, despite having to fight "five very high-profile cases." The reason? "People are willing to spend money to send bulk email."

In August 1997, Wallace claimed that Cyber Promotions had more than 11,000 customers. But the successful career of "Spamford Wallace," as he had taken to calling himself, abruptly collapsed a month later, when Apex Global Information Services (AGIS) terminated a high-speed connection it had been leasing to Wallace since 1994.

AGIS had long known that Wallace was sending unwanted junk email. But rather than terminate him in 1995 or 1996, the company had worked with Wallace to legitimize unsolicited direct marketing email. And Wallace was far from the only spammer using the company's facilities. Besides Cyber Promotions, AGIS had also provided high-speed connections to Integrated Media Promotions Corporation (IMPC) and Quantum Communications, Inc. Then, in September 1997, AGIS abruptly terminated the Internet connections of all its spamming customers. The reason—AGIS itself was being attacked by anti-spamming vigilantes.

Wallace had almost reached the end of his rope. Having become one of the most hated people on the Internet, there was no Internet backbone provider left that was willing to sell him a high-speed circuit from which to send junk email. But rather than give up, Wallace came up with a different solution. He decided to partner with Walt Rines, president of Quantum Communications, Inc., and build his own Internet backbone—the "spambone"—on which spam would be permitted and even encouraged.

The obvious problem with the idea of the "spambone" is that a network is valuable only if other organizations connect to it. Otherwise, the spambone's customers would simply be sending bulk email to themselves. But what Internet provider would willingly connect to the spambone? Any provider that needed cash, Wallace responded. Over the next four months, the Wallace/Rines partnership evolved into a company called Global Technology Marketing, Inc. (GTMI), which planned to give ISPs free high-speed connections and then pay the Internet providers for each spam message they accepted. Companies could then pass these savings along to their customers, effectively using spam to subsidize Internet access. The venture was similar in concept to Juno, a U.S. email provider that offers free access in exchange for the right to put an advertisement on each customer's screen.

Alas, GTMI never really got off the ground. A web site set up to publicize the company was shut down by anti-spam vigilantes. Other attempts to publicize the organization were similarly thwarted. But perhaps another reason was that GTMI's business model of paying ISPs between 1 and 2 cents for each message received would have dramatically increased the cost of sending spam messages. At a penny a message, it would cost $10,000 to send a million pieces of bulk email—still a bargain compared with conventional marketing techniques, but 20 times more expensive than hiring a spammer to send a million messages and 500 times more expensive than sending them out yourself. Realizing that it would have to appeal to a difference kind of customer, GTMI announced that it would not spam for "get rich quick" schemes or pornographers. Instead, the company hoped to attract legitimate businesses as its customers and hoped to be able to provide them with detailed demographics about the people who were being paid to receive the messages. But despite a $10 million contract signed with the ISP GetNet, it was clear that the business would take a long time to build.

Wallace wasn't up to the project. On April 13, 1998, Sanford Wallace announced he was retiring from the world of spam and would go back to his previous profession of marketing Philadelphia restaurants. A few weeks later, he also said he would be serving as a consultant in several anti-spam trials being pursued against other spammers. Appendix B, *Cyber Promotions Timeline*, provides a detailed history of Cyber Promotions.

But by that point, what Sanford Wallace did really didn't matter anymore. Spamming had been democratized. Hundreds, and perhaps thousands, of individuals had taken up the profession.

Usenet and the Spam Cancelers

Email is a one-to-one communications medium: each message is sent from one person and received by another. But Usenet is a one-to-many medium: each message that is sent is transmitted to every computer on the network. For this reason, spamming has always been a much larger threat to Usenet than it has been to email; because each message is duplicated tens of thousands of times, a single spammer can do far more damage.

Spam Canceling

Unlike with email, there is a powerful tool that Usenet users can use to counteract spam: *cancel messages.*

Under normal circumstances, sending an email message is irrevocable—once it has left the sender's computer and is en route to the recipient, it cannot be rescinded. But posted news articles can be canceled by sending a second message, called a "cancel message." Cancel messages allow people to change their minds and "cancel" something they've posted. Officially, only the author of a message or his news administrator should send the corresponding cancel message. But like normal Usenet messages, there is little security in cancel messages; because it is easy to forge messages, any person on the network can cancel an article posted by anyone else.

The ability of anyone on Usenet to cancel anyone else's messages left the network open to a certain amount of abuse. But for the most part, abuse was minimal: canceling other people's messages was seen as a rude thing to do, something that could get your account terminated.

With the rise of spam, some people argued that there was suddenly a legitimate reason for a person to cancel messages they did not originate. Clearly, spam should be canceled. Others argued that this was a slippery slope: how do you tell the difference between messages that are spam and messages that some people simply don't like? What was needed, these people said, was a content-neutral mechanism for measuring when a message was spam and when it wasn't.

In 1994, a programmer going by the moniker Cancelmoose wrote a program to cancel Usenet messages automatically. The program scanned the Usenet and automatically issued cancel messages for Usenet messages posted more than 50 times. Cancelmoose later created a system called NoCeM (No See 'Em), which allowed anyone on Usenet to issue cryptographically signed recommendations of messages to cancel or hide. NoCeM is discussed in greater detail in Chapter 6, *A User's Guide to Usenet Spam.*

Clearly, an article posted 50 times to 50 different newsgroups represents an abuse of Usenet. What about an article posted only 10 times, but where each copy is cross-posted to 9 different newsgroups so that the message is visible in 90 different newsgroups in all? Shouldn't the mechanism for measuring spam take into account cross-posting as well as the number of individual posts? In 1995, Dr. Seth Breidbart, a 20-year veteran of the Internet and an avid Usenet participant, invented such a mechanism: the Breidbart Index (BI).

To compute the BI of a news posting, simply add the square root of the number of newsgroups to which each copy of the article was posted. For example, if 10 copies of an article are cross-posted to 9 newsgroups each, the BI is 10 times the square root of 9, or 30. An article with a BI greater than 20 has come to be considered cancelable spam.*

Over the following years, a number of other cancel services started up. Some were automatic, while others were manual. The majority of the automatic services adopted the BI as their technique for deciding whether something was spam.

With the advent of canceling, spamming Usenet essentially became a race between the spammers and the cancelers. For the spammers, the goal was to flood Usenet with as many of their spams as possible before the messages got canceled. For the cancelers, the goal was to find all the spam as fast as possible and send the cancel messages so that—it was hoped—the spammers would realize the futility of their effort and give up. The only limiting factor in this war was the speed of Usenet—how many messages could be transmitted in a given amount of time.

The Usenet Death Penalty

The spam cancelers hoped that canceling would be an interim measure. They thought they had another weapon: *terms of service* agreements, adopted by ISPs, saying that users were prohibited from spamming. The real solution to spamming was to close spammers' accounts and charge them damage fees.

Some ISPs enforced these terms-of-service clauses, but others didn't, and the spamming problem continued unabated. By the middle of 1997, Usenet was showing serious strain. At one point, as many as 60% of all messages sent over the network were cancel messages for earlier spams. In many cases, different canceling agencies simultaneously issued cancel messages for the same spam. But what was most infuriating to the spam cancelers was that many ISPs who were not policing their own networks were getting a free ride from the community's efforts. Something had to be done.

---

* This means that a single article cross-posted to fewer than 400 groups is not considered spam. However, because of technical limitations in the Usenet software, such a cross-post is generally not possible anyway.

In July 1997, Ken Lucke, creator of the *stopspam.org* web site, organized a Usenet Death Penalty (UDP) against the UUNET ISP for not policing its news servers and for harboring spammers. The idea of the death penalty was simple: Lucke and others would simply run a program that would cancel *every* news message transmitted from UUNET's news servers, spam and nonspam alike. The self-appointed guardians of the greater Usenet community were simply turning their back on UUNET and excluding it from their community. By canceling every message sent from UUNET, they reasoned, the company's customers, no longer able to send their messages beyond UUNET's news server itself, would complain to UUNET, and the company would be forced to change its policy.

UUNET refused to back down, and the UDP went into effect on August 1, 1997. A few days later, UUNET gave in and said that it would start cracking down on spammers using its resources. But when Lucke attempted to post his message rescinding the UDP, that message itself was canceled—by pranksters, probably, or anti-spammers who didn't think that the penalty should have been rescinded just yet. Over the next few days, Lucke posted many more attempts to call off the UDP, but each one was canceled. Ultimately, he was forced to distribute the message through online news services such as *news.com* to get the message through.

After the UDP, the spam cancelers were generally happier with UUNET's behavior. But spammers were still getting access to Usenet through other ISPs. The next biggest spam source was CompuServe, which had the UDP imposed against it on November 18, 1997. The cancelers imposed the penalty out of sheer frustration when their attempts to communicate with the company's news administrator had been completely rebuffed. But the following day, with CompuServe's news servers effectively isolated from the rest of Usenet, the company was very eager to speak with the cancelers. With communication in place, the penalty was immediately lifted.

On February 19, 1998, Netcom was threatened with a UDP. This time the company addressed the cancelers' concerns, and the UDP didn't go into effect. In August 1998, a similar threat of UDP against *mci2000.com* was withdrawn.

The Cancel Moratorium

It was becoming apparent that the succession of death penalties was simply not working. Usenet was crumbling, the anti-spammers thought, and the only way to save it was to force the ISPs to police themselves. But ironically, the actions of the anti-spammers masked the extent of the problem. The answer was simple: the anti-spammers decided to go on strike to prove to the world how bad things were.

The strike started on April 3, 1998. Although they continued to issue NoCeM notices, many of the anti-spammers ceased issuing cancel messages, hoping to force ISPs to implement better means to prevent their users from spamming. Reporting on the results two weeks later, Chris Lewis, one of those involved in the moratorium, noted that during the moratorium, spam volume jumped substantially, overloading a number of news servers that did not have their own spam-filtering mechanisms. Other ISPs implemented spam filters on their news servers with excellent results. Although the Usenet spam moratorium officially ended on April 17, 1998, many of the spam cancelers decided to stop canceling indefinitely. But other cancelers continued to operate.

In Their Own Words

How do spammers justify their actions? Here is a selection of statements from well-known spammers and junk emailers:

From *How to Make a Fortune on the Information Superhighway*, by Canter and Siegel:

> ... some starry eyed individuals who access the Net think of Cyberspace as a community, with rules, regulations and codes of behavior. Don't you believe it!... Along your journey, someone may try to tell you that in order to be a good Net "citizen," you must follow the rules of the Cyberspace community. Don't listen. The only laws and rules with which you should concern yourself are those passed by the country, state and city in which you live. The only ethics you should adopt as you pursue wealth on the Iway are those dictated by the religious faith you have chosen to follow and your own good conscience.

A spammed advertisement for Jeff Slaton's spamming services said:

> I pulled ALL possible LIST SERVE MAILING LISTS and 14,000 NEWS GROUPS on the Internet. I send out "just one E-mail" ... LIST SERVERS act as a postman and deliver your message to ALL members of the mailing list ... NEWS GROUPS are used in a similar fashion. I simply PULL the E-mail addresses off the News Groups ... You can also "post your message" to the News Groups. Be prepared for Flames and Mail Bombs (large files designed to clog up the server) to both you and your Service Provider. However, I have found that the so called "Voices from the Net" is much overrated. Most people pay no attention if they have no interest. People simply hit the delete key thereby eliminating the message. I might add that this method is a whole lot better for the environment than filling up our landfills with paper junk mail. However, your SERVICE PROVIDER WILL react due to even the smallest amount of mail bombs it receives.

WHY you ask? Service Providers get UPSET due to the fact that mail bombs can overload, shut or slow down the Server. This temporarily deprives some of their customer's access. This tends to make them a LIT-TLE TESTY! However, this is not as bad as it seems . . .

A suggested time to send out your huge mass posting is on a Monday morning at 2:00 am. At that time there is less competition for bandwidth. Furthermore, the Syops (system operators serve as monitors) are usually not very awake on Monday morning. They are more likely to let your E-mail slip by due to dealing with hundreds of posting to their Mailing List from the weekend. It really pays to make your Subject Header something that is "very generic." Many Syops just look at the Subject header and NOT the content before posting. When that happens . . . You're in business!

This Tip is MOST important! Make sure that you have an address and phone number in your message for prospects to call or write. Remember that your Service Provider will bump you off. Therefore, don't count on receiving any replies via E-mail . . .

The Net is totally unregulated and governed by something called "Neti-quette." However, you can within reason, disregard Netiquette because of the constantly changing self imposed rules and hypocrisy of most of the users . . . .

From an interview with Sanford Wallace, President of Cyber Promotions, Inc., by Kathleen Murphy, in *Web Week* (September 29, 1997):

WW: Junk e-mail imposes costs on recipients for connect time and disk space. Why should recipients, in effect, buy and run printing presses for spammers instead of charging the sender?

Wallace: There are definitely cases where there are still people who pay hourly charges, but that is quickly disappearing. You're seeing most providers convert to unlimited access, and you're seeing POPs popping up all over the place so people now have local access. As far as disk space, there are filtering technologies being developed that eliminate junk mail at the server level so that disk space is not wasted.

WW: If so many people like to get spam, why is it that spammers so often forge their addresses and try to mask their identity and origin?

Wallace: What you're seeing is that on the Internet, it's so easy to com-plain. Let's say that a spammer sends out 20,000 messages from a $20-per-month account. If that service provider gets one out of 1,000 complaints on that mailing, that might be enough for the provider to say hey, this does not justify the $19.95 a month that we're getting. We're going to have to cancel this account. You're seeing recipients either complaining, or in some cases mail-bombing, the service providers of the advertisers. The only way that these advertisers have been able to stay in business is to go behind the scenes and hide a little. We all wish that would not have to be the case. And we are developing services that will allow advertisers to actually show who they are, to not hide behind the fake address. You're going to see more of that as this industry continues to get legitimized.

3

Spamming Today

Spamming has undergone a renaissance since the days of Canter and Siegel, Slaton, and Wallace. Spamming is no longer the province of a few rogue computer mavens. Instead, there is now a core of hundreds—and perhaps thousands—of individuals and small businesses selling spamming tools and services. Understanding their operation is critical to stamping out spamming.

The Players

A wide range of players is sending unsolicited messages on the Internet today. Spam has been used to sell merchandise, advertise Internet services, and recruit victims for scams. But it has also been used to raise money for the needy, promote political causes, and attack reputations. Like the Internet itself, spamming has quickly become a form of mass communication experienced by millions. Unfortunately, it's a form of communication that most of the participants would rather do without.

Spammers-for-Hire

Many spammers on the Internet today are lone operators. By spamming, they can reach millions of customers at very low cost. And the communication is decidedly one-way, as the only way for the recipient of the spam message to contact the sender is through a Post Office box number or a phone number that goes to a voicemail system. Spammers typically charge a few hundred dollars for their services.

A typical bulk mailer is Florida-based Eric Reinertsen, who operates the GOLF-PROMO mailing list. In June 1998, Reinertsen sent out a bulk mailing promoting his advertising services. We received one of his messages and engaged him in a dialogue about his operation. "I compile targeted lists (Over 3 million presently in our database) and send your ad to millions of Golf enthusiasts around the world or right in your town," he wrote in a follow-up email message. "I charge $250. per 100,000 mails with quantity discounts available. The lists are acquired through internet extraction with golf keywords and through newsgroups. There are 99.9% Golfers on our lists but from time to time we get a non-golfer and they are removed immediately."

Reinertsen claims his customers get a response rate between 0.2% and 4%. "Most are very happy to receive the mails because it is of interest to them as fellow golfers and sports enthusiasts."

Reinertsen frequently combines spamming with conventional web-based advertising. Of course, this can lead to some problems, because many web-hosting companies will terminate the account of a customer who also engages in spamming. But for Reinertsen, these policies are just another business opportunity. "We have had some remote problems with complaints to the webhosts and have resolved this problem by contracting with a bulk friendly server to host a mirror site for your pages. This is charged at a cost of $75 per month while your ad is being run or as long as you wish (1 month min.)."

Beyond golf, Reinertsen also claims to have 1.2 million travel-related names "and some other assorted subjects and lots by state and country." But because of the nature of the business, it is nearly impossible for customers to verify or validate the bulk mailer's claims. For example, we learned of Reinertsen because we received his spam, even though we had no interest in golf. Reinertsen's customers have no real way of knowing how many of his three million email addresses actually belong to golf enthusiasts—or how many actually work, for that matter.

Customers of lone spammers tend to be small businesses or individuals who do not know much about the Internet and are seeking a simple, low-cost way to advertise. But sometimes there are exceptions. In 1997, for example, an administrator at a university in New Jersey hired a small firm to promote a conference on the Internet that the university was hosting. Unknown to the administrator, the promoter he hired was a spammer. The spammer obtained an account with a small ISP in Maine and proceeded to send tens of thousands of email messages over the course of a weekend, each one with the name of the university. Although the promotion was effective, the kind of publicity the university received was ultimately unwanted.

Self-Spammers

Some small businesses engage in their own spamming. Two of the main kinds of companies in this area seem to be pornographers and multilevel marketing firms.

Pornographers

According to some estimates, there are now more than 100,000 X-rated sites on the World Wide Web, offering a wide assortment of pornography that is as varied as human sexuality itself. Each of these sites needs some way to stand out. Many of them employ spamming as one of their primary techniques for recruiting new customers. Some of the unsolicited messages have suggestive "From:" and "Subject:" lines. Other spam messages contain actual pornography.

In some states and countries, sending unsolicited pornography over the Internet, and especially sending it to children, may actually be a crime. But law enforcement has not taken the challenge. Instead, the primary legal challenges to pornographic spammers have been civil lawsuits from America Online.

Multilevel marketers

A multilevel marketing operation is one in which a business that manufactures a product recruits distributors to sell its product. But instead of having its distributors sell the product directly to end users, the distributors in turn recruit second-level distributors, who might in turn be told to recruit third-level distributors. Multilevel marketing dramatically increases costs to the end user. These business operations allegedly make money by controlling access to highly desirable goods for which consumers are willing to pay very high prices. They can also make money by finding a large number of second- and third-tier distributors who are willing to risk their capital by preordering large amounts of merchandise.

Some multilevel marketing schemes are legal in some countries but not in others. Others are always illegal. In general, the specific details of the particular scheme and the location of its operation determine whether soliciting new "distributors" is or is not a criminal offense.

Telefriend, based in Spokane, Washington, is one company that has used bulk email to find a group of distributors for a multilevel marketing opportunity. "We represent two companies: a uniquely mixed nutrient line and a cancer-ingredient free personal-use type line," says Dan O'Neil, a spokesperson for the company. In other words, upscale vitamins and "natural" beauty aids such as skin creams and deodorants.

In the spring of 1998, Telefriend sent out 150,000 email messages in the course of 6 weeks and recruited 31 people to represent its product. "In email marketing, that's not bad," says O'Neil.

AOL's 10 Most Wanted Spammer List

In March 1998, America Online published its "10 Most Wanted Spammer List." The list included the names of spammers "who have persisted in sending junk email to AOL members despite AOL's demands that they stop." The list included:

1. The "Notoriously Nasty" Spammer (pornography)
    Sample Text of Email: "FREE - Over 7400 Adult Sites you can access with just one password"

2. The LoseWeight Center (weight-loss gimmicks)
    Sample Text of Email: "Succeed in Achieving your #1 Resolution!"

3. Lovetoys Productions (pornography)
    Sample Text of Email: "FREE ADULT VIDEO WITH ANY PURCHASE!!!"

4. CN Productions (pornography)
    Sample Text of Email: "Our live sex shows will make your computer screens SIZZLE"

5. Internext (pornography)
    Sample Text of Email: "Live Florida Beach Babes do it all right in your browser . . . "

6. AMV, Inc. (pornography)
    Sample Text of Email: "8 ALL LIVE - ALL NUDE SHOWS"

7. Softcell Marketing, Inc. (pornography)
    Sample Text of Email: "The Mega Sex Site of All Time is Free"

8. Paragon Marketing (pornography and non-pornography)
    Sample Text of Email: "NEW ADULT WEB SITE WITH HOT LINKS!!!"

9. American Eagle/PMA (bulk-mail software)
    Sample Text of Email: "80 Million Addresses"

10. Springdale Publications (non-pornography)
    Sample Text of Email: "What Airlines Don't Want You To Know!!!"

Tools Vendors

A growing industry is feeding the spammers-for-hire and the self-spammers with spamming tools such as bulk-mail software, lists of email addresses, and software for "extracting" email addresses from the Usenet and web pages.

Newport Internet Marketing, based in northern California, is a typical bulk-mail tools vendor. Although Newport engages in bulk-mail operations, it does so only to advertise its software, which costs $129 "and allows you unlimited bulk emails for a lifetime," says Robert Alan, one of the company's owners.

Newport's software can be downloaded from the company's web site and set up in less than 15 minutes. Also on the company's web site are 35 million email addresses, broken down into 60 different files. Customers can download these files at will and use them for mailing purposes. Alternatively, they can extract their own email addresses.

Business was booming in the spring of 1998 for the three-person company, said Alan. "There is a demand for it," he said. "People want a good way to advertise. A free way to advertise. This is just like direct mail, except it is electronic."

"My opinion is that everyone doesn't like it [spam email] because they realize we are doing it for free. If they thought we had to pay to send it out, they wouldn't care."

The Technology

Despite the diversity of spammers today, the technology they employ is remarkably similar. To succeed in sending millions of unsolicited email messages, all a spammer really needs is a list of email addresses and a means to send the messages out. In practice, this translates to the following:

1. The spammer needs an Internet connection from which to collect addresses and send messages. The ideal Internet connection is a low-cost, flat-rate connection that doesn't charge per message sent or limit the amount of outgoing bandwidth the spammer can use. Most spammers prefer dial-up PPP connections because they are difficult to monitor and because it is easy for a PPP user to forge reply addresses. The ideal ISP is large enough to handle all the outgoing messages the spammer plans to send, but inexperienced enough not to have a policy against spamming or a way to recover damages written into its service contract.

2. Once a connection is secured, the spammer needs to collect a large list of valid email addresses or newsgroups. Email addresses can be harvested from a variety of publicly accessible places on the Internet. Popular sources of email addresses are headers of Usenet news messages, headers of messages on mailing lists to which the spammer subscribes, listings on web pages, and complete subscription lists from improperly managed mailing lists. Spammers also buy and trade lists. Putting together a list of newsgroups is much easier. A list of active newsgroups can be downloaded from any news server or by FTP from major Usenet sites.

3. The spammer now needs a message to send. Many spammers start business by sending a message advertising their spamming services.

4. The spammer needs a program that will send a message to every email address or newsgroup on the list. Such programs are easily written or can be purchased. The spammer can choose to send the messages directly from his machine to the recipient or, alternatively, vector the messages through a third party.

5. The spammer needs to provide a way for interested recipients to contact the spammer or send money. Most spamming services use P.O. boxes or voicemail boxes, which allow them to engage in two-way communications without revealing their real names or addresses.

6. If the spammer wants to stay in business, he needs some way to prevent complaints to his ISP. Complaints may result in the ISP's terminating his account, billing him for time spent responding to complaints, suing him, etc. One way to avoid complaints is to disguise (forge) the message sender or other delivery information so that simply replying to the message won't work. Another is to find a spam-friendly ISP that's willing to ignore complaints. Yet another is to promise that only one message will be sent or that recipients can "opt out" and remove themselves from the mailing list by replying to a special address.

Clearly, spamming is easy. That's why it's on the rise today. In the rest of this book, we describe ways to fight back, tactics that address each of the previously described steps: making ISPs less spam-friendly, keeping addresses private, preventing the mass mailing or posting itself, making it harder to contact spammers, and getting action from ISPs.

Spamming in the Future

Take a moment to imagine our nightmarish future if spamming continues to increase:

> You're planning a trip to New York City for Valentine's Day with your sweetheart. You call up your travel agent to make a reservation, then go out for lunch. When you return, you discover that your email box is filled. There are more than 5,000 restaurants in the Big Apple, and a third of them have sent you electronic coupons offering you 15% off your entrée if you visit them on your big trip.

> You pick up the phone to call your travel agent and yell at her for selling your name. But you don't have a chance: instead of hearing a dial tone, you find yourself speaking with a representative from MetroPol Airlines. Your travel agent ticketed you on American, the representative informs you. "We discovered it by scanning the reservation system. If you'll ticket your next business trip on MetroPol, we'll honor your American ticket and give you a complimentary upgrade to Business Class, as well."

It takes you five minutes to get the MetroPol representative off the phone. By that time, you've forgotten about your travel agent. But then the phone rings again. This time it's somebody from AirFlot Pacific, who is trying to interest you in their special "New York/Hong Kong" getaway package. "What a perfect way to extend your vacation," she says. "It's just $999."

A few days later, you find yourself besieged with mail-order catalogs. Companies selling everything from sharp "New York–style suits" to Mace® are trying to get your attention, offering to sell you precisely what you need for your upcoming trip. One of the catalogs shows boxes of chocolates that you can have gift-wrapped and delivered to your hotel room. The hotel is apparently the third business that has sold your name and your travel plans on the open market.

The constant marketing barrage doesn't let up. When your tickets show up, you discover a coupon printed on your boarding pass. Even on the plane, you look at the "air phone" on the back of the seat in front of you, and notice that it is displaying a tiny personalized advertisement for a jewelry store in Times Square. If you come in on February 14, they'll give you a 40% discount on engagement rings.

It seems that everybody knows you're going on this trip. But how did the jewelry store know you and your sweetie aren't married? Over the next few days you keep turning this question over and over in your mind. Then, when you and your darling get home, you discover that your house has been burglarized.

The world is filled with companies that want to sell us things. The dropping cost of communications, combined with the increased availability of personal information, makes it more than likely that many companies will be soliciting us simultaneously in the years to come. And this is not just a problem for people making Valentine's Day trips to New York City.

Soon businesses all over the nation, and even all over the world, will be vying for our attention and our money—a direct result of decreased transportation costs and globalized markets. Businesses must be convinced not to use unsolicited bulk mail as a way of finding new customers. The best way to prevent businesses from adopting spamming is to stop the practice today dead in its tracks.

4

Internet Basics

To understand spam, why it's a problem, and what you can do about it, you need to know how the Internet works. Many of the tactics in the fight against spam take advantage of the way email or news travels through the Internet; for example, to determine whether an email address is forged, you can look at the message's mail headers to see whether they match the address in the "From:" field.

In this chapter, we review the basics about how information travels through the Internet. We discuss how Internet computers identify one another by number or name and different ways that messages like email or news articles can travel between computers and reach their intended recipients. If you're already familiar with these ideas, you can skip ahead to the next chapter.

Addresses

Before two computers can communicate over the Internet, each must know how to reach the other. One way to locate a computer on the Internet is by its *Internet address*. Every computer on the Internet has an Internet address, just as companies in a city have phone numbers. Internet addresses are also called *IP addresses* because they are based on the Internet protocol. They are usually written as four numbers separated by periods, like 204.148.40.9, a notation sometimes called a *dotted octet*. Each of the numbers is between 0 and 255. A computer can have more than one Internet address, but two computers usually don't share the same Internet address at the same time.*

---

* The two main cases where two computers share the same Internet address are (1) when the address is part of a pool of addresses that are assigned to computers that dial up to a server, and (2) when one of the two computers is behind a firewall or otherwise isolated from direct communication with the rest of the Internet. In the first case, different computers may use the same address at different times. In the second, the computers use the same address at the same time, but because there is no direct route from one computer's network to the other's, there is no confusion about which computer receives data for the given address.

The numbers in an IP address are like the area code, prefix, and other parts of a phone number. Just as many different neighborhoods can share the same area code, many different computers and networks can share the "204." prefix in their IP addresses. Just as many different households in the same area code can share a prefix, many different computers and networks can share the "204.148." prefix, as well. And usually 255 computers can share the "204.148.40." prefix; often these are computers on the same network or managed by the same organization.

Large organizations, or those that were historically important to the development of the Internet, were allocated entire prefixes (e.g., the Xerox Palo Alto Research Center owns all IP addresses starting with "13."). Other major organizations control narrower blocks of addresses beginning with the same two-number prefix (e.g., the University of California, Berkeley owns IP addresses starting with "128.32."). Smaller organizations and Internet latecomers usually own one or more address blocks with three-number prefixes.

Internet address allocation is thus often a two-tier system. First-tier ISPs, like PSI and UUNET, control large blocks of IP addresses. They assign smaller blocks to second-tier ISPs or organizations, which assign them to individual computers— either computers in the organization itself or computers that dial up to the organization's modems. There may even be three tiers—UUNET may assign a block of addresses to a smaller ISP that may assign a block to a company that doles out the individual addresses to company PCs.

Naming Computers

Computers are very good at dealing with numbers; people prefer names. A second way to locate a computer on the Internet is to know its name. If one computer knows another's name, the first can look up the second's address, just as you can look up a friend's phone number in the phone book if you know her full name.

Names of computers on the Internet, like *www.berkeley.edu*, consist of a series of parts that provide information about the computer. The first part of the name, *www*, identifies a particular computer; the rest of the name, *berkeley.edu*, identifies the *domain* with which the computer is associated.

Domain names are hierarchical, with the broadest category (the *top-level domain*) last. For example, *berkeley.edu* is in the *edu* top-level domain, which signifies that it's used by an educational institution. Other top-level domains may signify a commercial organization (*.com*), a nonprofit organization (*.org*), a site that serves the Internet itself (*.net*), a U.S. government (*.gov*) or military (*.mil*) site, or the country in which the computer or its owner resides (*.uk*, for example, for the United Kingdom).

Many international domain names use the second part of the name, before the country code, to indicate the type of site. For example, *co.uk* sites are commercial sites in the U.K., and *ac.il* sites are academic sites in Israel.

The second-rightmost part of the domain name identifies a domain beneath the top-level domain. *berkeley.edu* is the domain belonging to the University of California, Berkeley; all computers whose names end in *berkeley.edu* are associated with UC Berkeley.

There may be further *subdomains* in the domain name. For example, *www.lcs.mit. edu* identifies the host *www* in the domain *lcs.mit.edu. edu* is the top-level education domain, *mit.edu* is the domain used by the Massachusetts Institute of Technology, and *lcs.mit.edu* is the subdomain used for MIT's Laboratory of Computer Science.

Initially, Internet addresses were associated with computer names by listing all the names and addresses in a file called *hosts* that every computer on the Internet needed to have. The *hosts* file was like a single large phone book. A central registry organization, called the InterNIC,* kept the master version of the file up-to-date; every computer had to update its copy from the InterNIC's. Soon, however, the file got too big and too difficult to keep consistent on all the Internet computers. Imagine having to keep every phone book from every city in the world in your house. Wouldn't it be easier to dial Information when you needed a number?

The solution used today is the *Domain Name System* (DNS), a distributed database that keeps track of names and addresses.† Instead of being kept in a single big file, different parts of the database are delegated to different computers, called *name servers.* It works like this:

- The *root* name servers know the Internet addresses of name servers that are responsible for each of the top-level domains. That is, the root name servers know the addresses of the *.com* name servers, the *.edu* name servers, the *.uk* name servers, etc. The InterNIC maintains the root name server databases. Other computers on the Internet transfer copies of the list of root name servers from the InterNIC. Fortunately, this list is short and rarely changes.

- The *edu* name servers know the Internet addresses of name servers for all the educational domains. For example, the *.edu* name servers know that a *berkeley.edu* name server (*ns1.berkeley.edu*) is located at 128.32.136.9. The InterNIC maintains the name servers for *.com*, *.org*, *.edu*, and *.net.* Other registry

---

* Short for "Internet Network Information Center."

† For much more information on DNS, see *DNS and BIND, 3rd Edition*, by Paul Albitz and Cricket Liu (O'Reilly & Associates, Inc.).

organizations maintain the name servers for *.gov*, *.mil*, and non-U.S. countries' domains. A list of these registries is available at *http://rs.internic.net/help/other-reg.html*.

- The *berkeley.edu* name servers know the Internet addresses for all the computers in the *berkeley.edu* domain. These name servers know how to find *www.berkeley.edu*. UC Berkeley maintains the *berkeley.edu* name servers and decides which computers can get *berkeley.edu* names.

When your computer wants to communicate with *www.berkeley.edu* and doesn't have its IP address, it asks the root name server where to get the address.* The root name server doesn't know it either, but knows the address of the *.edu* name server and tells your computer that address. Your computer then asks the *.edu* name server, which passes on the address of a *berkeley.edu* name server. Finally, your computer asks a *berkeley.edu* name server, which provides the IP address. Your computer saves the address for a while, along with the addresses of the *.edu* and *berkeley.edu* name servers, in case you need them again, but doesn't remember them forever. That way, if UC Berkeley decides to change the IP address associated with *www.berkeley.edu*, your computer will learn about the change.

DNS reduces the amount of information each system must keep and automatically keeps the information up-to-date. It also delegates responsibility appropriately: each organization gets to maintain its own domain name.

Internet RFCs

Internet standards are defined by documents called *Requests for Comment*, or more colloquially, *RFCs*, issued by the Internet Engineering Task Force (IETF). The Internet RFCs are numbered; RFC 1206, for example, is a list of frequently asked questions by new Internet users. RFCs 1032–1035 describe the basics of the Domain Name System.

You can get the RFCs mentioned in this book (or any other RFC) by FTP from *venera.isi.edu* in the *in-notes* directory or on the World Wide Web at *http://www.isi.edu/rfc-editor/rfc.html* or *http://www.cis.ohio-state.edu/hypertext/information/rfc.html*.

---

* In fact, your computer may not go to the root name server immediately. If your computer happens to know the address of a relevant, more specific name server (such as a *berkeley.edu* name server), it will ask that name server directly instead.

Ports

When you call a large organization on the phone, its phone number may not be enough to identify the department you want to speak with—you may have to dial an extension. Similarly, because computers on the Internet can offer many different services (email, Usenet news, web pages, etc.), it's important to be able to specify not only the address of the computer that you want to connect to, but the specific service you want to access. Services are associated with *port numbers*; well-known services are assigned standard port numbers on all Internet hosts.

RFC 1700 lists the port numbers associated with well-known services. Some of them include:

Port	Service
25	Mail servers listen for connections on port 25; other servers and mail readers connect to send email using the SMTP protocol (discussed later in this chapter).
80	Web servers listen for connections on port 80; web browsers connect to this port to request web pages.
110	Mail programs like Eudora Pro connect to this port to download email using the POP protocol (discussed later in this chapter).
119	Usenet news servers listen for connections on port 119; other news servers and news readers connect to exchange news articles, read news articles, or post news articles.

Protocols

Once two computers know each other's addresses, how do they communicate? What exactly do they say to one another?

Communication over the Internet is managed by a set of *protocols*. A protocol is a script for a structured conversation. For example, when you call a restaurant to make a reservation, the conversation might go like this:

> **Restaurant:** Chez Lui, may I help you?
> **You:** This is Sam Smith.
> **Restaurant:** Ah, hello Sam!
> **You:** I'd like to make a reservation for Thursday night.
> **Restaurant:** Very good!
> **You:** For a party of two.
> **Restaurant:** Very good!
> **You:** At seven o'clock.
> **Restaurant:** Very good, we'll see you Thursday at 7:00 p.m. Anything else?
> **You:** No, thanks. Bye!

The "reservation" protocol establishes a convention for how to get a reservation. First, the restaurant identifies itself; in response, you identify yourself and indicate your intention to make a reservation. In the next series of interactions, you provide detailed information about the reservation, and the restaurant acknowledges your requests ("Very good"). If, for example, the restaurant didn't accept reservations for parties of fewer than six, it would inform you that your request could not be met. Finally, you say good-bye and end the conversation.

Internet communications protocols work much the same way. The two computers agree on a series of interactions during which they pass information necessary to deliver a message or take some other action. Some of the Internet messaging protocols include:

SMTP

> The Simple Mail Transfer Protocol is the basic protocol used by mail servers to send messages to one another. A more advanced version of this protocol is the Enhanced Simple Mail Transfer Protocol, ESMTP.

POP

> The Post Office Protocol is a way for a computer to ask a mail server to send it any messages the server is holding for the computer.

IMAP

> The Internet Message Access Protocol can also be used to ask a mail server to send messages it's holding. In addition, a mail program that speaks IMAP can manipulate the mailboxes on the mail server.

NNTP

> The Network News Transfer Protocol is really two protocols in one. Usenet news servers use it to send news articles to one another. News reader software uses it to get articles from, and post articles to, news servers.

We'll take a look at the conversations defined by each of these protocols in the next sections, when we examine how email messages and Usenet news articles travel from system to system across the Internet.

Email

To illustrate the way email travels, imagine that you want to send an email message about a concert from your account, *you@earth.solar.net*, to a friend's account, *chris@jupiter.solar.net*. You compose your message using your Mail User Agent (MUA) software. Some common MUAs include Eudora Pro for Windows and Macintosh systems, Netscape Messenger and Microsoft Outlook Express for Windows systems, and *elm*, *pine*, *mutt*, and *mail* for Unix systems. When you compose it, your message might look like this:

```
Date: Sat, 9 May 1998 12:40:30 -0600
From: you@earth.solar.net
To: Chris <chris@jupiter.solar.net>
Subject: Steel Pulse concert date

Hi, Chris!

The next Steel Pulse concert is on Friday. See you there!
```

The email message has two parts: a *header* and a *body*. The header contains information that's important for message delivery; in this example, it includes the date the message was composed, the address of the sender, the address of the recipient, and the subject of the message. The body is the actual text of the message. A blank line separates the header and the body.

You may have noticed that there are a few different ways to write valid email addresses. According to RFC 822, the document that defines the standards for the format of Internet mail messages, any of the following formats are okay:*

```
gatsby@host.net
gatsby@host.net (The Great Gatsby)
The Great Gatsby <gatsby@host.net>
"The Great Gatsby" <gatsby@host.net>
```

When you tell your MUA to send the message, it adds a few new headers of its own. Most MUAs add a "Message-Id:" header that assigns the message a unique identifying string. This can make it easier to track down the message later on. Many MUAs add an "X-Mailer:" header that gives the name of the MUA software. The message that the MUA sends, then, might look like this (new headers are in **bold**):

```
Date: Sat, 9 May 1998 12:40:30 -0600
From: you@earth.solar.net
To: Chris <chris@jupiter.solar.net>
Subject: Steel Pulse concert date
Message-Id: <19980509124030.0113@earth.solar.net>
X-Mailer: QUALCOMM Windows Eudora Pro Version 4.0

Hi, Chris!

The next Steel Pulse concert is on Friday. See you there!
```

---

* RFC 822 actually permits more flexibility than the forms listed show. For example, spaces may be liberally inserted, so *<gatsby @ (my favorite) host . (on the) net >* is an acceptable RFC 822 email address, albeit an uncommon one.

Mail Transport Agents

In order to deliver the message, your Mail User Agent (MUA) must contact a Mail Transport Agent (MTA). Your MUA helps you read and write email, but the MTA, like a post office, is responsible for delivering the message across the Internet. Your MTA might be a program on your computer or a program on your organization's mail server, a central computer that manages email delivery.

Let's say that your email is handled by the MTA running at *earth.solar.net*, so it's a program on your computer. When the *earth* MTA receives the message, it initiates a connection to the MTA at *jupiter.solar.net* in order to deliver the message. The two MTAs speak to each other using the SMTP protocol. Here's what the conversation looks like. *earth*'s part of the conversation is written in **bold**; annotation is in *italic*:

```
earth's MTA connects to port 25 at jupiter.solar.net
jupiter's MTA announces that it's listening
220 jupiter.solar.net Sendmail 8.8.8/8.8.8 ready at Sat, 9 May 1998
    12:40:40 -600
HELO earth.solar.net
earth's MTA identifies itself
250 jupiter.solar.net Hello earth.solar.net, pleased to meet you
MAIL From:<you@earth.solar.net>
earth's MTA identifies the sender
250 <you@earth.solar.net>... Sender ok
RCPT To:<chris@jupiter.solar.net>
earth's MTA mailer identifies the recipient
250 <chris@jupiter.solar.net>... Recipient ok
DATA
earth's MTA is ready to send the message
354 Enter mail, end with "." on a line by itself
earth's MTA transmits the message headers and body
.
earth's MTA is done with the message
250 Ok
QUIT
earth's MTA is done with the connection
221 jupiter.solar.net closing connection
```

Just like the restaurant reservation conversation, the SMTP dialogue between *earth* and *jupiter* begins with *jupiter* and *earth* identifying themselves. Then *earth* provides information about the message, and *jupiter* acknowledges each piece of information.*

When the *jupiter* MTA receives the message by SMTP, it adds a new header to the message. This header, "Received:," is like a postmark: every computer that

---

* Notice that each of *jupiter*'s acknowledgments begins with a three-digit number. It's really these numbers that *earth* understands; the text following them is strictly for the benefit of people who might be monitoring the conversation in order to debug a problem.

receives the message adds a "Received:" header. Here's how the message looks after *jupiter.solar.net* has received it:

```
Received: from earth.solar.net (earth.solar.net [1.4.4.4])
    by jupiter.solar.net (8.8.8/8.8.8) with SMTP id MAA00395
    for <chris@jupiter.solar.net>; Sat, 9 May 1998 12:40:40 -0600
Date: Sat, 9 May 1998 12:40:30 -0600
From: you@earth.solar.net
To: Chris <chris@jupiter.solar.net>
Subject: Steel Pulse concert date
Message-Id: <19980509124030.0113@earth.solar.net>
X-Mailer: QUALCOMM Windows Eudora Pro Version 4.0

Hi, Chris!

The next Steel Pulse concert is on Friday. See you there!
```

The "Received:" header first shows from which host the message was received. The first hostname, *earth.solar.net*, is the name given after the HELO at the beginning of the SMTP conversation. Because the sending MTA could be trying to misidentify itself, *jupiter* also includes, in parentheses, the real IP address of the sending computer and the hostname associated with that address in the DNS.

Next, the header records the name of the receiving computer (*jupiter.solar.net*) and version information about its MTA software (in this example, 8.8.8/8.8.8). In the clause beginning "with," the header indicates the protocol used to receive the message (typically SMTP or ESMTP) and an ID number that *jupiter* will use to identify the message.* Some MTAs include a clause beginning with "for" that lists the address of the intended recipient, as given in the RCPT portion of the SMTP conversation. All conclude the "Received:" header with the time and date at which the message was received. The -0600 in the header means that the time is in a timezone that is six hours west of Greenwich Mean Time.

What if Chris has set up her account at *jupiter* to forward her mail to another account, *chrism@pluto.solar.net*? In this case, once *jupiter*'s MTA receives the message, it begins a new SMTP conversation with *pluto*'s MTA. *jupiter*'s part of the conversation is in **bold**:

```
220 pluto.solar.net Sendmail 8.8.7 ready at Sat, 9 May 1998 12:40:45 -600
HELO jupiter.solar.net
250 pluto.solar.net Hello jupiter.solar.net, pleased to meet you
MAIL From:<you@earth.solar.net>
250 <you@earth.solar.net>... Sender ok
RCPT To:<chrism@pluto.solar.net>
```

---

* This ID should not be confused with the "Message-Id:" header. Message-Id values should be permanent, universal, and unique; no two messages should have the same Message-Id. In contrast, the ID number in the "Received:" header is temporary, used only by the receiving computer, and may be reused later.

```
250 <chrism@pluto.solar.net>... Recipient ok
DATA
354 Enter mail, end with "." on a line by itself
jupiter's MTA transmits the message headers and body
.
250 Ok
QUIT
221 pluto.solar.net closing connection
```

Now *pluto* adds its own "Received:" header, and the message looks like this:

```
Received: from jupiter.solar.net (jupiter.solar.net [1.4.4.7])
    by pluto.solar.net (8.8.7/8.8.7) with SMTP id KAB00332
    for <chrism@pluto.solar.net>; Sat, 9 May 1998 12:40:45 -0600
Received: from earth.solar.net (earth.solar.net [1.4.4.4])
    by jupiter.solar.net (8.8.8/8.8.8) with SMTP id MAA00395
    for <chris@jupiter.solar.net>; Sat, 9 May 1998 12:40:40 -0600
Date: Sat, 9 May 1998 12:40:30 -0600
From: you@earth.solar.net
To: Chris <chris@jupiter.solar.net>
Subject: Steel Pulse concert date
Message-Id: <19980509124030.0113@earth.solar.net>
X-Mailer: QUALCOMM Windows Eudora Pro Version 4.0

Hi, Chris!

The next Steel Pulse concert is on Friday. See you there!
```

Because *pluto* is the final destination (Chris's mail isn't going to be forwarded else-where), *pluto* also adds another header, called the *envelope sender* or *SMTP From header*.

```
From you@earth.solar.net Sat May 9 12:40:45 1998
Received: from jupiter.solar.net (jupiter.solar.net [1.4.4.7])
    by pluto.solar.net (8.8.7/8.8.7) with SMTP id KAB00332
    for <chrism@pluto.solar.net>; Sat, 9 May 1998 12:40:45 -0600
Received: from earth.solar.net (earth.solar.net [1.4.4.4])
    by jupiter.solar.net (8.8.8/8.8.8) with SMTP id MAA00395
    for <chris@jupiter.solar.net>; Sat, 9 May 1998 12:40:40 -0600
Date: Sat, 9 May 1998 12:40:30 -0600
From: you@earth.solar.net
To: Chris <chris@jupiter.solar.net>
Subject: Steel Pulse concert date
Message-Id: <19980509124030.0113@earth.solar.net>
X-Mailer: QUALCOMM Windows Eudora Pro Version 4.0

Hi, Chris!

The next Steel Pulse concert is on Friday. See you there!
```

The SMTP From header lists the address given in the **MAIL** part of the final SMTP conversation, along with the date and time.* The SMTP From header does not include a colon (:) after the header name, which distinguishes it from the standard "From:" header set by the sender's MUA. Figure 4-1 graphically displays the way this message travels from *you@earth.solar.net* to *chrism@pluto.solar.net*'s mailbox.

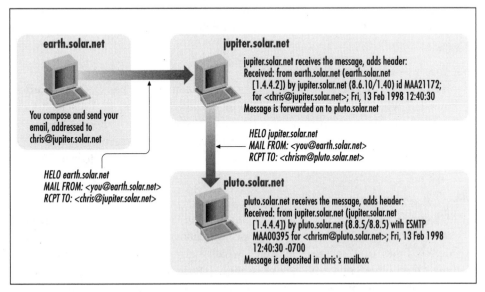

Figure 4-1: How email travels

Other Headers

From time to time, you may see other headers on a message. Here's a list of common headers:

Cc and Bcc

These list email addresses of people who were sent copies of the message. "Bcc" stands for "blind carbon copy." Recipients of the message don't see the "Bcc" header; it provides a way to send copies of a message without letting the recipients know who else received the message. Added in the sender's MUA.

Reply-To

An address where replies to the message should be sent. This is commonly used when people send email from one computer, but wish to receive replies on another computer. Added in the sender's MUA.

---

* Some MTAs store this information in a "Return-Path:" header instead of the SMTP From.

Sender

> According to RFC 822, this header should list the email address of the single person or computer that actually sent the message. It appears only when the "From:" header has been rewritten to show the name of the person who wished the message sent, instead of the actual sender. This practice is common when messages are sent out by mailing list software: the "From:" address shows the person who sent the message to the list, while the "Sender:" address is the address of the manager of the mailing list.* Added by mailing list software.

Resent-From and friends

> Headers that begin with "Resent-" indicate the message has been forwarded. In other words, an intermediate account received the mail and resent it to its final destination. These headers include "Resent-From," "Resent-Reply-To," and "Resent-To"; they provide information about the intermediate recipient who resent the message. Added by the MUA of the person forwarding the message.

Precedence

> This header can be used to instruct the sending computer that a message does not need immediate delivery. Large-scale mailings are often sent with "Precedence: bulk" or "Precedence: junk," which helps the sending computer manage the large number of messages. Programs like *vacation*, which automatically respond to email, often ignore low-precedence messages; if they didn't, mailing lists would be deluged with automatic "I'm on vacation" responses. Added by the sender's MUA or other sending software.

X- Headers that begin with "X-" are user-defined headers. No standard header begins with "X-," so people are free to make up headers that begin with "X-" without fear that any MTA will misinterpret the header. Examples include "X-Mailer," followed by the name of the email program that sent the message, "X-Face," followed by an encoded picture of the sender's face, and "X-Comment," followed by almost anything. Added at any stage.

Reading Mail with POP

What about Chris? Imagine that Chris reads mail using Eudora Pro on a PC called *pc1.solar.net*. Eudora is an MUA that uses the Post Office Protocol (POP) to transfer messages from a mail server (*pluto.solar.net* in our example).† When Chris

---

* Some mailing list programs purposefully misuse the "Sender:" header, setting it to the address of the list, rather than the list owner.

† POP can be used only to retrieve messages from a mail server; Eudora uses SMTP to send messages.

starts up Eudora and instructs it to check mail, Eudora's conversation with *pluto* looks like this (Eudora's part appears in **bold**):

```
Eudora connects to port 110 on pluto.solar.net
pluto's POP server announces that it's listening
+OK QPOP (version 2.2) at pluto.solar.net starting.
USER chrism
+OK Password required for chrism
PASS chrism's password
+OK chrism has 1 message (726 octets)
UIDL
+OK uidl command accepted.
1 179c97f481a77a5da1a8109409a00afe
RETR 1
+OK 726 octets
pluto sends the message
DELE 1
+OK Message 1 has been deleted.
QUIT
+OK Pop server at pluto.solar.net signing off.
```

First, *pluto*'s POP server announces that it's ready to converse. Eudora issues USER and PASS commands to send chrism's username and password to the POP server. The POP server checks chrism's mailbox and finds 1 message consisting of 726 "octets" (characters). Eudora then requests a "unique-ID listing" (UIDL) showing, for each message in the mailbox, a unique string that identifies it (in this case, "179c97f481a77a5da1a8109409a00afe" is message 1's unique ID). Eudora tells the POP server that it would like to retrieve (RETR) message 1, and the POP server obliges, sending the message. Now that Eudora has a copy of the message, it instructs the server to delete (DELE) the copy of the message in the server's mailbox, and the POP server acknowledges that the message has been marked for deletion.* Finally, Eudora lets the POP server know that it's done, and the POP server signs off.

Here's what the message might look like to Chris when she reads it in Eudora:†

```
From you@earth.solar.net Sat May 9 12:40:45 1998
Received: from jupiter.solar.net (jupiter.solar.net [1.4.4.7])
    by pluto.solar.net (8.8.7/8.8.7) with SMTP id KAB00332
    for <chrism@pluto.solar.net>; Sat, 9 May 1998 12:40:45 -0600
Received: from earth.solar.net (earth.solar.net [1.4.4.4])
    by jupiter.solar.net (8.8.8/8.8.8) with SMTP id MAA00395
    for <chris@jupiter.solar.net>; Sat, 9 May 1998 12:40:40 -0600
```

---

* For safety's sake, the message isn't actually deleted until and unless the MUA signs off with a QUIT command. If the connection should be broken for some other reason, the POP server would not delete the message.

† Some MUAs, like Eudora, don't show complete header information by default. In order to see all of the headers, you must configure the MUA to show them. See your MUA's help file or manual.

```
Date: Sat, 9 May 1998 12:40:30 -0600
From: you@earth.solar.net
To: Chris <chris@jupiter.solar.net>
Subject: Steel Pulse concert date
Message-Id: <19980509124030.0113@earth.solar.net>
X-Mailer: QUALCOMM Windows Eudora Pro Version 4.0
X-UIDL: 179c97f481a77a5da1a8109409a00afe

Hi, Chris!

The next Steel Pulse concert is on Friday. See you there!
```

The POP server has added the "X-UIDL:" header as a record of the unique id it assigned to the message.

The POP protocol is a simple one—the conversation it delineates allows the MUA only a few requests and the server only a few responses. Another protocol that is gaining increasing use in this context is IMAP. In its latest version, IMAP allows the MUA and server a much broader conversation. IMAP MUAs can manipulate mailboxes on the mail server as if they were local folders: the MUA can instruct the server to create new mailboxes, delete mailboxes, rename mailboxes, search for particular messages, etc. Recent versions of Eudora Pro, Netscape Messenger, and Microsoft Internet Explorer support both POP and IMAP.

Usenet News

Usenet news consists of articles organized into newsgroups. Newsgroups are named in a hierarchical fashion, with the broadest category first. For example, the newsgroup *comp.lang.perl.misc* is a newsgroup for miscellaneous articles about the Perl computer language. All the groups that begin *comp.* are about computers; all the groups that begin *comp.lang.* are about computer languages; all the groups that begin *comp.lang.perl.* are about Perl. This hierarchical organization often makes it easy to find newsgroups on topics of interest.

Like an email message, a news article includes a header and a body, separated by a blank line. Let's imagine you want to post an article from your account, *you@earth.solar.net*, to the newsgroup *rec.puzzles.crosswords*. You start up your news reader, which might be Netscape Collabra or Free Agent on a Windows system, Yet-Another-NewsWatcher on a Mac, or *trn* or *tin* on a Unix system. You compose your news article much like an email message:

```
From: you@earth.solar.net
Newsgroups: rec.puzzles.crosswords
Subject: Help with NY Times 5/10 puzzle?
Date: 10 May 1998 18:08:58 GMT

Does anyone know the answer to 1-down in the 5/10 NY Times puzzle?
```

Some of the news headers, like "From:," "Subject:," and "Date:" look very much like email headers. The formats of these headers, however, are often stricter. For example, there is only one correct way to format the date for Usenet; fortunately, your news reader knows this and will correctly format the date.

Other headers are specific to news. The most important is "Newsgroups," which lists the newsgroup or newsgroups to which the article should be posted. When more than one newsgroup is listed (e.g., *Newsgroups: rec.puzzles.crosswords,alt. crosswords*), the article is said to be *cross-posted* to the newsgroups. Most news-reading software will show you a cross-posted article only once, even if you read all the groups.

Posting an Article

What happens when you ask your news reader to post the article? First, it adds some important headers: "Message-ID:" and "Path:." A Message-ID for a news article serves much the same purpose as a Message-Id for an email message: it provides a means of keeping track of articles as they travel across the Internet. Message-IDs are even more important for news articles, however, because news servers reject any article with a Message-ID that matches an article the server has previously seen. It's crucial, therefore, that news Message-IDs be unique—otherwise, news servers might not accept your article!

The "Path:" header records the computers through which the article travels, much as the "Received:" headers in email show the route an email message takes. The Path consists of a series of news hostnames, separated by exclamation points (!), read from right to left. A news hostname is often the full DNS name of the news server, but can be any name that uniquely identifies the news server. The right-most Path entry is often the username of the sender.*

After the two new headers are added, the article looks like this:

```
Path: earth.solar.net!you
From: you@earth.solar.net
Newsgroups: rec.puzzles.crosswords
Subject: Help with NY Times 5/10 puzzle?
Date: 10 May 1998 18:08:58 GMT
Message-ID: <19980510180858.1230@earth.solar.net>

Does anyone know the answer to 1-down in the 5/10 NY Times puzzle?
```

---

* In the days of yore, the Path could be used to route email replies using UUCP, the Unix-to-Unix copying program. Because UUCP is rarely used for email now, many systems use "not-for-mail" as the rightmost element in the Path to emphasize that it should not be used to route replies. Others simply leave out the username and end the path with the hostname of the posting system.

Now the news reader contacts the local news server, *news.solar.net*. The news reader and the news server communicate with NNTP. In this example, the news reader's part of the conversation is in **bold**; annotation is in *italic*:

```
The news reader connects to news.solar.net at port 119
200 news.solar.net INN 1.5.1 17-Dec-1996 ready (posting ok).
POST
340 Ok to post. Send article followed by a ".".
earth's news reader transfers the article
.
240 Article posted successfully.
QUIT
205 news.solar.net closing connection. Goodbye.
```

The posting conversation is short and simple. The news server announces itself. The news reader requests to POST an article; the server acknowledges the request. The news reader transfers the article, followed by a period on a line by itself; the server acknowledges receipt. Finally, the news reader asks to QUIT, and the news server signs off.

Some Usenet newsgroups are *moderated*. In a moderated newsgroup, posted articles don't appear in the newsgroup immediately. Instead, the first news server that receives the article emails it to the newsgroup's moderator. The moderator (which may be a person, a team, or a program) decides whether the article is appropriate for the newsgroup and, if so, adds a special "Approved:" header to the article and reposts it to the group. When the moderator's news server receives the article with the "Approved:" header, it knows the article has been approved and adds it to the newsgroup.

Transferring News from Server to Server

Now *news.solar.net* has the new article. First, it checks to be sure it has not received this article before. The server does this in two ways. It checks to see whether it recognizes the Message-ID of the article, and it checks for its own name in the Path. In either case, it discards the article.

Once the news server is satisfied that the article is not a duplicate, it adds its name to the front of the Path. It may also add a header called "NNTP-Posting-Host:"* showing the hostname of the computer from which it received the article by NNTP. The article now looks like this:

```
Path: news.solar.net!earth.solar.net!you
From: you@earth.solar.net
Newsgroups: rec.puzzles.crosswords
Subject: Help with NY Times 5/10 puzzle?
```

---

* Some older news servers use "X-NNTP-Posting-Host:" instead.

```
Date: 10 May 1998 18:08:58 GMT
Message-ID: <19980510180858.1230@earth.solar.net>
```
NNTP-Posting-Host: earth.solar.net

```
Does anyone know the answer to 1-down in the 5/10 NY Times puzzle?
```

Now *news.solar.net* is ready to transfer the article to the other news servers with which it exchanges news. The administrator of each news server enters into agreements with other administrators to exchange news with their servers.

Let's say that *news.solar.net* exchanges news with *news.some-domain.org*. The two news servers communicate via NNTP. Here's what the conversation might look like (*news.solar.net*'s part is in **bold**, annotation is in *italic*):

```
news.solar.net connects to news.some-domain.org at port 119
201 news.some-domain.org NNTP server ready (no posting)
```
IHAVE <19980510180858.1230@earth.solar.net>
```
335 News to me! Send it!
news.solar.net sends the article
.
234 Article transferred.
```
QUIT
```
205 news.some-domain.org NNTP server waves goodbye.
```

Once *news.solar.net* connects, *news.some-domain.org* announces that it's ready. *news.solar.net* uses the IHAVE request to tell the other news server it has a new article and gives the Message-ID; the other server either declines the article because it has already received it from elsewhere or, as in our example, asks *news. solar.net* to send the article. *news.solar.net* does so and then asks to QUIT.

news.solar.net may transfer the new article to other news servers that have chosen to exchange news with it. Similarly, *news.some-domain.org* will now add its hostname to the front of the article's Path and offer it to other servers when it exchanges news. *news.some-domain.org* won't offer the article back to *news.solar. net*, because *news.solar.net* already appears in the article's Path.

Each news server that receives the article adds it to the server's database of news articles, filed by newsgroup.

Reading the Article

What happens when a user at *some-domain.org* reads *rec.puzzles.crosswords?* How does the article reach the newsgroup readers?

When a user at *sales.some-domain.org* runs his or her news reader, the news reader connects to the *news.some-domain.org* news server and enters into yet another NNTP conversation.* The news reader's part appears in **bold**; annotation is in *italic*:

```
The news reader connects to news.some-domain.org at port 119
200 news.some-domain.org NNTP server ready (posting ok)
NEWGROUPS 980509 140000
235 New newsgroups since 980509 follow
rec.music.classical.harpsichord
NEWNEWS * 980509 140000
230 New news since 980509 140000 follows
<19980510180858.1230@earth.solar.net>
ARTICLE <19980510180858.1230@earth.solar.net>
220 <19980510180858.1230@earth.solar.net> All of article follows
The news server sends the article
QUIT
205 news.some-domain.org NNTP server waves goodbye.
```

After receiving the news server's initial announcement, the news reader asks the server whether any new newsgroups have been created since the last time it checked, on May 9, 1998 at 2:00 p.m. (14:00:00).† The server responds that a new group, *rec.music.classical.harpsichord*, has been created, and the news reader adds this group to its list of available newsgroups. Then the news reader asks whether any new news has been received in any newsgroup since it last checked. The server responds by sending the Message-ID of the new article. The news reader hasn't seen this article before, so it uses the ARTICLE command to ask the server to send it. Once the server finishes sending the article, the news reader quits.

Here's what the article looks like when our user at *sales.some-domain.org* reads it:

```
Path: news.some-domain.org!news.solar.net!earth.solar.net!you
From: you@earth.solar.net
Newsgroups: rec.puzzles.crosswords
Subject: Help with NY Times 5/10 puzzle?
Date: 10 May 1998 18:08:58 GMT
Message-ID: <19980510180858.1230@earth.solar.net>
NNTP-Posting-Host: earth.solar.net
Xref: news.some-domain.org rec.puzzles.crosswords:36449

Does anyone know the answer to 1-down in the 5/10 NY Times puzzle?
```

The new "Xref:" header is added by the local news server (*news.some-domain.org*) and indicates the article's number in the local server's database of articles for each group on the server in which the article appears. Figure 4-2 graphically displays how news travels.

---

* If the user were logged in to *news.some-domain.org* itself and reading news there, it wouldn't be necessary to transfer the article by NNTP. Instead, the news reader would directly access the news server's article database.

† Newsgroup creation is discussed later in this chapter.

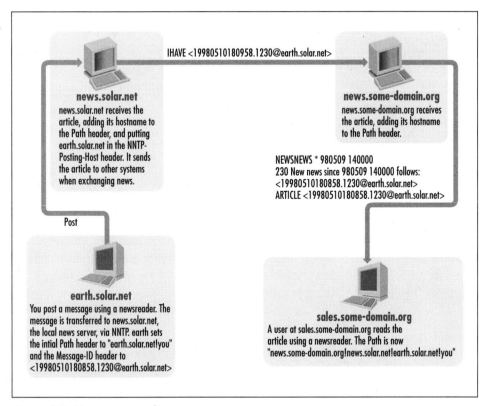

Figure 4-2: How news travels

Control Messages

In addition to exchanging news articles, news servers must learn which newsgroups have been newly created or removed and which articles have been canceled by their posters.* This kind of "metanews" is passed between news servers
in the form of *control messages*.

A control message is just like an ordinary news article except that it contains a
"Control:" header, a specially formatted subject line, and, in some cases, an
"Approved:" header. Although control messages are posted to relevant newsgroups, they don't usually show up when you read the newsgroups. Sometimes
they appear in the special newsgroup (or newsgroup hierarchy) *control*.

---

* As mentioned in Chapter 2, *The History of Spam*, under some conditions, people other than the
poster will cancel a message. This is controversial, and a relatively strict set of conditions must hold
before the Usenet community will accept a third-party cancel as legitimate. These conditions are discussed in Chapter 6, *A User's Guide to Usenet Spam*.

Three important control messages are *newgroup*, *rmgroup*, and *cancel*.

newgroup and rmgroup

Here's an example of a *newgroup* message, which calls for the creation of a new newsgroup:

```
Newsgroups: alt.config
Subject: cmsg newgroup alt.collecting.stamps.software
From: root@airmail.net
Date: Sat, 07 Feb 1998 15:12:03 EST
Message-ID: <MPG.f446154bb330408989681@news.mci2000.com>
Control: newgroup alt.collecting.stamps.software
Approved: root@airmail.net

cmsg newgroup alt.collecting.stamps.software
```

For a *newgroup* message, the "Control:" header must contain either `newgroup groupname`, to create an unmoderated group, or `newgroup groupname moderated`, to create a moderated group. The "Subject:" header is the same as the "Control:" header, with "cmsg" prepended. Finally, an "Approved:" header must appear and should show the email address of the person issuing the newgroup message.

An *rmgroup* message, which calls for the removal of a newsgroup, looks similar:

```
Newsgroups: rec.photo.help
Subject: cmsg rmgroup rec.photo.help
From: group-admin@isc.org (David C Lawrence)
Date: Mon, 23 Feb 1998 12:00:00 EST
Message-ID: <888251488.17018@isc.org>
Control: rmgroup rec.photo.help
Approved: group-admin@isc.org

rec.photo.help has been superseded by rec.photo.misc by a vote of
253:32 through a reorganization of the rec.photo hierarchy reported in
news.announce.newgroups on 19 Sep 1995.
```

Again, there must be a "Control:" header, reading `rmgroup groupname`, a similar "Subject:" header, and an "Approved:" header.

newgroup and *rmgroup* control messages are advisory, not binding. The news administrator at each news server decides which groups to create or remove based on the control messages.

In the "Big 8" Usenet newsgroup hierarchies (*comp, humanities, misc, news, rec, sci, soc,* and *talk*), all legitimate newgroup and rmgroup messages come from David Lawrence (as shown earlier in the "From:" header). Lawrence, also known as "tale," is the moderator of *news.announce.newgroups* and the one person designated by nearly all news administrators as trustworthy to make changes in the

Big 8. His work with Usenet is on a volunteer basis; he's employed by the Internet Software Consortium (*isc.org*), a nonprofit corporation that sponsors the development of reference implementations of Internet protocols.* Many news administrators configure their software to automatically accept *newgroup* messages that originate from Lawrence.

Other hierarchies have other suggested policies about *newgroup* and *rmgroup*, generally involving some sort of polling process to establish that people support the proposed action. The final decision always rests with the news administrator at each site.

Cancel messages

A cancel message requests the removal of an article. Here's an example:

```
Newsgroups: rec.arts.disney.parks
Subject:    cmsg cancel <scrapp59-2302980908060001@ppp-20.ts-1.stl.idt.net>
From:       scrapp59@idt.net (Scrappy)
Date:       Mon, 23 Feb 1998 12:00:00 EST
Message-ID: <scrapp59-2302980908550001@ppp-20.ts-1.stl.idt.net>
Control:    cancel <scrapp59-2302980908060001@ppp-20.ts-1.stl.idt.net>

cancel <scrapp59-2302980908060001@ppp-20.ts-1.stl.idt.net>
```

The crucial header is again "Control:," which must contain `cancel` *message-id*. "Subject:," as usual, looks like "Control:" with "cmsg" prepended. The "Sender:" address (or the "From:" address if there is no "Sender:") should match the address of the original message's poster in order for the cancel message to take effect.

When a news server accepts a cancel message for an article in its local database, it removes the article from the database. If a cancel message arrives before the article it was meant to cancel, some servers mark the article to be canceled as "already arrived" (so that attempts to send it are rejected); others ignore the cancel message. The cancel messages themselves are stored in the local database and are removed after a period of time. News administrators often configure their servers to honor or ignore cancel messages automatically; considering each individually would be far too much work.

Most newsreaders have a cancel command you can use to cancel your postings. Of course, if you cancel an article a week after you posted it, many people will have had time to read the article. Moreover, some administrators configure their news servers so they do not honor any cancel messages; your article will remain visible to news readers that use those news servers.

---

* Along with Henry Spencer, he's also written *Managing Usenet* (O'Reilly & Associates, Inc.), a comprehensive guide to running a Usenet news server.

Instant Messages

Email and news are both stored message systems: once transmitted, the message is stored until it can be read. The Internet also supports a variety of instant message systems. These services can be used for electronic "chat."

Instant Message Systems

The following are the main instant message services available on the Internet today.

IRC

Short for Internet Relay Chat, IRC was developed by Jarkko Oikarinen in Finland in the late 1980s. IRC is based on a client/server system. Participants in the chat connect to an IRC server using a special IRC client. Once connected, the user specifies an IRC channel. A typical channel is "#hack," used by computer crackers to discuss techniques for breaking into systems. After a channel is specified, any message typed on the client is automatically sent to all the other clients that are connected.

IRC servers can also connect to other IRC servers. In this manner, large numbers of people can communicate simultaneously across the world. Most IRC systems allow users to create new channels at will. A person who creates the channel has special privileges within that channel that allow them to purge unwanted users from the channel. A person with privilege can also give privilege to other participants inside the channel.

IRC users are identified by the handle they provide when they connect to the system. Each time an IRC user reconnects, they can choose the same handle or a new handle, provided no other user on the system is currently using that handle.

AOL Instant Messenger

A version of America Online's instant message system for the Internet, this system allows anyone on the Internet (who is running the AOL Instant Messenger application) to send an instant message to other users on the Internet or to users on AOL. All messages are sent from the user's computer to AOL and then to the intended recipients.

AOL Instant Messenger users are identified by a screen name, similar to an AOL screen name (username). Indeed, AOL encourages its users to use their actual AOL screen names when communicating over AOL Instant Messenger using the Internet.

ICQ

ICQ is another instant message system, originally developed by Mirabilis LTD, an Israeli firm that was purchased by America Online on June 8, 1998 for $287 million in cash.

To use ICQ, each user must register with Mirabilis, at which point he or she is given a unique ICQ number. Mirabilis maintains a directory of its ICQ users listing their email addresses, names, age, sex, and other demographic information, which is given at the time of registration. Users can control which pieces of information appear in the Mirabilis public directory and which remain private.

Like IRC and AOL's Instant Messenger, ICQ is a client/server system, with the server running at Mirabilis's headquarters and the client running on the customer's machine. But unlike the other systems, the ICQ server is used only for setting up the initial contact between users. After that point, messages travel directly from one client to another.

Instant Messages and Spamming

Instant message systems are important for spammers in two ways: as a source of email addresses and as an entirely new venue for sending out unsolicited advertisements.

As a source of email addresses, instant message systems provide less fertile ground than Usenet messages or web pages, which generally contain more email addresses and can be harvested very quickly. On the other hand, email addresses sent over instant message systems are likely to be valid and can be easily correlated with other kinds of information. Instant message directories, such as the ICQ listing, are a great source of information for spammers who can figure out how to extract the relevant information.

As a venue for spamming itself, instant message systems are generally uncharted territory: few spammers are using them today. This is likely to change as software is developed and sold that will specifically target instant message systems.

What is clear, however, is that advertisers are looking at chat rooms and instant message systems with open eyes. Recently, we were sent a message that read, in part, "We want to go to chat rooms and drop hints how great [our company] is to work for. Our only problem is that we are having a difficult time finding the appropriate chat rooms. We are looking for people primarily in Boston that are looking for jobs. If you have any ideas for us, would you be so kind as to email us back with any information you may have. We really appreciate it."

5

A User's Guide to Email Spam

Spam is not democratic. A lot of people have never gotten any spam, so they don't realize it is a problem. But once you get on a list and start getting spam, you usually start getting more and more of it. What can *you* do about junk mail? In this chapter, we look at three approaches to stopping email spam:

- Keeping your email address out of the hands of spammers in the first place

- Filtering your incoming email to remove spam

- Tracking down the spammer and complaining—to the spammer or to someone responsible for the spammer's Internet access

These tactics aren't exclusive: you can (and we often do) take advantage of all three to reduce the amount of junk mail you receive and to help make spamming unprofitable.

Safeguarding Your Email Address

The single best way to prevent yourself from receiving junk email is to keep your email address out of the hands of spammers in the first place. After all, nobody can email you without your address. Unfortunately, this is a lot harder than it sounds—after all, you probably *want* people to know your email address so they can send you legitimate email. And even if spammers don't know your email address, they can frequently guess it.

Spammers build their mailing lists by collecting addresses from legitimate mailing lists, web pages, and especially Usenet newsgroups. To prevent spam, you can conceal or disguise your email address whenever it appears in a public place. Email addresses are also harvested from chat rooms and ISP membership directories. This is especially a problem for AOL subscribers. If your ISP operates such a directory, you may ask to have your name removed to prevent your name from being harvested by a spammer.

An effective, if sometimes expensive, way to protect your email address is to open a second Internet account. Use one account as your "important" account and give this email address to family, friends, business contacts, and others whose mail you want to receive. Check this account for email on a regular basis. Whenever you subscribe to a mailing list, post a message to Usenet, or otherwise make your email address public, however, use the address of the second, "unimportant" account. Check this account for email now and then—you'll probably be able to delete anything that isn't obviously from a mailing list you've subscribed to.*

America Online subscribers may have up to five "screen names," each of which is a different email address. Using one of your screen names for newsgroup postings and other public exposures goes a long way toward avoiding unwanted email to your private screen name.

Hotmail offers free email addresses and a web-based interface with which to send and read email. Hotmail is advertiser-supported, so your web browser shows you ads from sponsors along with your email. Hotmail's URL is *http://www.hotmail. com*. A similar service is offered by Yahoo! (*http://www.yahoo.com*). Free email is also available from Juno (*http://www.juno.com*), which uses its own mail reader software, rather than a web browser.

Two particularly interesting places to get an email address are Junkproof (*http://www.junkproof.com*) and Bigfoot (*http://www.bigfoot.com*). Email to these addresses is filtered by the companies to remove spam and is then forwarded to another email address of your choosing. Junkproof charges $10 per month plus $10 per 100 MB forwarded per month if your mail volume exceeds 100 MB. Bigfoot's spam-mail filtering service is currently free, although the company may charge for the service in the future.

None of these services supports direct posting to newsgroups, but you can use your new account to register at DejaNews (*http://www.dejanews.com*), which supports posting to newsgroups, or to send email to a mail-to-news gateway. For a list of mail-to-news gateways, see *http://www.sabotage.org/~don/mail2news.html*.

Mailing Lists

Spammers have also been able to gather email addresses from Internet mailing lists. Many mailing lists on the Internet are managed by programs (e.g., LISTSERV or Majordomo) that can handle day-to-day tasks such as adding new members and

---

* In fact, you may want to use some of the filtering tactics described later to save mailing list messages and delete other messages sent to this account.

sending digests. These programs also support a feature called **who** that returns a list of email addresses subscribed to a particular list. If you subscribe to popular mailing lists, you're at risk from spammers who collect addresses by querying the list server.

Mailing list programs usually offer list managers the option of disabling the **who** feature. If you are on a mailing list, you should urge the list manager to disable the **who** feature.*

If you must subscribe to a list that doesn't disable **who**, you can often conceal your address from **who** requests:

*   If the list is managed by Listproc, send a message to *listproc* with the line `SET listname CONCEAL YES` in the message body.

*   If the list is managed by LISTSERV, send a message to *listserv* with the line `SET listname CONCEAL` in the message body.

*   If the list is managed by Majordomo, SmartList, or another mailing list server, you'll have to ask the list manager to restrict the **who** request to list subscribers. (Unfortunately, this really does not provide sufficient security because the spammer can add himself to the mailing list, execute the **who** command, and then remove himself from the mailing list when he is done.)

Newsgroup Postings

If you have only one Internet account and wish to post to a newsgroup, protecting your email address is more difficult. There are two commonly used tactics: anonymous remailers and address munging.

Anonymous remailers

An *anonymous remailer* allows you to send email anonymously. Mail that you send through the service is rewritten to remove your email address and other sending information. Some remailers have built-in support for anonymous newsgroup postings. Even those that don't can be used to post anonymously by sending newsgroup postings through the remailer to a mail-to-news gateway, discussed earlier.†

---

* If you *are* the manager of a list served by Listproc, LISTSERV, Majordomo, or SmartList, you can find more information about list management and configuration in Alan Schwartz's book *Managing Mailing Lists* (O'Reilly & Associates, Inc.).

† Anonymous remailers can be much fancier. Some of the most sophisticated support encrypted email and random timing of delivery (to prevent someone from determining that you sent the mail by comparing sending time to receiving time). You can also use a chain of remailers so that each remailer only knows the next remailer in the chain. (Later remailers don't know where the message came from, and earlier remailers don't know where the message's final destination is.) These privacy features go far beyond simply protecting your email address.

An easy-to-use remailer is *remailer@replay.com*. See *http://www.replay.com/ remailer/* for instructions on how to use the remailer to post news anonymously.

Some software makes anonymous posting even easier. The most popular free anonymous email package for Windows is Private Idaho, written by Joel McNamara and available at *http://www.eskimo.com/~joelm/pi.html*. Mac users might try anonAIMouS by Chris Riley (*http://hyperarchive.lcs.mit.edu/HyperArchive/Archive/ comm/inet/mail/*) or another popular choice, Yet-Another-NewsWatcher by Brian Clark (*ftp://ftp.acns.nwu.edu/pub/newswatcher/*). Unix users can look into premail by Raph Levien (*ftp://ftp.replay.com/pub/replay/pub/remailer/premail*).

One problem with anonymous remailers is that you're just that— anonymous. In some newsgroups, readers ignore or discount anonymous postings, because they are often used by spammers and "trolls"—people who post inflammatory messages to newsgroups just to provoke heated responses.

Some anonymous remailers are really pseudonymous—they assign you a pseudonymous email address and forward email sent to your pseudonym to your actual email address (*hotmail.com*, mentioned earlier, is another approach to pseudonymous email). Naturally, spammers can collect your pseudonymous address, so this tactic must be combined with some sort of email filtering (discussed later in this chapter) to avoid seeing unwanted messages. For example, you might filter your email so that all messages addressed to your pseudonymous address are filed in a "low-priority" folder, apart from your high-priority personal email.

Address munging

A second popular approach to protecting email addresses in newsgroup postings is *address munging*—replacing your email address with an address that doesn't work, but from which your true address could be easily determined by a human being (but not an address-harvesting program!). For example, replacing *john@nuts. com* with *john@remove-this-to-reply.nuts.com* tells a human reader your real address, but address-harvesting programs will be foiled.

 Address munging may violate the terms of your agreement with your ISP. You may wish to check with your provider before masquerading under a munged address.

How should an address be munged? Among the guidelines suggested by W.D. Baseley, in his "Address Munging FAQ" (posted regularly to *news.admin.net-abuse.policy*), are:

- Make it obvious to humans, but do not make it so obvious that it becomes easier for junk emailers to strip it out.

- Tell folks how to demunge your address somewhere in your message. The signature that gets added to the end of each message is a good place to do this.

- Do not make up domain names—someone may register that domain one day, and then they will receive all the spam sent to your munged address.

- Be sure to munge your domain name. Don't simply modify your username or mailbox (the part to the left of the "@" sign). If you use an invalid mailbox but a valid domain name, you'll still be forcing your mail server to process incoming junk mail and determine that it's to an unknown user. For example, if your real address is *alice@wonderland.org*, use something like *alice@delete.wonderland.org*. This limits the spammer's abuse of your resources to asking the *wonderland.org* name server if there's a host named *delete*. (In fact, Chris Lewis, a well-known spam canceler, strongly recommends that munged addresses use a bogus top-level domain name, like *.nospam* or *.seemysig*. This limits the spammer's resource abuse to asking a root name server about the *.nospam* domain.)

Good examples of munged addresses include *alice@unusual-string.wonderland. org* and *alice@nospam.nospam* (along with a signature file that says "replace the first nospam with wonderland and the second with org").

Bad examples include *alice@nospam.org* (*nospam.org* is a real domain name) and *alice-deletethis@wonderland.org* (*wonderland.org* must still use its resources to process the mail). *alice@nospam.wonderland.org* is probably not going to be a good choice for long—address harvesting software will soon learn to discard suspicious hostnames like "nospam" and "remove."

Munging is effective—it prevents unwanted email from reaching you by keeping your real email address out of the clutches of the address-harvesting programs. On the other hand, by munging your address, you make it difficult for people to reply to your postings using their news reader's default "reply" function. This may confuse people and cause you to miss important replies. It's a particularly bad idea to munge your address in email—save munging for Usenet, where people can post replies back to newsgroups.

Address munging is one tactic that's simpler for PC and Mac users than for Unix users. Most PC and Mac news-posting software allows you to identify yourself with any email address. Most Unix news-posting software, on the other hand, allows you to change the message's "From:" header, but if you do, inserts an "Originator:" header with your actual email address anyway!

Channels

Yet another approach to minimize spam mail from Usenet is to create a special email address that will be only used for a limited time. This technique was first proposed by Robert Hall, a researcher at AT&T Labs, as part of a system called *email channels*. Hall's system is for people to create different email addresses for different purposes: a public channel that would go on business cards, another channel for private communications, still another channel for Usenet postings—and to have software that automatically filters incoming email destined for different channels to different mailboxes. Channels used for Usenet postings can be deleted after a few weeks—long enough to receive legitimate replies, short enough to avoid spamming by all but the most aggressive spammers.

LPWA has developed a service based on this approach. You can find more information at *http://lpwa.com:8000*.

Thomas Erskine's *tms* (Tagged Message Sender) program can be used with the *qmail* MTA to automatically create outgoing addresses that are valid only for a limited time or for a particular sender, or that direct responses to a special mailbox. These email addresses can then be used as the "Reply-to:" address for Usenet postings. Alternatively, you can post to Usenet via a mail-to-news gateway.

Web Pages

Spammers frequently harvest email addresses from web pages by using a program to traverse the web and collect addresses. If you maintain web pages, protecting your address on the web can be important.

In some respects, keeping your address hidden on the web is harder than keeping it from Usenet. Usually, you *want* your web page to include your email address, so people can contact you. But if you must hide your address, here are a few tactics that may be helpful:

- Munge the address just as you would in a newsgroup posting. For example, write your email address as *slash@myhost-dot-com*, and instruct readers to replace "*-dot-*" with a period.

- Matthew "Indigo Jo" Smith suggests setting parts of the email address or hostname in bold or italic: many harvesters currently do not strip the HTML formatting codes from the addresses and will get confused. For example, you might format the domain name in italic, using HTML like this:

```
yourname@<I>yourhost.com</I>
```

- The Multimedia Marketing Group (*http://www.mmgco.com/nospam*) suggests inserting a %20 before your email address when it appears in a "mailto:" link, like this:

```
<A HREF="mailto:%20yourname@yourhost.com">Mail me!</A>
```

Browsers translate the %20 into a space when you follow the link, so the link works fine for web browsers, but most address harvesters, at least today, get an invalid email address instead.

- Create a graphical image that includes your email address and display the image on your page. This won't be usable by people who use text-only browsers or blind people who use screen readers, of course, but it won't be usable by harvesting programs, either.

- Collect comments and other messages by using a form and a CGI script, rather than a "mailto:" URL. This is probably the safest approach.

- If you manage the web server, give your address as *www@yourhost* or *http@yourhost*. Some spammers may be reluctant to send junk mail to these users and others who appear to be "in charge" (e.g., *postmaster*, *root*, etc.). On the other hand, spammers have added email addresses such as *abuse@vineyard.net* to their spam lists, so beware.

Opt-Out Lists

In the non-Internet world of direct marketing, mailing-list companies and telemarketers have developed a system called *opt-out* to let people who don't want to receive solicitations voluntarily take themselves off mailing and phone lists. The way the lists work is simple. If you don't want to receive junk email or junk phone calls, you write a letter to the Direct Marketing Association's (DMA) Mail Preference Service with your name and address. The DMA gives this information to the nation's largest direct-marketing companies, which then use this database to "clean" the mailing lists of their clients. The DMA's system isn't foolproof—you have to reregister with the service every three years and every time you move, and compliance by the mailing services is voluntary and at the discretion of the company that's actually sending the advertisements. But the Mail Preference Service works well enough that the marketing industry has been able to use its existence to successfully fight off increased federal regulation.

Seeing the DMA's success, many spammers have tried to emulate it. Today many electronic bulk mailings have a little note at the bottom:

```
To unsubscribe to "PuRe Power Marketing Tips" please reply to this
message and type in unsubscribe in the subject line.
```

Spambait

An interesting tactic to discourage email address harvesting from web pages is creating "spambait"—pages full of made-up email addresses. The goal of spambait is to tie up the junk mailer's computer with useless fake addresses from which mail will bounce.

John Harvey's *makebait* Perl script produces spambait pages. It can be downloaded from *http://linux.lan.com/spam/tools/makebait.txt*. Here's a short sample of *makebait*'s work, rendered in plain text:

```
            Vos Uber Djv Kfxe Kdz Efaqs

xkni@eiwbt.nl mom9g2@to5l.no zq@styhz.edu tulz@vz.edu
ippaaukc@vvisvppp.kwpdc.ffjxwnt.com dmqjircz@vgsrszb.no
uoutnpib@fkt.edu sdciikiw@akrjxuab.zgzas.com pjgbp@dwkmfcc.com
x9yei@m3dz.m7w8blo.com ycbbdx@bvtak.com ghnn@ydcrt.gov pgy@fw.edu
lvcvi@eovyd.edu svusjc@guqqnmj.wuwkt.ishqeer.edu lonnvb@cu.j2b9vf.de
ydque@stisbsd.de mxsqt@zqodgbdk.com fzr@innida.com
mcok@tzuty.esynof.gjyj.com
```

Each email address is also a "mailto:" link.

Another popular program for producing spambait is *wpoison*, a CGI script that generates pages containing a few fake addresses and many real-appearing links that generate additional spambait pages. You can download *wpoison* from *http://www.e-scrub.com/wpoison/*.

Spambait is a community approach to stopping spam. If many people put up spambait pages, the majority of the email addresses that spammers harvest from the Web will be fictitious. Unfortunately, spambait doesn't solve the problem of mail bounces—that is, what happens to the spam messages sent to the spambait addresses.

Spambait pages also present a problem for programs that index the Web. These "robots" or "spiders" can easily wind up indexing pages full of worthless addresses, reducing the usefulness of the search engines that use the indices. Web server administrators can direct robots to steer clear of spambait pages by creating a *robots.txt* file in the main web document directory (i.e., accessible with the URL *http://yoursite/robots.txt*) containing these lines:

```
User-agent: *
Disallow /cgi-bin/wpoison/
Disallow /spambait.html
```

Each "Disallow" line indicates a relative URL that robots should ignore. Of course, the downside of helping honest robots is that spammer address harvesters may check your *robots.txt* file themselves and avoid your spambait!

Whether spammers actually honor remove requests is questionable. Many spam messages are sent out from fraudulent addresses that can't be replied to. In other instances, some spammers have been known to collect the addresses of people who ask to be removed and sell them to other spammers as "confirmed" address lists!

More recently, some companies have offered global opt-out lists. You register your email address with the global list. Businesses that plan to send unsolicited email first send their mailing lists to the opt-out list site, where addresses of people who have chosen to opt out are removed. This "cleaned" list is then returned to the bulk mailer to use as a mailing list. The service is typically free to both you and the bulk mailer. Note that a spammer could, by comparing his original list and the cleaned list, come up with a list of working email addresses that have opted out, and use this list for further spamming. At least three global opt-out lists have been announced; all have since ceased operation.

America Online users may receive advertisements from companies to which AOL provides user information. If you're not interested in any ads from these companies, you can use the AOL "Marketing Preferences" keyword to keep your address out of these lists.

Opt-out lists might sound like a solution to the problem of unsolicited email, to the extent that spammers actually use the lists and don't abuse them to gather email addresses. On the other hand, the very principle of requiring people to opt out is considered unethical by some because it assumes that you'd like to receive junk mail unless you say otherwise.

But what's really not clear is whether the economics of spamming make opt-out lists financially workable. Building and maintaining a database of opt-out addresses is expensive. That's a worthwhile expense in the world of postal or telephone marketing, where it costs a company between 25 cents and a dollar to send each message. But with email marketing, where 100,000 messages can be sent out for a few pennies, the economics of running an opt-out service do not exist unless the bulk-mail firms have some ulterior motive for running the database. Preventing government regulation might be sufficient motivation for legitimate industry participants, but it's unlikely to be sufficient for all the bad actors in the world of bulk email today.

Filtering Junk Mail

A common suggestion for dealing with both unwanted email and inappropriate newsgroup postings is to "just click Delete"—to delete them from your mailbox after you've determined that you're not interested in what they have to say. This tactic has the advantage of being simple and requiring no special software.

Unfortunately, clicking Delete has many disadvantages. The junk email still interrupts your train of thought. You must then spend time determining which messages are unwanted and which are not. If you receive many unwanted email messages, they may fill up your mailbox, preventing you from receiving important messages. A better approach would be to have your computer delete the spam mail *automatically*, before you ever see it. You can do that with email filters.

Filters

A *filter* is a set of instructions for the disposition of email. For example, a mail filter might include instructions like:

1. If the mail is from *mom@home.org*, save it in the *family* mailbox.

2. If the mail is from *dracula@monster.com*, delete it.

3. Otherwise, leave it in my incoming mailbox.

The flexibility of the filter depends on the filtering software. Most filters can file messages to mailboxes, delete messages, or leave them untouched. Some can trigger external programs and pass the messages to those programs. All filters can make filtering decisions based on message headers; some can also scan message bodies.

There are many programs for filtering email. The popular Macintosh and Windows mail client Eudora Pro has filtering capabilities, as do Microsoft Outlook Express and Netscape Messenger. On Unix systems, the *elm* mail package includes a simple filtering utility called *filter*, but a more complex and powerful program called *procmail* has become the de facto standard for serious filtering jobs.* With these programs, it's usually the individual user who chooses what filters to apply to incoming email. Each user can have a different set of filters.

If you use America Online, you can enable AOL's mail filter in their "Mail Controls" dialog box, shown in Figure 5-1. Using the Mail Controls, you can allow email from only selected users, or you can allow email from all users except those you specify. When combined with multiple screen names, Mail Controls becomes a good tool for spam fighting—you can block all email sent to your public screen names and accept nearly all email sent to your private screen name.

Email filters typically check an incoming message against each filtering instruction, in order, and stop when the message matches one of the instructions.† This makes the order of the filtering instructions critical. For example, this filter, while it

---

* *procmail* is available at *ftp://ftp.informatik.rwth-aachen.de/pub/packages/procmail/*.

† Flexible filtering software like *procmail* can also be instructed to continue matching the message against instructions even after a match is found.

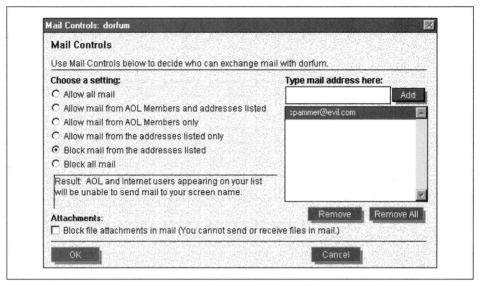

Figure 5-1: America Online's Mail Controls dialog box

appears correct, will actually delete a message from mom with "money" in the subject:

1. Delete messages with subject "money"

2. Save messages from mom to the *family* mailbox

3. Leave the rest in my incoming mailbox

A better filter might be:

1. Save messages from mom to the *family* mailbox

2. Delete messages with subject "money"

3. Leave the rest in my incoming mailbox

 Be very careful with filters that automatically delete messages. As this example shows, it is all too easy to have them accidentally delete messages that you really want.

A Filtering Example

To illustrate the configuration of email filters, let's set up the following filter using a few different mail clients:

1. If the mail is from *mom@home.org*, save it in the *family* mailbox.

2. If the mail is from *dracula@monster.com*, delete it.

3. Otherwise, leave it in my incoming mailbox.

Eudora Pro 4.0

In keeping with its easy-to-use design, Eudora's filtering configuration is straightforward. Here's how to set up our filter:

1. Select "Filters" from the "Tools" menu to bring up the Filters window.

2. Click the "New" button to create a new filter.

3. Make sure the checkbox for "incoming" is checked, so the filter will be applied to incoming email.

4. Using the pull-down menus and text boxes in the "Match" portion of the screen, select the header "From:," the "contains" relationship, and type in *mom@home.org*.

5. In the "Action" portion of the screen, select "Transfer To:" as the action, and click the button that appears next to the action to set the mailbox where the message should be transferred—in our example, *family*.

6. Repeat steps 2–5 for the dracula filter, choosing "Transfer To:" as the action, and "Trash" as the mailbox.

Figure 5-2 shows the Filters window after both filters have been added.

Outlook Express

The filtering feature of Microsoft Outlook Express is called the "Inbox Assistant" and is accessible from the "Tools" menu. The "Add" button in the Inbox Assistant brings up the dialog box for defining filters, shown in Figure 5-3.

Netscape Messenger 4.05

You can find Netscape Messenger's filtering features in the "Edit" menu as the "Mail Filters" option. The "New" button displays the dialog box for defining filters, shown in Figure 5-4.

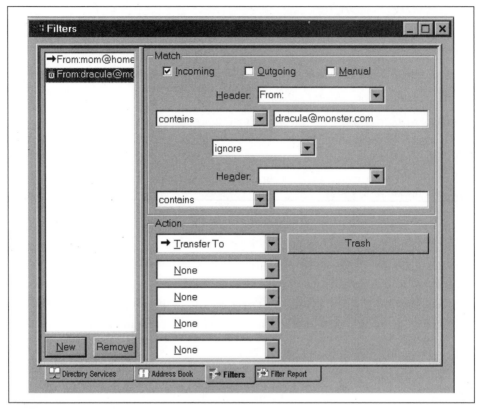

Figure 5-2: The Eudora Pro filters window

Outlook 98

Microsoft Outlook 98 (not to be confused with Outlook Express) includes the simple mail-filtering capabilities in Outlook Express, but also adds a sophisticated rule-based system, developed by Microsoft, to detect junk email and adult-oriented advertisements automatically and either move them to a special mailbox or delete the messages.

In order to prevent spammers from reverse-engineering its system, Microsoft does not publicize the particular rules that its system uses. Updates to the rules can be downloaded from the Web.

filter (Unix)

The *elm* mail system, available on many Unix systems, includes a mail-filtering program called *filter*. *filter* is simple to set up, but it's easy to exhaust its limited functionality. If you need only very basic filtering, however, *filter* may be for you.

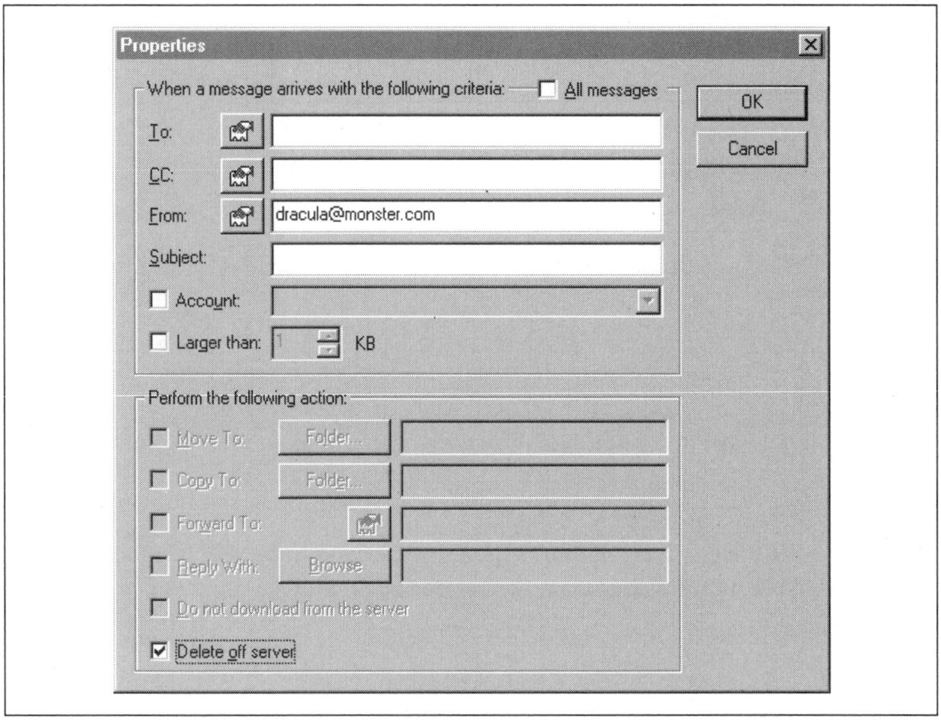

Figure 5-3: The Outlook Express Inbox Assistant

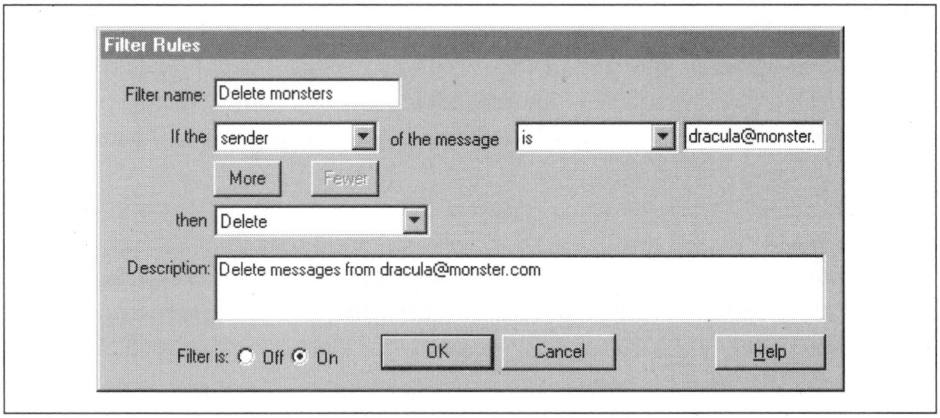

Figure 5-4: The Netscape Messenger 4.05 Mail Filters window

Here's how to set up *filter*:

1. Figure out where *filter* is installed by using a command like **which filter** or **whereis filter** or by asking your system administrator. Let's assume *filter* is in */usr/local/bin*.

2. Edit the file *.forward* in your home directory to contain the line:

```
|"IFS=' '; exec /usr/local/bin/filter -o /your/directory/filter.errors"
```

This instructs your system to forward your incoming email to the *filter* program* and tells *filter* that it should save any error messages it generates to */your/directory/filter.errors*.

3. Create the file *filter-rules* in the *.elm* subdirectory of your home directory. If you don't already use *elm*, you may have to create this directory. The *filter-rules* file contains the filtering instructions. For our example, it should contain:

```
if (from = "mom@home.org") then save "~/Mail/family"
if (from = "dracula@monster.com") then delete
```

4. Use the **filter -r** command to check your rules to be sure they're correctly written. The output of **filter -r** for our example is:

```
Rule 1: if (from = "mom@home.org") then
        Save ~/Mail/family
Rule 2: if (from = "dracula@monster.com") then
        Delete
```

Using *filter*, you can filter based on a combination of the headers "Sender:," "Subject:," "From:," and "To:," as well as the number of lines in the message. You can match the headers against simple strings (as shown earlier) or against more powerful regular expressions (described later). Matching messages may be deleted, saved into another folder, forwarded to another address, passed on to another program, or left in your mailbox.

Procmail

procmail is widely accepted as the most powerful and popular email filter for Unix systems. Its power comes at the cost of simplicity, however—if very simple filtering for a Unix account is all you need, you may find the *filter* program discussed earlier to be easier to use. Here's how to set up our filter using *procmail*:

1. Figure out where *procmail* is installed on your system. Commands like **which procmail** or **whereis procmail** should locate it; if they don't, ask your system administrator if *procmail* has been (or can be) installed. Let's assume that *procmail* is in */usr/local/bin*.

---

* This example, and the *procmail* example that follows, assumes that your system is using a mail delivery program that understands *.forward*, like *sendmail*. If you know that your system uses different mail software; ask your system administrator how to pass your email to a program.

2. Edit the file *.forward* in your home directory to contain the line:

```
|"IFS=' '; exec /usr/local/bin/procmail #your-login-name"
```

   This instructs your system's mail delivery program to forward your incoming email to the *procmail* program.

3. Create the file *.procmailrc* in your home directory. *.procmailrc* is *procmail*'s "recipe file"—the file that describes how *procmail* should filter messages—and is written in a special language. For our example, *.procmailrc* should contain:

```
:0
* ^From:.*mom@home.org
family

:0
* ^From:.*dracula@monster.com
/dev/null
```

The file contains two simple *procmail* recipes. Each consists of an initial line (beginning with `:0`), filtering criteria (each beginning with `*`), and an action to perform. The first recipe in our example checks the message headers to see whether any match the regular expression `^From:.*mom@home\.org`, which is read as "a line beginning `From:`, followed by any number of characters, followed by `mom@home.org`."[*] If the message matches, the action is performed—in this case, the message is deposited in the *family* mailbox. Actions can also include forwarding messages to other email addresses and piping messages to programs. As the second recipe shows, the way to delete a message is to save it to the special file */dev/null*.

Procmail can do much more than these simple filters. See the *procmail* manual pages for details and examples. A more extensive *procmail* tutorial is also available at *http://shell3.ba.best.com/~ariel/nospam/proctut.shtml*.

Filtering Strategies

What criteria should be used to filter email? When filtering to reduce the amount of junk mail, an obvious tactic is to focus on the message sender and try to avoid messages sent by spammers. But there are also other ways to recognize junk mail.

---

[*] For a complete treatment of regular expressions, see *Mastering Regular Expressions* by Jeffrey E. F. Friedl (O'Reilly & Associates, Inc.).

Where to Filter

If you filter spam messages with your mail client (Eudora, Outlook Express, or another program), each spam message must still be downloaded to your computer. If you filter on your mail server with *procmail*, spam messages are filtered before they reach your mailbox. As a result, they do not make you wait for your email to be downloaded.

Yet another place to filter is at your mail server's SMTP server. Filter here, and your spam messages are blocked as they travel over the Internet and never need be delivered to your mail server. Filtering at the SMTP server can be done only by system administrators. For information, see Chapter 7, *Spam Stopping for Administrators and ISPs*.

Filtering by sender

There are two basic approaches to filtering email by the message sender's address:

- With the "refuse villains, allow others" approach, filters are used to delete messages from known spammers. Messages from unknown senders are assumed to be okay and are allowed to pass through the filter. This approach prevents overfiltering, but you won't know whether unknown senders should be added to your villain list until they send you an unwanted message.

- With the "allow friends, refuse others" approach, filters allow messages only from preselected addresses to pass through and delete all others. This approach is unfriendly to strangers—only people whom you've decided you want messages from are able to reach you—but is almost totally effective against unwanted messages.

Because the second strategy makes communication so difficult, some variations may be more useful. With powerful filter software like *procmail* in Unix, instead of deleting messages from unknown senders, you could bounce the messages back to their senders, along with a "filter password," and accept messages that either are from friends or contain the filter password in their subject. Because spammers won't bother to read your rejection message and customize their junk mail to include your filter password, this provides good protection against unwanted email while permitting those who really want to reach you to do so. To illustrate the power of *procmail*, here's a *procmail* recipe that implements this system:

```
# Define important variables:
SHELL=/bin/sh
MYNAME=alansz                    # My login name
FRIEND_LIST=$HOME/.myfriends     # My file of friendly addresses
FILTER_PASSWD=oodles             # My filter password
```

```
:0
* !^FROM_DAEMON                   # Don't reply to daemons or myself
* !^From +$MYNAME
{
  FROM=`formail -rx "To:"`       # Get the sender's address

  :0                             # If it's a friend, keep the message
  * ? egrep $FROM $FRIEND_LIST
  $DEFAULT

  :0                             # If it has the password,
  * $ Subject:.*$FILTER_PASSWD
  {
    :0c                          # keep it and...
    $DEFAULT
    :0                           # make this person a friend
    |echo $FROM >> $FRIEND_LIST
  }

  :0                             # Otherwise bounce it.
  | (formail -rkA"Precedence: junk"; \
    echo "Your message is being returned. Due to the large amount of"; \
    echo "spam I've had to deal with, I now only accept email from"; \
    echo "people I've ok'd. How do you become a person I've ok'd?"; \
    echo "Easy. Just send your mail back to me with $FILTER_PASSWD in"; \
    echo "the Subject header. Once you do that once, my filter will"; \
    echo "recognize you, and you won't have to do it again unless you"; \
    echo "change email addresses. Sorry for the trouble."; \
    ) | $SENDMAIL -t
}
```

See the *procmail* manpages for help understanding and writing recipes like these.

Other Filtering Techniques

There are other useful ways to filter email:

- Filter by subject, to avoid messages with subjects written in ALL CAPITALS or containing many exclamation points or dollar signs, common tip-offs to junk mail.

- Filter out mail with "Priority:" or "X-Priority:" headers, since few people use these headers in genuine email.

- The "X-UIDL:" header is added by POP servers when a POP client asks for a unique ID listing (see Chapter 4, *Internet Basics*). If a message already has an "X-UIDL:" header before you download it, or if you don't use a POP client and the message has an "X-UIDL:" header, it's probably spam.

- The header "Comments: Authenticated sender is <*address*>" is added by the Pegasus mail client and by some spam programs. Pegasus also adds an "X-Mailer: Pegasus" header; any message that contains the "Comments:

Authenticated sender is *<address>*" header without the "X-Mailer: Pegasus" header is probably spam. Many spamming programs have similar "signatures" that can be used to identify their messages; because these change so quickly, you may be better off using filtering software that's updated often, such as the Spam Bouncer, discussed later in this chapter.

NoCeM-E

Chapter 6, *A User's Guide to Usenet Spam*, discusses the NoCeM system on Usenet—authenticated suggestions about messages to be deleted that can be issued by anyone and accepted selectively. There has been some interest in a similar approach to suppressing junk email. The NoCeM-E (NoCeM for Email) program allows people to distribute and receive authenticated *procmail* recipes for filtering junk mail. The recipes you receive can be automatically added to your *procmail* filter.

A beta version of the NoCeM-E software, written by Don Doumakes, is available at *http://www.novia.net/~doumakes/abuse/*. A mailing list for distributing NoCeM-E notices has been set up by Dougal Campbell; to subscribe, send email to *nocem-e-notices-request@advicom.net* with the word `subscribe` in the body of the message.

Other Filters

The Multimedia Marketing Group (*http://www.mmgco.com/nospam*) suggests creating a filter that files any message that doesn't contain your email address into a low-priority mailbox that you check only once in a while. Most spam won't have your email address in the "To:" or "Cc:" header, so this tactic works on many junk mail messages. Figure 5-5 shows what that filter looks like in Eudora.

Unfortunately, if you subscribe to mailing lists, they also may put the list address rather than your address in the "To:" header, and your filter will treat list messages as junk mail, too. You may need to add filters specifically to hold on to list mail before the MMG filter.

The Spam Bouncer, by Catherine Hampton, is a set of *procmail* recipes that perform extensive spam filtering and responding based on lists of known spammers and analyses of message headers and the message body. It's available at *http://www.best.com/~ariel/nospam*.

Mailjail (*http://www.mailjail.com*) is a commonly available plug-in filter that works with most POP-based mail clients. The program comes with a sophisticated set of filters that blocks much spam. New filters are available on a subscription basis.

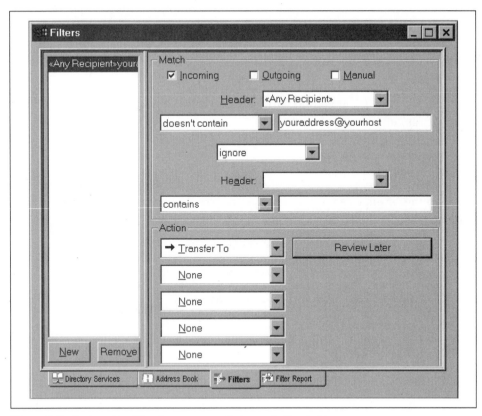

Figure 5-5: Eudora Pro filter for messages that aren't directed to you

Responding to Junk Mail

Hiding your address is inconvenient and far from foolproof, and filtering only avoids the problem. To stop spam, you must stop the spammer.

Most ISPs have rules that are supposed to prohibit their customers from spamming. Accordingly, if you can track down the site from which the spam originated, you can often get good results by complaining to the administrator at that site. The spammer's ISP may not know that its computers are being used to send spam; by alerting them, you enable them to take appropriate action—warn the spammer to stop, terminate the spammer's account, or even hit the spammer where it hurts by assessing cleanup fees to cover the cost of dealing with the results of the spam. Many ISPs will respond to complaints with alacrity; receiving a letter from an ISP informing you that they've terminated a spammer's account and are recovering damages is particularly gratifying.

Spam won't stop unless the victims complain. Complaining takes time, and you may not want to complain about every message you receive, but informing ISPs about spamming customers is a public service. If everyone assumes that someone else has complained, the result is that no one complains, and the spammer's methods are justified.

In this section, we show you how to track down junk emailers, identify their ISPs, and complain effectively.

Tracing Junk Email

To illustrate the process of determining the source of an email message, let's return to the example email message in Chapter 4, as received by *chrism@pluto. solar.net*:

```
From you@earth.solar.net Sat May 9 12:40:45 1998
Received: from jupiter.solar.net (jupiter.solar.net [1.4.4.7])
    by pluto.solar.net (8.8.7/8.8.7) with SMTP id KAB00332
    for <chrism@pluto.solar.net>; Sat, 9 May 1998 12:40:45 -0600
Received: from earth.solar.net (earth.solar.net [1.4.4.4])
    by jupiter.solar.net (8.8.8/8.8.8) with SMTP id MAA00395
    for <chris@jupiter.solar.net>; Sat, 9 May 1998 12:40:40 -0600
Date: Sat, 9 May 1998 12:40:30 -0600
From: you@earth.solar.net
To: Chris <chris@jupiter.solar.net>
Subject: Steel Pulse concert date
Message-Id: <19980509124030.0113@earth.solar.net>
X-Mailer: QUALCOMM Windows Eudora Pro Version 4.0
X-UIDL: 179c97f481a77a5da1a8109409a00afe

Hi, Chris!

The next Steel Pulse concert is on Friday. See you there!
```

How does Chris know who sent the messsage? In the message, there are four indications:

- The "From:" header lists *you@earth.solar.net* as the sender. For legitimate email, this usually suffices—legitimate senders want you to know they sent the message. But the value of the "From:" header can easily be set to any email address, valid or not. Accordingly, it is not a reliable way to determine the message sender.

- The "SMTP From:" header (the first line) also lists *you@earth.solar.net* as the sender. Again, for legitimate email, this usually suffices, though it can differ from the "From:" header when the latter is used to identify the address to which replies should be sent, and the former to identify the actual host and account from which the message was sent. But the value of the "SMTP From:" header is taken from the MAIL command in the SMTP conversation, and a knowledgeable spammer or a clever spamming program can easily set it to an incorrect address as well. "SMTP From:" is not a reliable way to determine the message sender.

- The "Message-Id:" header indicates the message originated at *earth.solar.net*; since most mail software adds a Message-Id based on the sending host, this header also usually points to where the message originated. But again, a spammer can easily insert a bogus Message-Id to throw you off, so the Message-Id is not a reliable way to determine the message sender.

- Finally, the "Received:" headers show the mail traveled from *earth.solar.net* to *jupiter.solar.net* and then to *pluto.solar.net*. Because Chris has accounts on both *jupiter* and *pluto*, she knows the message really did travel as the first "Received:" header indicates. Moreover, because the second "Received:" header was added by *jupiter*, a trustworthy host, Chris knows *jupiter* received the message from *earth.solar.net*.

Only the "Received:" headers added by trustworthy hosts are truly reliable for determining the source of a message. Unfortunately, they don't identify the user who sent the message, but they do lead back to the originating site.

Spammers don't want you to track them down and complain about their activities before they can garner some results from their messages. There are a variety of tricks that spammers use to obfuscate their message headers and slow down identification. Three prominent spammer tricks are forging common headers, adding bogus "Received:" headers, and using open relay sites. We describe these tricks in the following sections. Just about any header in an email message can be forged by the sender. A naive spammer may change only the "From:" header; a more sophisticated one will try to ensure that the other headers—such as the "Message-Id:" and the envelope sender—present either a consistent but wrong picture of the origin of the message or a wildly inconsistent and confusing picture. The headers may point to a completely bogus email address or may suggest an actual user's email address, perhaps in an attempt to damage the user's reputation in revenge for anti-spam actions.

Here's a simple example:

```
From newsrelease@the18th.com  Sat May  2 05:23:36 1998
Received: from 207.181.72.204 (van-bc6-12.netcom.ca [207.181.72.204])
      by earth.solar.net (8.8.8/8.8.8) with SMTP id FAA16164
      for <you@earth.solar.net>; Sat, 2 May 1998 05:23:34 -0500 (CDT)
Date: Sat, 2 May 1998 05:23:34 -0500 (CDT)
From: newsrelease@the18th.com
Message-Id: <199805021023.FAA16164@earth.solar.net>
To: you@earth.solar.net
Subject: Significant New Venture....
```

```
Historic Joint Venture.
After 2 years preparation, this
* World Presence Pre-Launch *
captures small and big Players.
```

Although the "Received:" header shows the message arrived from *van-bc6-12.net-com.ca*, the "From:" header and the envelope sender (the first "From" line) are written to suggest that the source of the message is *newsrelease@the18th.com*. Although this may not be a forgery in the legal sense—*newsrelease@the18th.com* may indeed be the email address of the sender—it illustrates that spammers can easily rewrite headers to mislead the reader as to their service provider.

Adding bogus "Received:" headers

Because the "Received:" headers are often the most useful clues to the source of an unwanted message, some spammers try to hide their tracks by adding fake "Received:" headers, in the hope that you'll track them to a site in the fake header. Here's an extreme example:

```
From e54b533@mci.com  Sun May  3 07:06:02 1998
Received: from akscorpio.komatsu.co.jp (akscorpio.komatsu.co.jp
          [202.221.199.1]) by earth.solar.net (8.8.8/8.8.8) with
          SMTP id HAA23960
          for <you@earth.solar.net>; Sun, 3 May 1998 07:06:00 -0500 (CDT)
Received: from 1Cust108.tnt14.lax3.da.uu.net
          by akscorpio.komatsu.co.jp; (5.65v3.2/1.1.8.2/31Jan96-0159PM)
          id AA32103; Sun, 3 May 1998 20:54:40 +0900
Date: Sun, 3 May 1998 20:54:40 +0900
From: e54b533 <e54b533@mci.com>
To: <you@earth.solar.net>
Received: from SMTP.XServer (Smail4.1.19.1 #20) id m0wBzN7-009vdR;
          Sunday, May 24th, 1998
Received: from mail.apache.net(really [164/187])
          by relay.comanche.com Friday, May 22nd, 1998
Received: from 32776.21445(really [80110/80111])
          by relay.denmark.nl Wednesday, May 20th, 1998
Received: from local.nethost.org(really [24553/24554])
          by relay.SS621.net Tuesday, May 19th, 1998
Message-Id: <19943672.886214@relay.comanche.denmark.eu>
          Monday, May 25th, 1998
Reply-To: e54b533@mci.com
MIME-Version: 1.0
Content-Type: text/plain; charset=unknown-8bit
Content-Transfer-Encoding: 8bit
Status: RO
Content-Length: 4859
Lines: 123

Authenticated sender is <e54b533@mci.com>
Subject:  e5
Mime-Version: 1.0
Content-Type: text/plain; charset="us-ascii"
```

```
Content-Transfer-Encoding: 7bit

EMAIL MARKETING WORKS!!

Bull's Eye Gold is the PREMIER email address collection tool.
```

The first "Received:" header is trustworthy, because it was added by *earth.solar. net*, the recipient's system. The second header may be trustworthy and suggests that the spammer connected to a *uu.net* dial-up account and relayed his message through *akscorpio.komatsu.co.jp* (see a discussion of relays later in this chapter).

The remaining "Received:" headers appearing below the "To:" header are clearly forgeries. Not only don't they show a connected path the mail followed, they are often incomplete (some don't include IDs, some don't include who the message was received by), and the dates are often incorrect (in this case, they are future dates!). These headers were added solely to confuse people and programs attempting to trace the spammer's site of origin.

Not all added "Received:" headers are so obvious, but an invalid "Received:" header is always suspicious. Recall from Chapter 4 that a valid "Received:" header has this format:

```
Received: from sending host [(sending-hostname sending-IP-address)]
    by receiving host [(MTA version)]
    with protocol and id [for recipient]; date
```

Obvious clues to forged "Received:" headers are an invalid format, invalid host-names, invalid IP addresses, and wildly incorrect dates. The **recipient** should match an email address you recognize; if it doesn't, the header is probably forged. Hosts that receive an email message prepend their "Received:" header to the set of "Received:" headers already present; when other headers appear between "Received:" headers, it's often a tip-off that one of the sets of "Received:" headers is bogus.

The very informative Frequently Asked Questions list for the SPAM-L mailing list, maintained by Doug Muth and others, reports that some "stealth mailers" use the same SMTP ID in all forged "Received:" headers (which typically begin with "XAA" or "GAA") and report the **sending host** as *alt1* at some domain. It also notes that if you receive your email through a forwarder or firewall,* the forwarding system may add suspicious-looking "Received:" headers, so check a valid piece of

---

* A *firewall* is a system that sits between the Internet and an internal network, and prevents most data from flowing between them. Many companies use firewalls to protect their internal networks against crackers from the Internet or to restrict their employees' access to the Internet. When email is allowed between the internal network and the Internet, the mail is often received at the firewall machine, which forwards it to its final destination. For more information about firewalls, see Brent Chapman and Elizabeth Zwicky's *Building Internet Firewalls* (O'Reilly & Associates, Inc.).

mail to see what you should expect. The SPAM-L FAQ is available from *http://bounce.to/spam-l.**

Relay sites

Another way spammers try to hide the source of their spam is by asking an unrelated system's Mail Transport Agent (MTA), rather than the spammer's own agent, to deliver the email. Although more and more MTAs are being configured to disallow this practice by accepting email only to or from a user at the MTA's site, a February 1998 survey by the Internet Mail Consortium (*http://www.imc.org*) found that 55% of the mail servers they tested were still open to abuse.

A relay site is generally easy to recognize from the "Received:" headers. If there's a relay in use, the headers will show your site receiving the message from the relay site and the relay site receiving the message from elsewhere, like this:

```
Received: from relay.site.org (RELAY.SITE.ORG [128.250.200.51])
          by araw.uic.edu (8.8.8/8.8.8) with ESMTP id PAA25284
          for <alansz@araw.uic.edu>; Mon, 23 Feb 1998 15:41:43 -0600 (CST)
Received: from spammer.evil.com (SPAMMER.EVIL.COM [129.23.99.26])
          by relay.site.org (8.8.5/8.8.5) with ESMTP id PAA17600
          for alansz@araw.uic.edu; Mon, 23 Feb 1998 15:37:15 -0600
```

Working backward, we see that *araw.uic.edu* received the message from *relay.site.org*. We know this header is accurate. We also see that *relay.site.org* received the message from *spammer.evil.com*. Either *relay* is being abused as a relay by *spammer.evil.com* or, if the second "Received:" header is bogus, the spam came from *relay.site.org*. Either way, we're going to want to let *relay*'s administrator know about this message.

There are many legitimate uses for email relaying. Most notably, in organizations where the users have desktop PCs that don't have their own MTAs, email from the PCs is relayed by a central mail server. The mail server must allow the PCs to relay messages, but should not allow unknown computers to do the same, lest a spammer take advantage of the server to hide his tracks.

The only way to be sure that a site allows relaying, however, is to test it by relaying a message to yourself. Here's how:

1. Connect to the site's SMTP (Simple Mail Transport Protocol) port, using your telnet program to telnet to port 25 on the site. You should see a response like:

```
220 relay.site.org ESMTP Sendmail 8.8.8/8.8.8; Wed, 25 Feb 1998
11:46:28 -0600 (CST)
```

---

* Note that *.to* isn't a typo; it's the top-level domain for the Kingdom of Tonga. *bounce.to*, however, is run by an Australian company.

2. Identify yourself to the site with the HELO command:

HELO mysite.mydomain
```
250 relay.site.org Hello mysite.mydomain [IP address]
```

3. Identify yourself as the mail sender with the MAIL FROM: command:

MAIL FROM: myname@mysite.mydomain
```
250 myname@mysite.mydomain... Sender ok
```

4. Ask to send email to yourself with the RCPT TO: command:

RCPT TO: myname@mysite.mydomain

If the remote site allows relaying, it will return a message like this:

```
250 myname@mysite.mydomain... Recipient ok
```

If relaying is prohibited, the message will read something like:

```
571 myname@mysite.mydomain... We do not relay
```

After you've received one of these messages, send the QUIT command to end the conversation without sending a message. The MAPS Transport Security Initiative web page (*http://maps.vix.com/tsi*) contains an online tool system administrators can use to check their own MTAs to ensure that they will not relay messages for anyone who asks.

 Testing a site for relaying may constitute theft of service from that site, particularly if you actually send a relayed message.

If you discover that a site is allowing open relaying, contact the site's *postmaster* (as described later in this chapter). It's quite likely that the site isn't aware that they are serving as an accessory to spam.

A real-life example

Here's an example of a real unsolicited commercial email message:*

```
From www.callb4u.com/phone/oleg.htm@kaja.octonline.com
     Mon Dec 29 03:28:51 1997
Received: from kaja.octonline.com ([207.6.35.100])
     by earth.solar.net (8.8.8/8.8.8) with ESMTP id DAA22945
     for <alansz@earth.solar.net>; Mon, 29 Dec 1997 03:28:46 -0600 (CST)
```

---

* Your mail or news reader may not show you all the message headers by default. There should be a command or option that allows you to see the headers in their entirety. This is crucial for tracking down the source of spam.

```
Received: from jusko.kaja ([209.29.187.214] (may be forged))
    by kaja.octonline.com (2.5 Build 2626 (Berkeley 8.8.6)/8.8.4)
    with SMTP id AAA02487; Mon, 29 Dec 1997 00:40:46 -0500
Message-Id: <199712290540.AAA02487@kaja.octonline.com>
Comments: Authenticated sender is <jusko@kaja.octonline.com>
From: "http://www.callb4u.com/phone/oleg.htm"
    <www.callb4u.com/phone/oleg.htm@octonline.com>
To: logic@octonline.com
Date: Mon, 29 Dec 1997 00:25:50 +0000
Subject: free international ..
Reply-to: truedate@octonline.com
X-Confirm-Reading-To: truedate@octonline.com
X-pmrqc: 1
Return-receipt-to: truedate@octonline.com
Priority: urgent
X-mailer: Pegasus Mail for Windows (v2.42a)
Status: RO
Content-Length: 4616
Lines: 113

>>>>  Here is the information  you've   requested . Best choice on the Net.

1) Take a break and join  INTERNATIONAL DATING CLUB -->> FREE .
   ...etc...
```

From what we've learned, only the "Received:" headers may be reliable.* It certainly appears that other headers have been forged: the "Reply-To:," "X-Confirm-Reading-To:," and "Return-receipt-to:" headers are likely forgeries. The email address listed in the "From" and "From:" headers isn't a legitimate Internet email address—the username has been replaced with a web address.

The first "Received:" header shows that *earth.solar.net* received this message from *kaja.octonline.com*, which has IP address 207.6.35.100. Because that header was added by *earth.solar.net*, it should be trustworthy. Therefore, the message probably came from *kaja.octonline.com*.†

The other "Received:" header claims to show that the message originated from a host called "jusko.kaja" and was only passed on by *kaja.octonline.com*. Since *.kaja* isn't a valid top-level domain, this must be the result of a misconfiguration (perhaps *jusko.kaja.octonline.com* is what's meant) or a forgery. In fact, the "Received:" header added by *kaja.octonline.com* even warns us that this host name may be a forgery. Is there a *jusko.kaja.octonline.com*?

---

* Some spammers have also started forging "Received:" headers to throw ambitious spam trackers off the trail. When looking at "Received:" headers, look carefully at dates. If a date seems wrong or the header seems otherwise suspicious, it may be a fraud.

† Strictly speaking, a computer could impersonate *kaja.octonline.com*, but its IP address would have to match *kaja*'s IP address because the receiving machine knows which IP address the data is coming from and can compare it to *kaja*'s registered IP address, by looking *kaja* up in the Domain Name System. This is possible to achieve, but very difficult to achieve reliably and beyond the means of most spammers.

The Unix *nslookup* program can look up a hostname in the Domain Name System (DNS). On other systems, the program may be called something else, or may be part of the *ping* program, but nearly all Internet software includes a utility that can do DNS lookups.* A lookup of *jusko.kaja.octonline.com* shows that there is no such host. What about that IP address, 209.29.187.214? Some DNS lookup programs can look up a DNS name from an IP address (a so-called *reverse lookup*) just by typing in the IP address. For others, you must reverse the address and add ".in-addr.arpa" (i.e., *214.187.29.209.in-addr.arpa*). It's not uncommon for reverse lookups to fail; people who manage name servers don't always remember to add reverse entries to their DNS tables. In this case, however, the reverse lookup succeeds. 209.29.187.214 is *ppp101-group1.toronto.octonline.com*, which, from its name, could be a PPP dial-up connection in *octonline.com*'s Toronto operation.

Perhaps the mail came from *jusko@kaja.octonline.com*, and jusko's mail software identified itself as *jusko.kaja*. This might be supported by the "Comments:" header. The Pegasus Mail program, which is free and thus popular with spammers, inserts the header `Comments: Authenticated sender is email address at which sender checks mail`. Moreover, Pegasus Mail does add an `X-mailer: Pegagus Mail . . .`, and such a header appears in this message. On the other hand, both of these headers are easily forged and can't be relied on.

From the headers alone, we've identified a likely suspect—whoever runs *kaja.octonline.com* is hosting this spammer or being used by him. If the latter, we know from the "Received:" headers the exact time at which the message passed to *kaja*, so *kaja*'s system administrator can track the message back further, particularly if the Message-Id is also legitimate. We also suspect—with less reliable evidence—that *jusko@kaja.octonline.com* may be the message sender.

The message body, by the way, included many different World Wide Web site URLs. The owners of these sites may be paying the spammer for the advertising, and they may not know they are going to get a bad reputation on the Net from this spam. If you choose to respond to the spam, they're good people to inform, as well.

The message also included the Ontario postal address of someone whose first name is Jusko (to whom you are asked to send money for a CD-ROM). Not every email message will be this informative or easy to trace, but in most cases, you can at least determine the site at which the message was injected and the address (postal or email) where the spammer would like to receive your inquiries or money.

---

* If you don't have any DNS lookup software, there are some sites on the World Wide Web that will do lookups for you. Try *http://consumer.net/tracert.asp*, or search *http://www.yahoo.com* for "DNS lookup."

Finding a Responsible Person

Using these techniques, you can usually identify the site from which the spam originated, as well as sites advertised in the message and sites that are being used as relays. If you want to complain about the message, or alert sites that they are being abused, how can you determine whom to contact at each site?

Verifying sites with DNS lookups

First, you'll have to separate real sites from phony sites. Spammers often forge headers so that they appear to be mailing from bogus sites. The easiest way to tell whether a site is a genuine Internet host is to perform a DNS lookup on its hostname, as described earlier. Here are the results of a DNS lookup of the web server for Williams College, *web.williams.edu*, using *nslookup*:

```
Non-authoritative answer:
web.williams.edu        internet address = 137.165.4.29

Authoritative answers can be found from:
williams.EDU    nameserver = lee.williams.EDU
williams.EDU    nameserver = lenox.williams.EDU
williams.EDU    nameserver = nic.near.net
lee.williams.EDU          internet address = 137.165.4.2
lenox.williams.EDU        internet address = 137.165.4.21
nic.near.net    internet address = 192.52.71.4
```

In addition to listing the site's Internet address (thus proving it is a real host), this *nslookup* listing includes information about which name servers are providing name service for the domain.* If you look up a spammer's host, knowing who provides name service may suggest who provides Internet service to the spammer.

In two cases, you won't see the site's IP address. First, the host you're looking up may not be a real host, but an alternative name for a real host. For example, a lookup of *www.williams.edu* returns this:

```
www.williams.edu  canonical name = web.williams.edu
```

This lets you know that the host's real name is *web.williams.edu*; a DNS lookup on that name should return the IP address information.

Another possibility is that the host you're looking up doesn't handle its own email—another host, called a *mail exchanger* or *MX* host, handles its email.

```
sjdm.org  preference = 10, mail exchanger = mail.sjdm.org
```

---

* You may have to set options in your lookup program to get it to show you name servers and other DNS information associated with a hostname. For *nslookup*, creating the *.nslookuprc* file in your home directory and adding the line `type=any` will do this.

Mail sent to *sjdm.org* is actually handled by *mail.sjdm.org*; a DNS lookup on that name should return its IP address. This arrangement is quite common when sites want email to *user@domain.com* to be passed to a central mail server.

Research domains with whois

If you have trouble finding the host in the DNS, another possibility is to look up the domain name in the InterNIC's domain name registry. The program or command for this lookup on most systems is called *whois*, or you can access the registry on the Web from *http://whois.internic.net/cgi-bin/whois*.

Here's an example of a *whois* lookup on *pennmush.org*:

```
Alan Schwartz (PENNMUSH-DOM)
    808 S. Wood St., 986 CME
    Chicago, IL 60612-7309
    US

    Domain Name: PENNMUSH.ORG

    Administrative Contact:
        Schwartz, Alan  (AS4130)  alansz@ARAW.MEDE.UIC.EDU
        (312) 996-2070 (FAX) (312) 413-2048
    Technical Contact, Zone Contact:
        Natvig, Thorvald  (TN752)  xeno@MIX.HIVE.NO
        +47 33 07 01 77
    Billing Contact:
        Schwartz, Alan  (AS4130)  alansz@ARAW.MEDE.UIC.EDU
        (312) 996-2070 (FAX) (312) 413-2048

    Record last updated on 20-Sep-97.
    Record created on 20-Sep-97.
    Database last updated on 12-May-98 03:41:01 EDT.

    Domain servers in listed order:

    BIMBO.HIVE.NO               128.39.114.191
    NS.SJDM.ORG                 128.248.90.226
    NS.SNUGHARBOR.COM           205.179.241.244
```

In addition to proving that *pennmush.org* is a registered domain name, we learn the email addresses of people responsible for the domain:

- The *administrative contact* is the person formally "in charge" of the domain. If you're being spammed from or about a domain and are looking for a person at the domain to complain to, the administrative contact may be a reasonable choice.

- The *technical contact* or *zone contact* is the person who's responsible for maintaining the DNS database for the domain. If an ISP provides name service, the ISP's personnel are usually listed as the technical contact. If you can't get action from the spamming site itself, complaining to its service provider may produce results, especially if spamming violates the provider's terms of service.

- The *billing contact* is the person who pays the $35 yearly registration fee for the domain. This person might also be responsive to complaints, since they're paying for the benefit of having the domain name and they'll suffer if it gets a bad reputation.

Postmasters

The people listed as DNS contacts may be responsible for assigning hostnames within the domain, but may not actually be the system administrators for the computers with those hostnames. For example, Thorvald Natvig is the DNS administrator for *pennmush.org*, and assigns names to all *pennmush.org* hosts, but doesn't actually manage the *www.pennmush.org* computer.

Any site that receives email should have an address called *postmaster* that delivers mail to the person responsible for email at the site. If the site is a news server, it should have an address called *news* or *usenet* that reaches the news administrator. Nearly all ISPs will have these addresses, and many also have an address called *abuse* for reporting abuse of their services.

If mail to *postmaster* bounces, you can use the DNS contact information to contact someone associated with the domain and inform them that the host doesn't have a *postmaster* alias. If the DNS contact information is also out of date, you can try to identify the host's ISP with *traceroute*, discussed in the next section.

Identifying service providers with traceroute

If the spammer has registered his own domain and runs his own name servers, all the *whois* contact information may direct you right back to the spammer. One way to make a good guess about who's providing Internet service to a spamming site is to see the route by which data travels to the site. The company that owns the last router before the spamming site may be providing the spammer's Internet service.

The *traceroute* (Unix) or *tracert.exe* (DOS/Windows) program, available in some form on most Internet-connected computers or through the World Wide Web at *http://consumer.net/tracert.asp*, provides a picture of how data travels through the network to reach the remote system. It's useful for learning about the structure of the Internet, diagnosing sluggish network connections or other problems, and determining who provides Internet service to a spamming site.

traceroute works by sending a data packet with a very short "time to live." When a router on the way to the remote system encounters a packet after its time to live has been exceeded, the router sends back a message notifying the originating

---

abuse.net

You've tracked down a spam to the site *some-isp.com*. Now to whom should you report the spam: *postmaster@some-isp.com* or *abuse@some-isp.com* or maybe *support@some-isp.com*? The best addresses to report junk mail or spam vary from provider to provider, and it's difficult to keep track of them. Fortunately, you don't have to. *abuse.net* does it for you.

abuse.net, the Network Abuse Clearinghouse, maintains a master list of abuse-reporting addresses for ISPs. Moreover, if you register with *abuse.net*, you can simply send email to *domain@abuse.net* (e.g., *some-isp.com@abuse.net*), and it will be forwarded to the appropriate abuse-reporting address, or to *postmaster* if *abuse.net* doesn't know a better address.

To register with *abuse.net*, send email to *news@abuse.net*. It will send back a message containing the terms of service for using *abuse.net* and instructions on how to register.

---

system of this fact. By gradually increasing the time to live on the packets and noting which routers send back notification, *traceroute* finds all the routers between your site and the remote system.

Here's the output of a traceroute to *www.nsf.gov* from a *uic.edu* host:

```
traceroute to www.nsf.gov (206.235.18.84), 30 hops max, 40 byte packets
 1  HSW.GW.UIC.EDU (128.248.89.1)  2 ms  2 ms  2 ms
 2  UIC-FDDI-16.GW.UIC.EDU (128.248.100.16)  3 ms  2 ms  3 ms
 3  207.227.0.177 (207.227.0.177)  4 ms  2 ms  3 ms
 4  207.112.247.141 (207.112.247.141)  43 ms  30 ms  42 ms
 5  mae-east.psi.net (192.41.177.245)  46 ms  44 ms  95 ms
 6  38.1.4.5 (38.1.4.5)  80 ms  56 ms  65 ms
 7  rc5.southeast.us.psi.net (38.1.25.5)  49 ms  64 ms  54 ms
 8  rc5.southeast.us.psi.net (38.1.25.5)  55 ms  82 ms  74 ms
 9  38.146.148.44 (38.146.148.44)  73 ms  56 ms  75 ms
10  ahaz.nsf.gov (206.2.78.9)  48 ms  41 ms  63 ms
11  www.nsf.gov (206.235.18.84)  48 ms  *  65 ms
```

Each line in the output represents a host through which the data passed. If the host has a DNS hostname, the name is shown; if not, its IP address is shown. Then the host's IP address is shown for all hosts. Finally, three times are listed: these are the round-trip times in milliseconds for packets to be returned from three attempts that reached the router.*

---

* A * signifies a case when a router didn't return a packet from the *ping* request.

The last line in the output is the site to which we're tracing the route. Reading backward, the first line that doesn't end in the same domain name (*nsf.gov* in our example) is usually the router that connects that site to the rest of the Internet. Although you may find that packets take different routes when you run *traceroute*s at different times, many smaller sites only have a single router between them and the Internet, so the routing information rarely changes.

In this example, we can see that *abaz.nsf.gov* receives packets from 38.146.148.44. We can use *whois* to try to determine who is responsible for this IP address by looking it up in one of the DNS registries. If we can't find an entry for that specific IP address, we can also try to look up a block of IP addresses that includes 38.146.148.44. A block of addresses is specified by replacing elements of the address, starting from the right, with zero: 38.146.148.0 represents the block of 255 addresses ranging from 38.146.148.1 to 38.146.148.255. Similarly, 38.146.0.0 is the much larger block of addresses ranging from 38.146.0.1 to 38.146.255.255.

The American Registry for Internet Numbers (ARIN) *whois* server, *whois.arin.net*, provides information about the owners of IP address blocks.* In this case, there's no entry for 38.146.148.44, 38.146.148.0, or 38.146.0.0, but there is an entry for 38.0.0.0:

```
% whois -h whois.arin.net 38.0.0.0
Performance Systems International (NET-PSINETA)
    510 Huntmar Park Drive
          Herndon, VA   22070

    Netname: PSINETA
    Netnumber: 38.0.0.0

    Coordinator:
        Network Information and Support Center   (PSI-NISC-ARIN)
        hostinfo@psi.com
        (518) 283-8860

    Domain System inverse mapping provided by:

    NS.PSI.NET                    192.33.4.10
    NS2.PSI.NET                   38.8.50.2
    NS5.PSI.NET                   38.8.5.2

    Record last updated on 21-Sep-94.
    Database last updated on 21-May-98 16:09:46 EDT.
```

It looks as if *nsf.gov* gets its Internet service from PSI, a major U.S. East Coast ISP that controls the allocation of all IP addresses beginning with 38.

---

* Check the documentation for your *whois* program to learn how to specify a different registry from InterNIC's, which is usually the default. For the Unix *whois* program, either whois -h *registry-host address-to-look-up* or whois *address-to-look-up@registry-host* usually works.

Whom to Talk To

Often you can send complaints to the spammer's sending address, the address of the site where the spam originated, addresses advertised in the spam, or the service providers for addresses advertised in the spam. When should you complain to each? Although there are no hard and fast rules, here are some suggestions:

- Complain to the *spammer's* sending address if you think it's a valid address and you think complaining will do more good than harm. For example, if it seems that the spammer genuinely might not know their spam is bad for you, for them, and for the Internet as a whole, you might complain to enlighten them. If the spammer claims that by replying to them you can be removed from their mailing list, you might reply on the off chance that they're telling the truth—this will save you from future spam. On the other hand, replying gives the spammer proof that your email address works and reaches a potential target for future spam; for this reason, America Online and many spam fighters suggest not replying to spammers. In addition, don't reply to the sender if you're afraid they'll strike back at you in some fashion.

- Complain to the *address advertised in the spam* under the same conditions. The company responsible for that address may have hired the spammer to send the advertisement, and may be relatively naive about spam. In any case, this address is likely to be valid, and the more complaints about their spam the spammer receives, the harder it will be for them to pick out any genuine responses to their ad.*

- Complain to the *abuse-reporting address of the site where the spam originated* anytime that it isn't obviously under the spammer's control. Often, sites don't realize they've got their mail server configured to allow anyone to relay mail through it. The administrators of these sites will usually be sympathetic and will want to secure their sites to prevent further abuse.

- Complaining to the *abuse-reporting address of the service provider of the advertised site* is a matter of taste. Some people prefer to save this only for the second or subsequent spams; others send their first complaints to the service provider as well as the spammer. The service provider is generally the organization with the most power over the spammer: it can restrict or terminate the spammer's account and even try to sue the spammer for damages.

---

* This is not to suggest that you should complain more than once about each email or posting that you receive—sending a barrage of messages could constitute harassment, which is illegal in many jurisdictions. Further, if you send so much email that the user or the site can no longer receive messages because its mailbox is full, you have probably committed an illegal denial-of-service attack. If everyone who received the spam message complains just once, however, the results should be sufficiently effective; spammers rarely enjoy having their own mailboxes full of unwanted (but not, in this case, unsolicited) email.

Other places to send spam

If the spammed message is itself illegal, consider sending a copy to a relevant government agency (see the sidebar entitled "U.S. Government Agencies").

U.S. Government Agencies

If the spam originated in the United States and violates a U.S. law, you may want to report it to one of these agencies:

- If the spam might constitute securities fraud, you can forward it to the Securities and Exchange Commission at *enforcement@sec.gov*.

- Consumer fraud, including pyramid schemes, can be reported to the Federal Trade Commission at *consumerline@ftc.gov* or *uce@ftc.gov*. In February 1998, the FTC began contacting companies and individuals who have messages that may constitute fraud and has initiated at least one civil lawsuit against a junk emailer. Consumer fraud can also be reported to the nonprofit National Fraud Information Center (NFIC) using their Internet Fraud Report Form at *http://www.fraud.org/info/repoform. htm*.

- Tax fraud can be reported to the Internal Revenue Service by calling your local IRS office.

- "Make Money Fast" chain letters can be reported to the IRS, as well, at *abuse@nocs.insp.irs.gov*. If the spammers ask for money to be sent by postal mail, they violate the Postal Lottery Act and can be reported to your local Postal Inspector's office.

- Advertisements for child pornography or other illegal businesses can be brought to the attention of the Federal Bureau of Investigation by calling your local FBI office.

Another place that spam sightings can be reported is the newsgroup *news.admin. net-abuse.sightings*. This newsgroup is robomoderated; all postings must follow a standard format in order to be accepted by the robomoderator. The formatting requirements are:

- Lines must be 78 characters long or shorter.

- The "Subject:" header should begin with a word enclosed in square brackets indicating the type of abuse. The most common are [UBE] for unsolicited bulk email, [UCE] for unsolicited commercial email, and [email] for other unwanted email messages. This is usually followed by the subject from the unwanted message.

- The "Followup-To:" header must list an appropriate, unmoderated *news. admin.net-abuse.* group, such as *news.admin.net-abuse.email* or *news.admin. net-abuse.misc.* These groups are discussed in Chapter 8, *Community Action*.

- The message must contain the full headers and body of the unwanted message.

Here's an example of a posting to *news.admin.net-abuse.sightings*:

```
From: Alan J. Claffie <aclaffie@bgnn.com>
Newsgroups: news.admin.net-abuse.sightings
Subject: [email] YOUR CLASSIFIED / 333 NEWSPAPERS !!!!!!!!!
Followup-To: news.admin.net-abuse.email
Date: 21 May 1998 11:58:46 GMT

Complaint sent to postmaster @ rmi.net, rkd @ rmi.net

[A copy of this complaint was posted to the newsgroup
news.admin.net-abuse.sightings]

If this was bounced off your mail server, I can't tell where it came
from. If this originated from your system, then you've got a luser to
kill.

Received: from shell.rmi.net (root@shell.rmi.net [166.93.8.17]) by
adams.berk.net (8.8.8/8.6.12) with SMTP id EAA02244 for
<aclaffie@bgnn.com>; Thu, 21 May 1998 04:23:11 -0400 (EDT)
From: sysop@hk.super.net
Received: from shell.rmi.net
        by shell.rmi.net with smtp
        (Smail-3.1.29.1 #11) id m0ycM2X-001BT2C; Wed, 20 May 98 21:29 MDT
Received: from sysop@hk.super.net by  (8.8.5/8.6.5) with SMTP id
GAA02435 for <>; Wed, 20 May 1998 23:23:29 -0600 (EST)
Date: Wed, 20 May 98 23:23:29 EST
To: Friend@public.com
Subject: YOUR CLASSIFIED / 333 NEWSPAPERS !!!!!!!!!
Message-ID: < <199804211656.JAA11443@hk.super.net>>
Comments: Authenticated sender is
<<199804211656.JAA11443@hk.super.net>>
X-UIDL: cb519e73365a3e54a6b51cc0a2173616
X-PMFLAGS: 33554560


> From:          sysop@hk.super.net
> Date:          Wed, 20 May 98 23:23:29 EST
> To:            Friend@public.com
> Subject:       YOUR CLASSIFIED / 333 NEWSPAPERS !!!!!!!!!

> YOUR AD IN 333 NEWSPAPERS !!!!!!!!!!
> *********************************************
spam message body continues
```

Before reporting sightings to *news.admin.net-abuse.sightings*, read the previous messages in the group and be sure that no one else has already reported the message in question. If it's already been reported, you may want to follow the discussion about the message in the follow-up group to learn how others are dealing with the abuse, or follow up the report yourself to explain actions you take.

Finally, America Online users should forward any junk mail they receive to the address *TOSSpam@aol.com*, especially if the mail appears to be from another AOL user.

What to Say

You've decided to whom you'll complain. What should you say? For maximum effect, complaints should:

- *Be polite.* Identifying spammers isn't a perfect science, and there's a chance that you might make a mistake and send an unwarranted complaint. Moreover, when you're sending copies of complaints to system administrators, they respond much more favorably to polite, informative complaints that don't demand a particular response.

- *Include the offending message, with all headers.* Message headers are crucially important in helping a system administrator track down the message sender in log files.

- *Assert that the message is harmful.* Indicate that the message was unsolicited and that you do not want to receive unsolicited email. Explain how spam harms you, and state that you will never do business with a company that uses spam in its advertising.

- *Offer alternatives.* Mention *http://www.sendmail.org/antispam.html* and *http://maps.vix.com/tsi* to a site that's being used as a relay for junk mail.

- *Cite applicable laws, if any.* If the message violates a law in your country or state, say so. Ideally, provide a specific reference.

Here's a sample response to unsolicited commercial email:

```
TO THE SENDER:

I have received unsolicited commercial email from you.

I have to pay for my email, like most people. My private email
facilities are not your advertising medium. You abused my resources
and wasted my time, which is valuable to me.

You are shifting the cost of your advertisement to your recipients,
without their permission. That's like sending your junk postal mail
postage-due, or like telemarketing collect. Or sending a junk
```

fax—oops, those were made illegal in the United States (under the Federal Telephone Consumer Protection Act of 1991). Why? Because the Congress and the courts felt that forcing the recipient to pay the cost of advertising was wrong. I agree. Therefore, I will never do business with you or anyone associated with you. Any further communication from you will be considered harassment, and will be dealt with accordingly.

I will also be informing your Internet Service Provider of your abuse of resources. All legitimate ISPs prohibit this sort of abuse.

TO THE POSTMASTER:

A user on your system has sent me (and apparently many others) the included unsolicited commercial email. You are being contacted either because the message originated at your site, used your SMTP mailer, has replies directed to your site, or solicited visits to a web page hosted by your site.

Even if the sender purports to honor requests to remove my address from their unwelcome mailing list, that does not make this cost-shifting acceptable—I did not sign up to any sort of LISTSERV or Majordomo list in the first place, nor did I request any information from this user. It is abuse and forgery to put someone's email address on a mailing list without their permission or knowledge.

Likewise, if the sender's message claims that I will receive no other messages from them, it is still completely unacceptable that I (and other recipients) have been forced to subsidize the cost of this advertisement. I have received nothing of value in return for this unauthorized commercial use of my email resources.

I respectfully request that you, as sysop, take whatever steps are necessary to prevent this from happening to me or anyone else again.

Thanks.

If the spam was a chain letter, you might add:

This sort of chain letter is a pyramid scheme, which in turn is a form of fraud. It violates a U.S. federal statute, 18 U.S.C. sec. 1343, which reads:

"Whoever, having devised or intending to devise any scheme or artifice to defraud, or for obtaining money or property by means of false or fraudulent pretenses, representations, or promises, transmits or causes to be transmitted by means of wire, radio, or television communication in interstate or foreign commerce, any writings, signs, signals, pictures, or sounds for the purpose of executing such scheme or artifice, shall be fined not more than $1,000 or imprisoned not more than five years, or both. If the violation affects a financial institution, such person shall be fined not more than $1,000,000 or imprisoned not more than 30 years, or both."

```
If at any point the U.S. Mail is used, you also violate 18 U.S.C. sec.
1302, the Postal Lottery Statute. See

    http://www.usps.gov/websites/depart/inspect/chainlet.htm

This sort of chain letter is outlawed in Canada under the Section 206(1)(e)
of the Criminal Code and under Section 55 of the Competition Act.
```

Spam canceler Chris Lewis prefers to just send the text of the U.S. Postal Service web site verbatim. Phil Agre's article, "How to Complain About Spam, or Put a Spammer in the Slammer," available at *http://dlis.gseis.ucla.edu/people/pagre/spam.html*, offers other useful tips about what to say in response to unwanted messages.

Responding by phone

Doug Muth and others offer the following suggestions in the SPAM-L Frequently Asked Questions List:

```
Calling an ISP voice is one of the best ways for dealing with spamming
problems involving their site. For one thing, a phone call will get an
ISP's attention much more than an email will as phone calls generally
take more time. Any legit business will always take the time to listen
to complaints against them.

When calling an ISP voice, you should be sitting in front of your
system with all the necessary information handy before you place the
phone call. Nothing frustrates an anti-spam ISP more than a clueless
complaint.

Keeping calm and collected also cannot be emphasized enough. If you
call up an ISP and start yelling at them, they will brush you off as
some sort of lunatic instead of taking your complaint seriously...

A good place to get ISP phone numbers from is either by using
whois or by visiting [http://www.]thelist.com
```

 If you're tempted to call an 800 number listed in a spam, you should do so from a pay phone. Even if you have call blocking on your home phone, 800-number subscribers can always see the phone number from which they receive a call.

Responses to avoid

Although it's often tempting, never deluge a spammer with repeated or enormous responses. This tactic, called *mailbombing*, makes you liable for a charge of harassment from the spammer and is an illegal denial-of-service attack against the spammer's provider, since it may bring down the provider's mail system. A good rule of thumb is to send no more than one message per unwanted message.

Similarly, don't make threats in your responses. Threatening email also leaves you open to civil and criminal actions. Remember, you might have made a mistake in your identification of the spammer.

Automating the Process

Most of the work of tracking down and replying to an unwanted message can be automated, and some useful programs make complaining about spam a snap. Here is a smattering of currently available programs that may work for you; because each operates differently, there is no single "right" program for everyone.

The Spam Bouncer

A set of *procmail* recipes by Catherine Hampton that recognize spam email using a list of known spammers and spam sites, and analysis of the message headers and body. In additional to filtering, the Spam Bouncer can automatically notify upstream providers, send a fake "bounced mail" message back to the spammer, and do other tricks. The Spam Bouncer is updated regularly in an attempt to keep pace with new spamming software. Available at *http://www.best.com/~ariel/nospam*.

Antispam

A utility for Microsoft Exchange that generates automatic complaints about spam messages that you select. Available at *http://www.bsitech.com/antispam/antispam.zip*.

Spam Hater

A Windows program that generates automatic complaints about unwanted email or news postings. It works directly with a wide assortment of commonly used Windows Internet software, including America Online, Eudora, Netscape, and Pegasus Mail, and works with other software via the clipboard. It can also perform *whois* and *traceroute* searches. Available at *http://www.cix.co.uk/~net-services/spam/spam_hater.htm*.

adcomplain

A Perl script by Bill McFadden that generates complaints via *abuse.net* about unwanted email or news postings, with special text for "Make Money Fast" chain letters. Available at *http://agora.rdrop.com/users/billmc/adcomplain.html*.

mspam

A Perl script by John Levine that generates complaints via *abuse.net* about unwanted email messages. Available at *http://www.abuse.net/mspam.txt*. A modified version is available from Dougal Campbell at *http://advicom.net/~dougal/antispam/mymspam.txt*.

jmfilter

John Harvey's *jmfilter* is a complete spam filtering and responding system that automatically blocks future messages from users that it receives spam from and sends them and their administrators a complaint. It uses a sophisticated scoring system based on both header and body content. It's available at *http://www.io.com/˜johnbob/jm/jmfilter.html*.

Just as forged headers can confuse people about the source of spam, they can also confuse these programs at times. It's always wise to double-check the addresses to which the program intends to send complaints and ensure that they're the addresses you'd choose.

6

A User's Guide
to Usenet Spam

The ideal Usenet newsgroup may be a lively discussion, a central place to post important announcements, or a source of cogent solutions to readers' problems. Spam wrecks newsgroups by overshadowing interesting, on-topic, and useful postings with useless "noise." In this chapter, we look at what you can do to reduce the amount of spam on Usenet newsgroups.

Filtering News

It's often possible to reduce the volume of spam in a newsgroup with some kind of filtering—screening out spam and possibly even off-topic postings and keeping the useful messages. Someone, or some program, may already be filtering the newsgroup or newsgroup hierarchy you're interested in to remove spam and misplaced binary postings. But often you can establish your own filters as well.

Moderation

The easiest way to avoid unwanted messages in newsgroups is to have someone else filter the group for you. *Moderated newsgroups* are newsgroups in which a moderator (or a group of moderators) decides whether to accept or reject each posting. Because the moderator rejects postings that are off-topic, moderated newsgroups are usually of high quality. Usenet moderators are almost always unpaid volunteers.

For example, in the one-year period from April 1997 to April 1998, the moderator for the newsgroup *rec.games.mud.announce* approved 1,062 messages, rejected 708 messages as on-topic but incomplete, and rejected about 425 off-topic postings and 103 "Make Money Fast" (MMF) chain letters. Roughly 25% of the messages sent to this group were spam; less than 50% of the messages sent met with the moderator's approval and were posted. Readers of the newsgroup see only the approved messages.

Two variations on moderation are robomoderation and retromoderation. A *robo-moderated newsgroup* is a moderated group in which the moderator is a computer program instead of or in addition to a human being. In a robomoderated group, the human moderator sets up a computer program to approve or reject articles. Typically, a robomoderator maintains a list of preapproved posters and accepts any posting from a preapproved poster. It also maintains a list of banned posters and rejects any posting from a banned poster. New posters who aren't on either list have their messages passed on to the human moderator or bounced back with a password to use to submit their first article and join the preapproved list.

Retromoderation, on the other hand, is the practice of "cleaning up" unmoderated groups by issuing cancel messages for off-topic postings. Retromoderation is extremely controversial—because the newsgroup was chartered as unmoderated, few people recognize a retromoderator's right to impose her will on the group.

Moderated newsgroups offer relatively spam-free environments for announcements and discussion; it's not surprising that the rise in the amount of spam has been paralleled by more and more moderated newsgroups—even many previously unmoderated newsgroup hierarchies are reorganizing to add moderated groups. Moderation does have its disadvantages, however. Human-moderated groups rarely have the lively feel of unmoderated groups, due to the time lag between when an article is sent to the moderator and when the moderator approves it for posting. Although robomoderation can alleviate this problem, robomoderators are not as adept at rejecting off-topic postings or enforcing substantive aspects of the newsgroup's charter.

Killfiles

Killfiles are filters built into news reader software. They typically allow you to kill or select messages based on their subject, author, or the discussion thread* they appear in. A killed message is treated as if you'd already read it—it's still available to you, but it won't appear in your article listing by default. A selected message appears highlighted in some fashion.

Some Windows and Macintosh news readers let you create killfiles with dialog boxes. Figure 6-1 shows how a filter to kill messages with the subject "MAKE MONEY FAST" can be added via the "Tools/Newsgroup Filters/Add" dialog box in Microsoft Outlook Express. Figure 6-2 shows the Newsgroup Filters window after the filter has been added.

---

* A *thread* is an initial article and any articles posted as follow-ups to the initial article, follow-ups to the follow-ups, etc. Intuitively, a thread usually represents a discussion. Technically, a thread is constructed by the news reader based on the "Message-ID:" and "References:" headers in articles.

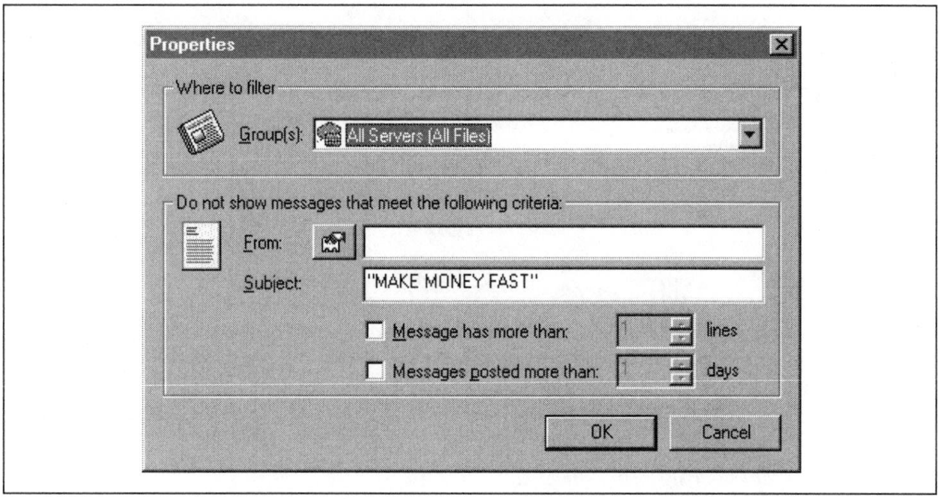

Figure 6-1: Adding a killfile entry in Outlook Express

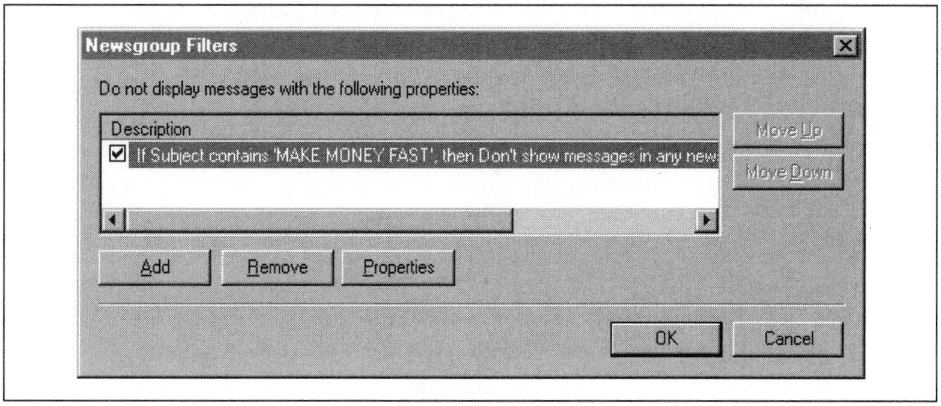

Figure 6-2: The Newsgroup Filters window in Outlook Express

Other PC news readers offer simpler *mark thread* and *kill thread* commands. For example, Free Agent 1.11, a popular freeware Windows news reader, offers "Watch Thread" and "Ignore Thread" options. Figure 6-3 shows how the options are used. Netscape Collabra appears to use the same "Mail Filters" dialog box to watch and ignore newsgroup threads as it uses for mail filtering. See Chapter 5, *A User's Guide to Email Spam*, for an example of mail filtering with Netscape's Communicator suite.

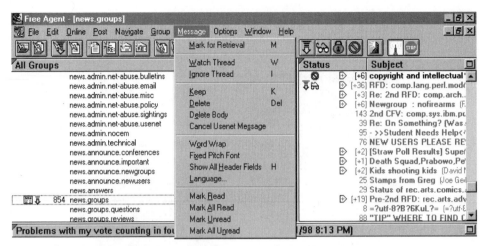

Figure 6-3: Watching or ignoring threads in Free Agent 1.11

Unix news readers are apt to use files of instructions as killfiles, allowing the user either to use *mark thread* and *kill thread* commands to add instructions to the files, or to actually edit the files themselves. The format of the killfiles is described in the news reader's manual page.

For example, here's part of a *trn* news reader killfile for *news.groups*, the news-group devoted to proposing, discussing, and voting on new newsgroups:

```
/CFV/:+
/perl/:T+
*X
```

The first two lines match regular expression patterns in the Subject lines of articles. `/CFV/` matches the letters "CFV" ("call for votes" in Usenet parlance); the `:+` instructs *trn* to select these articles for reading. Similarly, the next line instructs *trn* to select the entire message thread when the subject contains "perl." The final line tells *trn* to kill anything that hasn't been selected. The end result is that the reader sees articles only with subjects containing "CFV" or in threads with subjects containing "perl" when reading *news.groups*.

trn also has a global killfile that is applied to every article in every newsgroup. Here's what Alan's looks like:

```
/,.*,.*,.*,.*,.*,.*,.*,.*,.*,.*,/HNewsgroups:,
```

The regular expression matches a line that contains at least 12 commas. The `HNewsgroups:` instructs the news reader to look for this pattern in the "News-group:" header. The final comma (`,`) instructs the news reader to kill matching articles. This killfile entry thus serves as a filter against excessive cross-posting. Alan doesn't want to read any article that's been cross-posted to more than 12 groups—such articles are rarely on-topic. The number 12 is arbitrary; you might have a higher or lower threshold for cross-posting.

You can use your news reader's killfile capability to automatically select discussions that interest you and kill those that don't. You can also use it to reduce the amount of spam you have to deal with by instructing your news reader to kill articles by spammers whenever it sees them, but this requires that you get a list of spammer addresses (see Chapter 7, *Spam Stopping for Administrators and ISPs*, for information about how you might do this) or add them to the killfile individually, as you see spam posted. It may be more effective to try to eliminate spam based on the article's subject. If your news reader allows you kill articles based on patterns in the "Subject:" header, some things to look for include:

- Subjects in ALL CAPITALS

- Subjects with many !!! or $$$

- Subjects that mention "money fast" (as in "make money fast," "earn money fast," etc.

As always, be aware that when you automatically kill articles based on a simplistic rule, you run the risk of accidently hiding a message you would like to see.

NoCeM

Maintaining a useful killfile can be time-consuming. Wouldn't it be nice if you could just follow the advice of someone you trust and let them decide which articles should be marked already read (and thus hidden)?

NoCeM (pronounced "No-See-Um") is a way for anyone to suggest articles that should be hidden and for anyone to use those suggestions. Well, not quite anyone—NoCeM is currently available only for use with the AOL news reader (see later in this chapter), *rn*-like Unix news readers, and the GNU Emacs news reader.* NoCeM was invented by Cancelmoose; you can find out more about it at Cancelmoose's web site, *http://www.cm.org*.

Here's how NoCeM works. A NoCeM issuer posts a NoCeM notice to the newsgroup *news.lists.filters*. A typical NoCeM notice looks like this:

```
Newsgroups: news.lists.filters
From: rec.games.mud.admin NoCeM issuer <rgma-nocem@pennmush.tinymush.org>
Organization: rgma-nocem
Subject: NoCeM notice rgma-7392-880741507 in newsgroup @@rec.games.mud.admin
```

---

* Because NoCeM is written in Perl, it probably wouldn't be difficult to make it work with Windows news readers that use a newsgroup file format similar to the Unix *.newsrc* file (such as Netscape and WinVN). As of this writing, however, nobody has ported the system.

```
-----BEGIN PGP SIGNED MESSAGE-----


This is an automatically generated NoCeM ("no-see-um") notice for
the newsgroup rec.games.mud.admin. This notice is generated for
postings which do not have subject lines that meet the rgm.admin
posting guidelines. The guidelines are available at
http://pennmush.tinymush.org/~nocem/guidelines.txt

This is a NoCeM notice - it is purely advisory and does not
cancel the message listed below. It's a convenience for Usenet
readers who may choose to mark these articles as "already read."

@@BEGIN NCM HEADERS
Version: 0.93
Issuer: rec.games.mud.admin NoCeM issuer <rgma-nocem@pennmush.tinymush.org>
Type: bad-subject
Action: hide
Newsgroup: rec.games.mud.admin
Count: 3
Notice-ID: rgma-7392-880741507
@@BEGIN NCM BODY
<346558A5.39C6ED6F@hooked.net>          rec.games.mud.admin
<634sif$d5i$1@elektron.et.tudelft.nl> rec.games.mud.admin
<346587B8.21B6@concentric.net>          rec.games.mud.admin
@@END NCM BODY


-----BEGIN PGP SIGNATURE-----
Version: 2.6.2

iQCVAwUBNH8MhaypDMJ/DQthAQF5FwQAq7YJ7qddAldo2cLMSS0sSRVG6F59li1e
9XNaEAx2V79EAOvSlg+cCHmhqPSMu2+bTr/d37TUyxSc2cxuE8aWbL5ZovP7NBZ9
leWbAGjKHWpkfUXQOoHDeEaFes1A5aWCAs4NxHZ3GVPrBiRdDvzzSBNlslQENyJW
jt6N7FlYS+M=
=eYQR
-----END PGP SIGNATURE-----
```

The NoCeM notice gives some information about the issuer and then lists the Message-IDs of messages that the issuer recommends marking as already read. The notice is signed using the issuer's PGP key; this ensures that the notice really came from the issuer and hasn't been modified or tampered with.*

Using NoCeM

The NoCeM client software reads *news.lists.filters*, looking for NoCeM notices. When it finds a notice, it checks the PGP signature against a list of issuers from

---

* PGP stands for "Pretty Good Privacy." Despite its modest name, PGP is the de facto Internet standard for securely encrypting or digitally signing messages. For more information about PGP, see Simson Garfinkel's *PGP: Pretty Good Privacy* (O'Reilly & Associates, Inc.) or *The Official PGP User's Guide*, by Philip Zimmermann, author of PGP (MIT Press).

whom you have chosen to accept NoCeM notices. If a notice is by an issuer whose notices you honor, NoCeM modifies your news reader's files to mark the messages as read, and you don't see them when you read news.

If you're using a Unix news reader or GNU emacs, you choose whose notices you want to honor: your system administrator's, your girlfriend's, a well-known news administrator who issues notices for binaries posted to nonbinary newsgroups— it's up to you.

America Online users can also take advantage of the most important NoCeM notices by checking the "Filter Junk Posts" checkbox on the "Set Preferences" dialog box in the "Newsgroups" section. When you turn on filtering, AOL applies NoCeMs issued by the dozen or so most active anti-spam issuers, greatly reducing the number of unwanted messages you'll see.* In addition, AOL issues and applies its own NoCeM notices for its internal newsgroups, hiding spam, advertisements, off-topic postings, test messages, and duplicate postings. Figure 6-4 shows the "Global Newsgroup Preferences" dialog box.

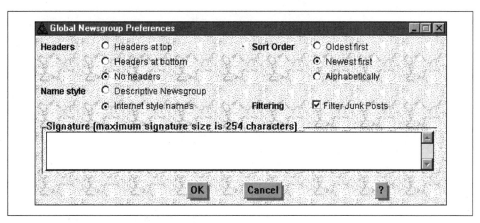

Figure 6-4: Filtering junk posts on AOL

Who issues NoCeMs?

People issue NoCeM notices for different reasons. Many spam cancelers issue NoCeM notices for the spam they cancel; other despammers issue NoCeM notices for articles that don't meet the spam threshold of BI >= 20, but that still have a BI greater than 10 or 15. (Chapter 2, *The History of Spam*, describes the BI, or Breidbart Index.) In addition, a number of individuals issue NoCeM notices for off-topic postings in specific newsgroups or hierarchies.

---

* In fact, a look at AOL's newsgroups list shows, for each group, both the total number of messages in the group and the number filtered out as junk. You quickly appreciate the junk post filter when you compare these numbers.

Rosalind Hengeveld maintains a registry of NoCeM issuers at *http://www.xs4all.
nl/~rosalind/nocemreg/nocemreg.html*. The registry lists many NoCeM issuers and
their issuing policies (which are often also posted to *news.admin.nocem*). The
NoCeM Registry also indicates which NoCeM notices are suitable for use "on-
spool." NoCeM-on-spool is software that allows news administrators to apply
NoCeM notices to incoming news articles and to delete offending articles before
they can be stored in the news database. Even if you don't use a news reader that
supports NoCeM, your ISP may be using NoCeM notices to filter out spam for you.

NoCeM versus cancel

NoCeM notices are sometimes confused with cancel messages, particularly with
the advent of NoCeM-on-spool. They're different.

Canceling an article always removes it from the news server's database, completely
and irrevocably. Only the author of an article is supposed to cancel it. The conditions under which third parties may issue cancel messages that the news system
will accept are strict; they're discussed later in this chapter.

A NoCeM notice, if accepted by an individual user and not applied "on-spool,"
simply marks messages as read by that user. The messages remain on the news
spool, and the user can still read them by asking her news software to show her
already read articles. Anyone can issue a NoCeM notice.

When NoCeM notices are applied "on-spool," they do function like cancel messages. But a big advantage of NoCeM-on-spool over cancels is that NoCeM notices
are authenticated with the issuer's PGP key—it's not possible to forge a NoCeM
notice, and the news administrator who accepts one always knows from whom it
came. In addition, a single NoCeM notice can be used to hide multiple articles (e.
g., all 200 copies of a spam). The same is not true of cancel messages: they can be
forged, and a separate cancel message must be transmitted for each article to be
canceled. For these reasons, many believe that NoCeM will one day replace cancel messages entirely.

Responding to Spam

Filtering can be effective at keeping Usenet spam out of your news reader, but you
can also address the problem at the source by taking action against spam and the
spammer. In this section, we show you how to track down the originating site of a
Usenet spam and complain about the spam to the site's ISP or issue your own cancel message or NoCeM notice.

Tracing Spam

To illustrate the process of determining the source of a news article, consider the example article in Chapter 4, *Internet Basics*, as read from *sales.some-domain.org*:

```
Path: news.some-domain.org!news.solar.net!earth.solar.net!you
From: you@earth.solar.net
Newsgroups: rec.puzzles.crosswords
Subject: Help with NY Times 5/10 puzzle?
Date: 10 May 1998 18:08:58 GMT
Message-ID: <19980510180858.1230@earth.solar.net>
NNTP-Posting-Host: earth.solar.net
Xref: news.some-domain.org rec.puzzles.crosswords:36449

Does anyone know the answer to 1-down in the 5/10 NY Times puzzle?
```

In this news article, there are four indications of the originating site:

- The "From:" header lists *you@earth.solar.net* as the poster, and if this is a legitimate news article, that's likely to be correct.* But this header can be set to any value that resembles an email address, so it's not always a reliable indicator of the originating site.

- The "Message-ID:" header has a similar deficiency; it can be set by the poster and thus isn't totally trustworthy.

- The "NNTP-Posting-Host:" header is usually added by the first host to receive the message by NNTP and set to the hostname of the posting host. But this header, too, can be forged, or the posting host might be an open NNTP server (see the section "Open NNTP servers" later in this chapter). Accordingly, the "NNTP-Posting-Host" header cannot always be trusted.

- The "Path:" header shows that the article originated from *earth.solar.net* and traveled through *news.solar.net* on the way to *news.some-domain.org*, from which we read it. A spammer can't forge an entire "Path:" header, because once the article leaves the spammer's control, news sites that receive it add their names to the front of the path. In short, we can work through the path from the leftmost news system—ours—rightward, to news systems that had the article before we did. If we can verify each step in the Path, we can track the message back to its origin.

Spammers don't want you to track them down and complain about their activities. Accordingly, they often use three tactics to confuse would-be complainants: forging article headers, adding bogus sites to the end of the Path, and posting through open NNTP servers. We describe these in the following sections.

---

* Unless the poster is munging his/her address to avoid junk mail, as discussed in Chapter 5.

Forging headers

Most headers in news articles can be forged by the poster. As with junk mail, an experienced spammer will try to ensure that all the headers either give a consistent but incorrect impression of the originating site or present a panoply of different possible originating sites to engender confusion. Moreover, a spammer may try to forge the headers to implicate another user specifically, in order to damage the user's reputation. Here's a simple example:

```
Path: popocat.d-and-d.com!news7.digex.net!digex!erinet.com!inquo!
      news.alt.net!su-news-hub1.bbnplanet.com!news.bbnplanet.com!
      newsfeed.direct.ca!news-xfer.netaxs.com!news-xfer.epix.net!
      nntp.epix.net!epix-news
From: xrated_videofeeds.com <webmaster@xrated_videofeeds.com>
Newsgroups: rec.music.makers.saxophone,rec.music.makers.songwriting,
            rec.music.makers.squeezebox,rec.music.makers.synth
Subject: !~Free X-Rated Videofeeds
Date: 12 May 98 14:09:20 +0000
Organization: xrated_videofeeds.com
Lines: 3
Message-ID: <8c57.c710.35c@default>
Reply-To: webmaster@xrated_videofeeds.com
NNTP-Posting-Host: qrv1209-74-47ppp49.epix.net
X-Newsposter: AtomicPost/32 (http://204.57.78.110) Registered
X-No-Archive: Yes
content-length: 83
Xref: popocat.d-and-d.com rec.music.makers.saxophone:9460 rec.music.makers.
+     songwriting:29613 rec.music.makers.squeezebox:16412 rec.music.makers.
+     synth:77304
etc.
```

The "Path:" header suggests that the message originated from a customer of *epix. net*, as does the "NNTP-Posting-Host:," but the "From:" and "Message-ID:" headers have been forged in an attempt to disguise the source of the article.

Adding bogus sites to the Path

A more sophisticated spammer, knowing that the "Path:" header is the surest clue to the source of an article, may try to hide by adding sites to the end of the Path. For example, a spam posting from *some-isp.com* might normally result in a Path like this:

```
Path: news.some-domain.org!news.solar.net!some-isp.com!not-for-mail
```

To make it more difficult to track down the spam, the spammer might post the article with a Path initially set to:

```
Path: fakesite.com!not-for-mail
```

By the time this article is read at *some-domain.org*, the Path contains:

```
Path: news.some-domain.org!news.solar.net!some-isp.com!fakesite.com!
    not-for-mail
```

The spammer couldn't prevent *some-isp.com* from adding itself to the Path, but has now implicated *fakesite.com*, the rightmost host, and buried the true originating site in the middle of the Path.

We can detect this tactic if we know that even though *news.some-domain.org* does receive news from *news.solar.net*, and *news.solar.net* does receive news from *some-isp.com*, *some-isp.com* does *not* exchange news with *fakesite.com*. We could then conclude that the article was actually sent from *some-isp.com*.

How would you know that *fakesite.com* doesn't feed *some-isp.com*? You can observe the paths that (unforged) news articles have taken in the past. AltaVista's (*http://www.altavista.digital.com*) Usenet search will show you the Paths that articles take to reach AltaVista if you click on the "B" (download binaries) link next to articles you find with it; unfortunately, you can't search by the "Path:" header itself.

If the article is being posted from an open NNTP server (see the next section), you could connect to the server and ask for a copy of the article as the server sees it. If that server sends back an article with a preinitialized and misleading "Path:" header, it's pretty solid proof of Path forgery.

Here's a recent example discovered by Dave Ritz and reported to *news.admin.net-abuse.sightings*. Dave connected to the open NNTP server and retrieved the spam article. He received these headers:

```
From: nobody@nowhere33.yet
Newsgroups: alt.sex
Subject: the (*R)(*A)(*P)(E*)  site 47139
Message-ID: <10059813.3538@nowhere33.yet>
Date: Sunday, 10 May 1998 13:35:38 -0600
Organization: <no organization>
NNTP-Posting-Host: 204.189.163.115
X-Trace: 10 May 1998 01:36:04 -0600, 204.189.163.115
Lines: 4
Path: news.mci2000.com!nowhere33.yet
```

Note that the Path has been set to *news.mci2000.com!nowhere33.yet*, implicating MCI, although the article had not been received from MCI. The "NNTP-Posting-Host:" header is also forged to appear to be from an MCI site.

Finally, you can ask *some-isp.com*'s news administrator; this is probably your best source of information.

Here's another example. Try to figure out the source of this article before you read
further:

```
From: bca34@hotmail.com
Subject: Win Cash, Win Cash, Win Cash (easily)
Date: Mon, 09 Feb 1998 12:13:31 -0600
Message-ID: <887046639.1093402632@dejanews.com>
Newsgroups: alt.bitterness,alt.biz.misc,alt.butts,
            alt.callahans,alt.comedy-standup
Organization: Deja News Posting Service
Path: news1.ee.net!news2.ee.net!news-chi-1.sprintlink.net!
      news-east.sprintlink.net!news-peer.sprintlink.net!
      news.sprintlink.net!Sprint!newsfeed.nacamar.de!
      newsfeed.ecrc.net!nntp2.dejanews.com!grunt.dejanews.com!not-for-mail
X-Article-Creation-Date: Mon Feb 09 17:50:39 1998 GMT
X-Authenticated-Sender: bca34@hotmail.com
X-Http-User-Agent: Mozilla/4.03 [en] (Win95; I)
X-Originating-IP-Addr: 204.32.158.113 (mod-ca3-17.ix.netcom.com)
Xref: news1.ee.net alt.bitterness:58601 alt.butts:21619
      alt.callahans:227311

Win Cash, Win Cash, Win Cash (easly)
etc
```

The "From:" header suggests a user at *hotmail.com*, but because you can't post
news from *hotmail.com*, that can't be the site from which the article was posted.
Nevertheless, *bca34@hotmail.com* is a viable candidate for some kind of anti-spam
action.

The "Organization:" and "Message-ID:" headers suggest that the message was
posted from DejaNews (*http://www.dejanews.com*), a web-based news reading and
posting service. A look at DejaNews' information for posters reveals that
DejaNews adds the headers "X-Article-Creation-Date:," "X-Http-User-Agent:," and
"X-Originating-IP-Addr:" when it posts articles. The "X-Originating-IP-Addr:" suggests that the connection to DejaNews was made from a *netcom.com* dial-up
modem.

In addition, DejaNews requires people who wish to post to register with a working email address at which they can receive replies, and it always inserts this
address as the "From:" header. A plausible interpretation of these headers is that
the sender dialed up to *netcom.com*, created an email address at *hotmail.com*,
used that to register at DejaNews, and posted the spam using DejaNews.

Both DejaNews and Hotmail are serious about keeping people from spamming;
complaints to them with the header information will likely result in the user's losing the Hotmail account and its DejaNews posting privileges. Of course, it's trivial
for the spammer to get another Hotmail account and reregister with DejaNews, so
informing Netcom, the spammer's service provider, is also important.

It's not impossible, however, that this interpretation could be wrong. A sufficiently clever spammer operating from *ecrc.net* or *nacamar.de* could have forged all the previous headers, including forging the Path by adding likely-looking DejaNews sites.

Open NNTP servers

As a public service, some sites run their news servers configured to allow anyone on the Internet to read news from them. Although this isn't normally a problem, some of these open NNTP servers also allow anyone to *post* news from them, which makes them particularly attractive to spammers seeking to hide their tracks.

News posted from an open NNTP server appears to originate from that server: the NNTP-Posting-Host, the Message-ID, and the Path can list the open server's address. If you trace spam back to an open server, it's a good idea to contact the news administrator at the server (try *news@site*, *usenet@site* or see Chapter 5 to learn how to locate this person). She may not know that her server is being abused. Once informed, she can disable open posting and may be able to track down the spammer from news server log files.

Recall from Chapter 4 that news servers receive news in two ways: from news readers via the `POST` command and from other news servers via the `IHAVE` command. Either can be abused by spammers. How can you determine whether an NNTP server allows open posting?

The NNTP port is 119; telnet to a news server's port 119 should result in one of the following:

- If the server does not allow open access at all, even to read news, you should see a message like:

  ```
  502 You have no permission to talk. Goodbye.
  ```

- If the server allows open access for reading, but not posting, you'll get a banner beginning with "201" from the server that looks something like:

  ```
  201 InterNetNews NNRP server INN 1.4 22-Dec-93 ready (no posting).
  ```

- If the server allows open posting, you'll get a banner begining with "200," like this:

  ```
  200 NNTP Service Version:5.0.0.7739 Posting Allowed
  ```

The only way to determine whether a server allows open `IHAVE` access is to try issuing an `IHAVE` command and see if it responds with a request for the article.

Connecting to other organizations' news servers to determine
whether they allow open posting or `IHAVE` access may violate your
terms of service with your ISP or may be illegal, particularly if you
actually post an article to the server.

Complaining About Spam

A straightforward way to respond to a Usenet spam is to complain about it by
sending email to the spammer or the spammer's ISP. Since most ISPs have policies
that prohibit their users from sending inappropriate messages, including spam to
newsgroups, this can be an effective way to stop a spammer. News administrators
are expressly authorized to cancel any inappropriate postings originating from
their site.

Whom to talk to

Once you've determined the spammer's posting site, you can send email to *abuse,
usenet,* or *news* at the site, or take advantage of *abuse.net,* described in Chapter 5.
You can also complain directly to the spammer or to sites advertised in the spam.
When should you complain to each?

- Complain to the *spammer's* posting address if you think it's a valid address
  and you think complaining will do more good than harm. For example, if it
  seems that the spammer genuinely might not know their spam is bad for you,
  for them, and for the Internet as a whole, you might complain to enlighten
  them. Don't reply to spammers if you're afraid they'll strike back at you in
  some fashion.

- Complain to the *address advertised in the spam* under the same conditions.
  The company responsible for that address may have hired the spammer to
  send the ad and may be relatively naive about spam. You might also complain
  to these companies' ISP if you feel they are knowingly abusing Usenet.

- Complain to the *abuse-reporting address of the site where the spam originated*
  unless it seems to be under the spammer's control. The news administrator
  may not realize that the NNTP server is configured to allow open posting or
  that a user is spamming from their site.

news.admin.net-abuse.sightings

Spam can also be reported to *news.admin.net-abuse.sightings.* Chapter 5 describes
the format that postings to this newsgroup should follow. For reports of Usenet
spam, the "Subject:" header should begin with `[usenet]`, and the "Followup-To:"
header should list *news.admin.net-abuse.usenet.*

Before reporting sightings to *news.admin.net-abuse.sightings*, read the group and be sure that no one else has already reported the article in question. If it's already been reported, you may want to follow the discussion about it in *news.admin.net-abuse.usenet.*

What to say

As with complaints about junk mail, a good complaint about Usenet spam should:

- *Be polite*, because you might be wrong about the source, and the news administrator is more likely to listen to you if you're friendly.

- *Include the spammed article, with all headers, especially the Path.* This will help the news administrator track down the message sender.

- *Cite any spam thresholds that have been violated.* If you can compute the BI for the articles, that information is helpful. Definitely indicate in which newsgroups the article appeared and how often.

- *Assert that the message is harmful.* Explain that the message appeared in an excessive number of groups and that it was off-topic for many. Explain how spam harms you, and state that you will never do business with a company that uses spam in its advertising.

- *Offer alternatives.* You might suggest that a spammer investigate the *biz.marketplace* or *ads* newsgroups, which allow advertising.

Here's a sample response to a Usenet spam:

```
POSTER:

Your message, posted and cross-posted multiple times to many
newsgroups, constitutes abuse of Usenet. It is off-topic for most of
the groups in which it appears, making it more difficult for people to
use Usenet for its intended purpose. It also wastes resources on news
servers worldwide. You may have posted a sufficient number of copies
to warrant anyone on Usenet issuing cancel messages to prevent your
article from appearing. You certainly have damaged your reputation -
I will never do business with you or anyone associated with you. Any
further communication from you will be considered harassment and will
be dealt with accordingly.

It is likely that your ISP prohibits this kind of abuse, and I am
informing them of your actions.

NEWS ADMINISTRATOR:

I have attached a representative copy of an article that has been
multiply posted and cross-posted to over 100 Usenet newsgroups at least
twice this week. You are being contacted because the article appears
to have been posted from your site, either by one of your users or by
someone abusing your NNTP server.
```

```
Please take whatever steps are necessary to prevent this from
happening again. If you feel it is appropriate, I hope you will issue
cancel messages for these articles (and charge the cost of your time
to the poster!).
```

```
Thanks.
```

Many other suggestions in Chapter 5 also hold for Usenet spam, such as what to say when contacting an ISP by phone, and how not to respond to spammers.

Canceling Spam

Another way to respond to inappropriate newsgroup postings is to take direct action by issuing a cancel message against the offending article. Because of the design of Usenet, any user may forge a cancel message for any other user. However, the Usenet community has developed standards as to when it is appropriate for a person to issue a cancel message and when it is inappropriate.

The standard reference to cancel messages is Tim Skirvin's Cancel Messages FAQ, which is regularly posted to *news.admin.net-abuse.usenet* and *news.answers* and is also available at *http://www.uiuc.edu/ph/www/tskirvin/faqs/cancel.html*.

As discussed in Chapter 4, *Internet Basics*, the cancel control message is used when a poster wishes to remove an article he's posted from a newsgroup. Most news readers have a cancel command you can use when you're reading one of your own articles.

Third-party cancel messages—cancel messages issued for *someone else's* article— are a controversial practice, and issuing third-party cancel messages indiscriminately is itself a form of Usenet abuse. There are only a few generally accepted reasons for issuing a cancel message for someone else's article:

- The news administrator at the site from which an article was posted may cancel the article in any circumstance. This is sometimes referred to as a "second-party cancel."

- You may cancel an article forged in your name.

- The moderator of a moderated Usenet newsgroup may cancel any article that appears in the newsgroup. Moderators generally cancel articles that bypassed them by forging moderator approval.

- Anyone may issue a cancel message for spam that exceeds the agreed-upon threshold. This threshold is currently a BI >= 20. See Chapter 1, *What's Spam and What's the Problem?* for an explanation of the BI, and see Tim Skirvin's Current Usenet Spam Thresholds and Guidelines FAQ, which is regularly posted to *news.admin.net-abuse.announce* and *news.answers* and is also available at *http://www.uiuc.edu/ph/www/tskirvin/faqs/spam.html*.

- Anyone may issue a cancel message for a *spew*—the same messages posted repeatedly by broken news software. Usually, the system administrator of the spewing system takes responsibility for cleaning up the results of the spew, but until the system administrator can be reached, it's open season.

- In theory, anyone may issue a cancel message for a large binary posted to a newsgroup that does not accept binary messages. In practice, however, it can be difficult to determine what constitutes "large" and how to handle other types of non-plain-text postings like HTML, RTF, or encoded text.*

If the article fits in one of these categories and you cancel it, you can be reasonably certain that your cancel message will be accepted by news administrators and the Usenet community at large.

Writing a cancel message

Third-party cancel messages must adhere to some special conventions, designed to increase accountability and visibility:

- As with any cancel message, there must be a `Control: cancel <original-message-ID>` header and the subject of the cancel message should be `cmsg cancel <original-message-ID>`.

- As with any cancel message, there should be an `Approved:` *address of issuer* header.

- The "Sender:" header of the cancel message must match the "Sender:" header of the original article exactly, or its "From:" header if it didn't have a "Sender:" header. The "From:" header of the cancel message should contain the issuer's address. Some news software strips out "Sender:" headers from postings—if yours does, don't issue cancel messages.

- The "Newsgroups:" header of the cancel message must match the "Newsgroups:" header of the original message exactly. You can't cancel a cross-posted message from only some of the groups it appeared in—it's all or none.

- The message must include the header `X-Cancelled-By:` *address of issuer*. This provides accountability—you can easily determine who issued the cancel message. This should be an email address that you check frequently and can respond to promptly, should someone write to question your cancel message. (Of course, this field, like the others, can be forged as well.)

- The Message-ID of the cancel message must begin with `cancel.`, followed by the Message-ID for the original article. For example, if the original article contained `Message-ID: <34E231EE.7A4C@hotmail.com>`, the cancel

---

* Shaun Davis-Gluyas's Bincancel FAQ, available at *http://www.southcom.com.au/~geniac/binfull.txt*, provides detailed information about cancelling binaries.

message should include the header `Message-ID: <cancel.34E231EE. 7A4C@hotmail.com>`. In addition to identifying the message as a cancel message, this header prevents news servers from accepting multiple cancel messages for the same article. It's referred to as the $alz [sic] convention, in honor of Richard Salz, author of the INN news server.

- Normally, the "Path:" header of a news article contains the list of news sites through which the article traveled, separated by exclamation points. It's built up automatically as the article passes from site to site.

When writing a cancel message, you must set the initial "Path:" header to include some *pseudo-sites*. Pseudo-sites aren't real news sites, but they allow other news administrators to decide whether they want to accept cancel messages or not. News servers can be configured to ignore articles that contain certain sites in their "Path:" header (recall from Chapter 4 that this is used to prevent article loops), so each server can choose whether to accept each kind of cancel message. The most common pseudo-sites are:

`cyberspam!usenet`
> A spam (excessive cross-posting/excessive multiposting) with a BI >= 20 over the last 45 days

`spewcancel!cyberspam!usenet`
> A spew

`mmfcancel!cyberspam!usenet`
> A "Make Money Fast" chain letter posting

`bincancel!cyberspam!usenet`
> A large binary in a nonbinary group

The use of the `usenet` pseudo-site isn't strictly necessary as long as something appears to the right of the `cyberspam` pseudo-site that clearly indicates that the last thing in the path isn't the name of the article sender and thus shouldn't be used to reply to the sender by email. Often, `not-for-mail` is used in place of `usenet`.

- Offer a brief explanation of the reason for the cancel message in the body of the article or in a "Summary:" header. If you're canceling spam, you should indicate whether it's EMP (excessive multi-posting) or ECP/EMP (excessive cross-posting/excessive multi-posting), and give the BI value and number of individual copies of the message that were posted. If you're canceling a chain letter, simply noting that it's an MMF, and including the portion of the article that asks readers to post it to a huge number of newsgroups, is sufficient.

- If you're so inclined, you may want to add a "Cc:" header and send a copy of your cancel message to the original article's author. If you plan to do this, your explanation of the reason for the cancel may have to be more explicit. Rosalind Hengeveld gives this example:

```
You posted a binary to a non-binary newsgroup. This is not allowed and
is eligible for cancellation in all non-binary newsgroups.

Please post to newsgroups like this only plain ascii text and nothing
encoded such as pictures, executables, sound files, et cetera.
Appropriate newsgroups to post binaries are those in alt.binaries.*.

The reason most of Usenet disallows binaries is that they usually take
up much more storage space than plain text articles (even though there
is no upper size limit for the latter). Sites with limited storage
capacity may choose to not carry the special binaries newsgroups.

This notice is a copy of a Usenet control message suggesting to sites
or their administrators that they drop your post from the newsgroup.
```

Here's an example of a complete cancel message from Tim Skirvin's "Cancel Messages: Frequently Asked Questions" article. Important conventions are **bold**:

<pre>
Date: 8 Jun 1997 15:43:37 GMT
Path: vixen.cso.uiuc.edu!ais.net!newsfeed.direct.ca!
      News1.Vancouver.iSTAR.net!news.istar.net!n1van.istar!
      hammer.uoregon.edu!nrchh45.rich.nt.com!bcarh8ac.bnr.ca!
      despams.ocunix.on.ca!cyberspam!not-for-mail
From: clewis@ferret.ocunix.on.ca (Chris Lewis)
Approved: clewis@ferret.ocunix.on.ca
X-Cancelled-by: clewis@ferret.ocunix.on.ca
Sender: Photorep45@ibm.net
Newsgroups: alt.recovery.aa
Subject: cmsg cancel <5ne625$f2b$25@news.internetmci.com>
Control: cancel <5ne625$f2b$25@news.internetmci.com>
Message-ID: <cancel.5ne625$f2b$25@news.internetmci.com>
X-No-Archive: Yes
X-Spam-Type: WOODSIDE
Lines: 7

WOODSIDE spam cancelled by clewis@ferret.ocunix.on.ca
Original Subject: Sell YourPhotosNYC.Agency
Total spams this type to date: 1888
Total this spam type for this user: 1041
Total this spam type for this user today: 503
Originating site: internetmci.com
Complaint addresses: spamcomplaints@mci.net postmaster@mci.net
</pre>

It's not necessary, or even a good idea, to include a copy of the canceled message; if you've adhered to the $alz convention, anyone who needs to find the canceled message can determine its Message-ID and search DejaNews or AltaVista for the message.

You can issue a cancel message manually using a news reader that allows you to edit headers. Or on Unix systems, you can write a cancel message in a separate file and then inject it into the news system with the *inews* command. Rosalind Hengeveld's "Newsgroup Care Cancel Cookbook" (available at *http://www.xs4all. nl/~rosalind/faq-care.html*) lists some Windows and Macintosh news readers that can create properly formatted third-party cancel messages.

You should be aware, however, that issuing a cancel message may upset the original article's poster, and they may retaliate. Spam canceling can be a thankless job. You may instead prefer to issue NoCeM notices, discussed later in this chapter.

Censorship

People who issue cancel messages often face charges of censorship. Issuing a cancel message does remove someone else's words from Usenet: does it also violate their rights?

Current thinking is that cancel messages based solely on quantity—that is, the number of newsgroups to which the article was posted—do not constitute censorship. As Tim Skirvin writes in the Cancel Messages FAQ (available from *http://www.uiuc.edu/ph/www/tskirvin/faqs/cancel.html*):

> Common practice says that non-content-based cancels are not censorship. Instead, they are based on how "loud" the message was said; it's not censorship to stop someone from blaring their message out in the middle of the night using a megaphone.

Canceling binaries in nonbinary newsgroups is handled much the same way: cancelations based solely on the size of the article, and not its content (other than that it's not plain text), are regarded as acceptable.

In addition, cancel messages are effectively prohibited in some Usenet newsgroups. In the *news.admin.net-abuse* newsgroups, a program called "Dave the Resurrector" automatically reposts canceled articles.

On the other hand, a few newsgroups, such as *alt.sex.cancel*, exist specifically so that the postings in them can be canceled. If you're looking to test a cancel message, you're free to cancel anything that appears in one of those groups. These "spam traps" are discussed in greater length in Chapter 8, *Community Action*.

Reporting your cancels

If you're canceling articles regularly, it's a good idea to publish a human-readable report of the third-party cancel messages you issue. *news.admin.net-abuse.bulletins* is specifically chartered for reports of action against spammers and is an ideal place to publish cancel reports. Cancel reports in this group must include a "Followup-To:" header listing *news.admin.net-abuse.usenet.* You may also want to cross-post your cancel reports to the affected newsgroups if there are only a few.

A cancel report should list all the articles you canceled, including their "Message-ID:," "Subject:," "From:," and "Newsgroup:" headers. It should also explain why you canceled the articles.

Here's an example of a cancel report issued by Frontier GlobalCenter, an ISP that takes its acceptable use policy seriously and cancels spam originating from its users:

```
Newsgroups: news.admin.net-abuse.bulletins
From: Frontier GlobalCenter Abuse Response Team <abuse@globalcenter.net>
Subject: Spam from foobar@primenet.com canceled
Followup-To: news.admin.net-abuse.usenet
Date: 11 May 1998 00:15:00 -0700

The following 71 articles of spam with the subject
"Pentium Computer System for Sale" have been canceled as per the
Frontier GlobalCenter user agreement
(http://www.globalcenter.net/aup/).

A sample instance of the canceled article is included at the
end of the list.

<35569965.6111786@news.primenet.com> ak.forsale
<35569a9a.6420468@news.primenet.com> alt.ads.forsale.computers
<35569a46.6336804@news.primenet.com> alabama.birmingham.forsale
 ...etc...
```

Automating the process

Writing cancel messages by hand is tedious. If you expect to issue many cancel messages (and are prepared for the consequences!), you'll probably prefer using a cancel program or a cancelbot. Almost all of these are written for Unix users.

A cancel program accepts a newsgroup message as input and produces a properly formatted third-party cancel message. It may output the cancel message to a file or send it directly to a news server. Cancel programs are ideal for occasional cancelers, like newsgroup moderators, who need to issue cancel messages infrequently and on a case-by-case basis. Many such programs are available from the Usenet Moderators Archive at *http://www.landfield.com/moderators/.*

A *cancelbot* is a program that runs continuously, scanning a newsgroup for messages that meet its criteria and issuing cancel messages for them. The major Usenet spam cancelers use cancelbots to automatically cancel spam, spew, and misplaced binaries. Running a cancelbot requires a very good understanding of the news

system; accordingly, cancelbots are not generally available. A capable news administrator could probably make a cancelbot out of Chris Lewis's *spamfind* program,
which notifies a news administrator if someone appears to be posting too many
articles. It's available as part of *http://spam.abuse.net/spam/tools/cancel.txt*.

Issuing NoCeM Notices

As discussed earlier in this chapter, a NoCeM notice is a suggestion that a set of
articles be marked "already read" by a news reader and thus not presented to the
user. A NoCeM message is a purely voluntary suggestion to a Usenet user or news
administrator; they must actively choose to honor your notice. Accordingly, it's
acceptable to issue a NoCeM message for any reason at all, although there's little
point in wasting Usenet bandwidth to issue messages no one else will use. In particular, content-based NoCeM notices (e.g., for off-topic postings to a particular
newsgroup) are acceptable if clearly marked as such.

Writing a NoCeM notice

A NoCeM notice should be posted to *news.lists.filters*, at a minimum, because that
is where the NoCeM program expects to read notices. Issuers who are writing
NoCeM notices for individual newsgroups (rather than for spam control) sometimes also post their notices to the affected newsgroups, but this practice can add
unwelcome noise to the newsgroup. The Subject of the notice should contain
either `@@NCM` (if it's intended to hide spam or spew) or `@@newsgroup` (if it's
intended to hide off-topic postings). NoCeM notices should not contain a "References:" header.

Here is the format that the body of a NoCeM message must take:

- The first part of the body is usually a human-readable explanation of the
  notice and NoCeM itself. You can head off a lot of angry responses by
  explaining that the notice is advisory and doesn't cancel any of the articles
  mentioned.

- The notice itself begins with the line `@@BEGIN NCM HEADERS`.

- The NoCeM "headers" come next. These should include at least:

  ```
  Version: the NoCeM version number, currently 0.9
  Issuer: issuer's address
  Type: reason for the notice
  Action: hide or show
  Newsgroup: name of newsgroup for which notice is issued
  Count: the number of articles this notice applies to
  Notice-ID: a unique identifier for this NoCeM notice
  ```

  Some common "Type:" values are "spam," "spew," "mmf," "content-based,"
  etc. The "Action:" header determines whether the articles should be marked as

already read ("hide") or selected for reading ("show"). The "Newsgroup:" header is included only when the notice pertains to a particular newsgroup; spam notices, for example, inherently apply to many newsgroups and thus don't contain a "Newsgroup:" NoCeM header.

- The NoCeM body begins with the line `@@BEGIN NCM BODY`.

- The list of articles to which the notice applies is given in the body. Each line begins with the Message-ID of an article, followed by a tab, and then a space-separated list of the newsgroups in which the article appeared. To keep lines from getting too long, you can break up the list of newsgroups into new lines that begin with a tab.

- The NoCeM body ends with the line `@@END NCM BODY`.

- The message itself must be signed with a PGP key. The signature should be applied using PGP's text mode so that it doesn't contain any unprintable characters.

Here's an example of a NoCeM notice issued for the *rec.games.mud.admin* newsgroup:

```
Newsgroups: news.lists.filters
From: rec.games.mud.admin NoCeM issuer <rgma-nocem@pennmush.tinymush.org>
Subject: NoCeM notice rgma-13826-888528304 @@rec.games.mud.admin

-----BEGIN PGP SIGNED MESSAGE-----

This is an automatically generated NoCeM ("no-see-um") notice for
the newsgroup rec.games.mud.admin. This notice is generated for
postings which do not have subject lines that meet the rgm.admin
posting guidelines. The guidelines are available at
http://pennmush.tinymush.org/~nocem/guidelines.txt

This is a NoCeM notice - it is purely advisory and does not
cancel the message listed below. It's a convenience for Usenet
readers who may choose to mark these articles as "already read."

@@BEGIN NCM HEADERS
Version: 0.93
Issuer: rgm.admin NoCeM issuer <rgma-nocem@pennmush.tinymush.org>
Type: bad-subject
Action: hide
Newsgroup: rec.games.mud.admin
Count: 10
Notice-ID: rgma-13826-888528304
@@BEGIN NCM BODY
<34f03def.0@news.cc.umr.edu>   rec.games.mud.admin
<6cpgt7$kmn@mozo.cc.purdue.edu>        rec.games.mud.admin
<01bd3f20$b0ca6740$5604d0cf@default>  rec.games.mud.admin
<6cnqaj$9o4$1@news3.microserve.net>   rec.games.mud.admin
 ...etc...
```

```
@@END NCM BODY
```

For reference purposes, the messages above had the following
Subject headers:
```
<34f03def.0@news.cc.umr.edu> had subject:
        >Re: mordor on mac
<6cpgt7$kmn@mozo.cc.purdue.edu> had subject:
        >Re: mordor on mac
```

 ...etc...

```
-----BEGIN PGP SIGNATURE-----
Version: 2.6.3a
Charset: noconv

iQCVAwUBNPXdsqypDMJ/DQthAQGKIgP9HVbGgULq5V3ewJRvVeV/ETj9u/z+kHr9
zLcB3CdMcVnJecD+ixWsZnMksjMkIZqCYW8yi2J/w+tZ+jm8L/ihtv8QyhFy9EUb
u4cBqmuEWap4rZROqEl/gOvSFn63SgPQqByB5RBFflSYgu3e1abW8HaCNIUxdlFI
Wy7D3mwZ4LM=
=XJo2
-----END PGP SIGNATURE-----
```

Before you issue your first NoCeM message, it's a good idea to post a notice to *news.admin.nocem* and any affected newsgroups stating your intention to issue NoCeM messages and the conditions under which you'll issue a message. This "notice of intentions" should be signed with the PGP key with which you'll sign notices. You should also submit your notice to Rosalind Hengeveld's NoCeM Registry at *http://www 4all.nl/~rosalind/nocemreg/nocemreg.html*, especially if you believe that your notices are suitable for application "on-spool" by news administrators.

Automating the process

Constructing NoCeM notices by hand can be tedious. Here's a Perl program that accepts a newsgroup message or a mailbox file of newgroup messages on its standard input and produces a NoCeM notice to hide the message(s) on its standard output:

```perl
#!/usr/local/bin/perl -w
#
# Given a news article or mbox file of news articles on stdin,
# issue a NoCeM notice for those articles
#
# Copyright (c) 1998 by Alan Schwartz
#
use strict 'subs';
use strict 'refs';
use English;
use Mail::Header;
require 'ctime.pl';
require 5;
```

```
######################################################################
# USER CONFIGURATION: VARIABLES YOU MUST SET
######################################################################

# Your email address
my $issuer = 'myname@myhost';

# Location of the pgp program:

my $pgp = '/usr/local/bin/pgp';

# The id of the PGP key to sign messages with
my $pgpid = 'myname@myhost';

# Put your PGP key pass phrase here if you don't want to be
# prompted for it.
$ENV{'PGPPASS'} = 'pgp pass phrase here';

# The tag to go at the end of the Subject: header:
# Use "@@NCM" if you're hiding spam/spew
# Use "@@<newsgroup name>" if you're hiding off-topic postings
my $subjecttag = '@@NCM';

# The "type" of notice. Example: spam, spew, mmf
my $type = "spam";

# You can put an explanation here of the purpose of these notices.
# The paragraph must end with the string EOP, on a line by itself.
my $explanation = <<'EOP';
This is an automatically generated NoCeM ("no-see-um") notice.  It is
purely advisory and does not cancel the message listed below. It's a
convenience for Usenet readers who may choose to mark these articles as
"already read".
EOP

######################################################################
# END OF USER CONFIGURATION
######################################################################

sub read_mbox_stdin;

my @messages = read_mbox_stdin();
die "No articles to process\n" unless @messages;
my @nocems;
my $newsgroup;
my $id = "$issuer-$$-" . time;
unless ($subjecttag eq '@@NCM') {
  $newsgroup = $subjecttag;
  $newsgroup =~ s/\@\@//;
}
my $nltab = "\n\t";
foreach my $msgref (@messages) {
  my $header = new Mail::Header $msgref, MailFrom => 'IGNORE';
  my $messageid = $header->get("Message-ID");
```

```perl
  chomp($messageid);
  my $newsgroups = $header->get("Newsgroups");
  chomp($newsgroups);
  $newsgroups =~ s/,/$nltab/og;
  push(@nocems,"$messageid\t$newsgroups\n");
}

my $headers = <<EOP;
Newsgroups: news.lists.filters
From: $issuer
Subject: NoCeM notice $id $subjecttag

EOP

my $tempfile = "/tmp/mknocem.$$";
open(OUT,">$tempfile") or
  die "Unable to open temporary file $tempfile: $!\n";
print OUT <<EOP;
$explanation

\@\@BEGIN NCM HEADERS
Version: 0.93
Issuer: $issuer
Type: $type
Action: hide
EOP

print OUT "Newsgroup: $newsgroup\n" if $newsgroup;
print OUT "Count: ", scalar(@nocems), "\n";
print OUT '@@BEGIN NCM BODY', "\n";
print OUT join("",@nocems);
print OUT '@@END NCM BODY', "\n";
close(OUT);

system("$pgp -s $tempfile -u $pgpid");
open(OUT,"$tempfile.asc") or
  die "Unable to open pgp-signed temporary file $tempfile.asc: $!\n";
print $headers;
print <OUT>;
close(OUT);
unlink("$tempfile");
unlink("$tempfile.asc");
exit 0;


# Based on read_mbox in Graham Barr's MailTools module
# Returns an array of references to messages, where each
# message is an array of lines.
sub read_mbox_stdin {
  my @mail  = ();
  my $mail  = [];
  my $blank = 1;

  while(<STDIN>) {
```

```
  if($blank && /\AFrom .*\d{4}/) {
   push(@mail, $mail) if scalar(@{$mail});
    $mail = [ $_ ];
    $blank = 0;
  } else {
    $blank = m#\A\Z#o ? 1 : 0;
   push(@{$mail}, $_);
  }
 }
 push(@mail, $mail) if scalar(@{$mail});
 return wantarray ? @mail : \@mail;
}
```

See "Getting the Scripts" in the Preface for information on downloading this script.

7

In this chapter:
- *Policy Choices*
- *Blocking Incoming Spam*
- *Stopping Outgoing Spam*

Spam Stopping for Administrators and ISPs

When you're running an Internet host or providing Internet service to others, spam is of particular concern to you. Not only might your users receive unwanted postings, but your users might send spam themselves, or a spammer elsewhere might try to use your site to disguise the source of his messages. If you're the mail or news administrator for your organization, you'll have to deal with the effects of unwanted messages on your mail or news system.

Because this chapter is directed at system administrators, it often assumes more technical knowledge than the other chapters in this book. However, the "Policy Choices" section should be useful to managers of ISPs, as well as administrators.

When it comes to providing Internet service or running a mail hub or news server, Unix remains the operating system of choice. Accordingly, most of the examples in this chapter assume you're using a Unix system to provide mail or news service to users (who probably use PC or Macintosh systems to connect to your hubs). If you're using a Windows NT server as your mail hub, some of the details of this chapter may not apply exactly, but the concepts should still be useful.

Policy Choices

One of the most important decisions you must make as a system administrator or ISP is what policies you will enforce. Some questions to ask yourself in formulating policies are:

- What is my security philosophy? How much time am I willing to spend to protect my system from being a target or relay for spam?

- How do I want to deal with spam that might be sent to users at my system?

- How do I want to deal with complaints against my users? If the complaints prove true, what action will I take against the users?

- How do I want to disseminate information about my policies and ensure that users agree to uphold them?

- What do I consider my responsibilities to other sites on the Internet and other Usenet news hosts?

Let's look at each of these questions in turn.

Security Philosophy

When your users begin receiving spam, or when a spammer disguises the source of his spam by suggesting that it originated at your site, your reaction will depend in part on how much time and energy you can spend protecting your site, educating your users, or tracking down abusers. The time and personnel available to you will determine whether you can actively hunt down spammers, complain to their providers, sue the spammers, etc.

If you anticipate having little time and few free resources, your best use of your time may be to establish strong controls from the start. An initial investment in securing your mail server and news server so they won't relay messages from outsiders can save a lot of time later.

If, on the other hand, you have the resources to help your users go after spammers, more power to you.

Spam to Your Users

There are three basic approaches to dealing with spam that your users receive:

- *Identify spammers and block them at the system level.* This relieves your system from having to spend its resources delivering or storing unwanted messages, and saves all your users from the possibility of unwanted messages from that spammer. On the other hand, this approach effectively prevents any user who *wants* to receive mail or read newsgroup postings from the spammer from doing so easily. This approach also runs the risk of accidentally blocking legitimate messages—and risking the anger of your users as a result.

- *Provide tools for your users, but don't get actively involved.* With this approach, you make your users aware of existing tools and information about how to identify, filter, or respond to spam. Each user chooses how to deal with her own mail and news reading. This approach wastes more of your system's resources and forces users to handle spam on their own, but it allows your system to behave as an impartial carrier of data without monitoring the nature of the data.

- *Use a hybrid approach.* Perhaps you block particularly obvious or egregious spam at the system level and provide tools for the users to do further filtering. Or like America Online, perhaps you maintain a filter than any user can choose to use or not use.

Whatever approach you choose, you'll want to be clear about it to your users to avoid misunderstandings. If your users sign up for service with you, expecting to receive their mail or news unadulterated, they may not be pleased if you're blocking spam. On the other hand, if they think you'll be shielding them from spam and you're leaving it up to them, they'll also be displeased.

Spam by Your Users

What process will you follow if you receive a complaint alleging that one of your users has been sending unsolicited bulk email (UBE) or posting spam to Usenet newsgroups? Will you have appropriate log files with which to determine when the user sent email messages, how many messages were sent, and to whom? Will you ask the user for an explanation? Will you lock out the user's account until you resolve the situation?

If the complaint proves to be well founded, what action will you take against the user? Will you provide a warning, terminate the user's account, assess cleanup fees, or seek legal redress against the user? What if the same user has more than one account? Terminating the offending account is the most common response; assessing cleanup fees to cover the cost of administrator time and system resources wasted by the spammer is one of the most effective. Again, you'll need to spell this out somehow.

Disseminating Policy Information

How will you let your users know about the policies you set? An ideal approach is to formulate a policy against spamming as part of your system's *Acceptable Use Policy* (AUP), a document that describes what constitutes acceptable and unacceptable use of your system, and how you will respond to unacceptable use. The AUP can constitute a legal contract between you and the user so that violators can be pursued legally for breach of contact.

A well-written AUP on spamming should contain, at a minimum:

- A specific description of what constitutes unacceptable use of email or newsgroups. The description should address as many of the types of spam described in Chapter 1, *What's Spam and What's the Problem?*, as are applicable. It's a good idea to think broadly here.

- If you provide Internet service to other ISPs, a clear statement that you hold them accountable for their own customers' actions. This gives you cause to act against a customer who sets up a "spam haven" domain for other spammers to use.

- A statement of action that you will take against users who engage in unacceptable practices. Your administrators should be able to suspend a user's access without approval from superiors. After review of the user's actions, if the user is at fault, you should be able to terminate the user's account and assess cleanup fees to recover damages to your system due to the spam (including use of system resources, administrator time spent answering complaints, etc.). Indicate that the policy outlines typical actions you may take, but it does not limit your actions.

- A statement about whether you will block spam at the system level.

- A contact address or phone number for users who have questions about the policy.

For example, here's MCI's policy on spamming:

MCI and its affiliates provide to business and consumer users several information technology related services, including such services as Internet access, various electronic mail (email) packages and services, World Wide Web website hosting arrangements, and other online and Internet-related services.

It is contrary to MCI policy for any user of any of these services to effect or participate in any of the following activities through an MCI-provided service:

1. To post ten (10) or more messages similar in content to Usenet or other newsgroups, forums, e-mail mailing lists or other similar groups or lists;
2. To post to any Usenet or other newsgroup, forum, e-mail mailing list or other similar group or list articles which are off-topic according to the charter or other owner-published FAQ or description of the group or list;
3. To send unsolicited e-mailings to more than twenty-five (25) e-mail users, if such unsolicited e-mailings could reasonably be expected to provoke complaints;
4. To falsify user information provided to MCI or to other users of the service in connection with use of an MCI service; and
5. To engage in any of the foregoing activities by using the service of another provider, but channeling such activities through an MCI account, remailer, or otherwise through an MCI service or using an MCI account as a maildrop for responses or otherwise using the services of another provider for the purpose of facilitating the foregoing activities if such use of another party's service could reasonably be expected to adversely affect an MCI service.

```
MCI considers the above practices to constitute abuse of our service
and of the recipients of such unsolicited mailings and/or postings,
who often bear the expense. Therefore, these practices are prohibited
by MCI's terms and conditions of service. Engaging in one or more of
these practices will result in termination of the offender's account
and/or access to MCI services.

In addition, MCI reserves the right, where feasible, to implement
technical mechanisms which block multiple postings as described above
before they are forwarded or otherwise sent to their intended
recipients.

This policy addresses only the kinds of network abuse specifically
enumerated above. In addition to these activities, MCI's terms and
conditions of service also prohibit other forms of abuse such as
harassment and the posting of illegal or unlawful materials, and MCI
will respond as appropriate to these other activities as well.

Nothing contained in this policy shall be construed to limit MCI's
actions or remedies in any way with respect to any of the foregoing
activities, and MCI reserves the right to take any and all additional
actions it may deem appropriate with respect to such activities,
including without limitation taking action to recover the costs and
expenses of identifying offenders and removing them from the MCI
service, and levying cancelation charges to cover MCI's costs in the
event of disconnection of dedicated access for the causes outlined
above. In addition, MCI reserves at all times all rights and remedies
available to it with respect to such activities at law or in equity.

If you have any questions regarding this Policy on Spamming, please
contact policies@internetmci.com.
```

Formulating and enforcing an AUP is an important step in keeping your system from becoming a haven for spammers. For other examples of AUPs, see Netcom (*http://www.netcom.com/netcom/aug.html*), Demon Internet, Ltd. (*http://www.demon.net/connect/aup/*), Sprintlink (*http://www.sprint.net/acceptableuse.htm*), or America Online (*ftp://ftp.aol.com/pub/usenet/aol-usenet-aup.txt*).

Remember that an AUP is a contract, and you are not limited to restricting your users from using *your* site to send spam. Many providers require that their customers not engage in spam in any part of their business in order to maintain their account. A policy like this enables you to take action if a user doesn't spam from your site, but lists his address at your site in his spam as a place to reach him.

Responsibility to the Net

No Internet host is an island. As an Internet system administrator, you depend on other hosts and their administrators to facilitate the routing of your data and your email and the exchange of Usenet news. Your responsibility to these hosts is a final policy consideration. Some anti-spam tactics, discussed in Chapter 8,

Community Action, rely on a united community of administrators who see the preservation of the Internet or Usenet as part of their responsibilities.

A responsible system administrator shouldn't provide free accounts without a reliable ID, such as a credit card number. If a spammer uses one of your free accounts, having a credit card number can make recovering the costs of the spam much easier; having to provide verifiable identification may deter spammers from abusing your site.

A responsible system administrator should retain system logging information from her news server, SMTP server, and POP server for at least seven days. Having a week's worth of logs allows you to confirm complaints of spam leveled against your users—if a spammer tries to implicate one of your users in revenge for a complaint, your logs will verify the accusation or prove it false.

Blocking Incoming Spam

There are a number of different approaches to system-level blocking of spam. Some rely on more or less sophisticated pattern-matching heuristics to determine whether a given message might be spam. Others focus on identifying and blocking known spammers or the sites from which they spam.

At the Mail Transport Agent

The most obvious place to block incoming spam email is at the Mail Transport Agent (MTA). Because the MTA has a complete copy of the message, it has access to all the relevant information that would help decide if the message is spam.

Most major Internet MTAs provide ways to block spam; implementing these blocks often requires considerable knowledge of the workings of your MTA. *sendmail* 8.9, released in May 1998, offers anti-spam and anti-relay rules built in, as well as powerful regular-expression-based filtering. Rule sets for blocking spam in *sendmail* 8.8 are available at *http://www.sendmail.org/antispam.html* and *http://www. informatik.uni-kiel.de/%7Eca/email/check.html*. Patches for blocking spam in the *qmail* MTA are available at *http://www.qmail.org/#addons*.

When you are blocking spam at the MTA, an important decision is what to do with messages that get classified as spam. There are four main options:

- *Accept and drop the message.* With this approach, your MTA accepts the message from the spammer and then deletes it or files it somewhere unimportant. Unless you need copies of spam messages (for example, to complain about), this is usually not a good choice, because it wastes system resources processing the messages. Moreover, because you provide no feedback to the spammer, you can expect to continue to receive spam.

- *Accept and bounce the message.* With this approach, your MTA accepts the message from the spammer and passes it to a filtering package that returns a bounce message to the spammer. Many MTA/filtering package combinations use this approach. Like *accept and drop,* this approach requires your system to process the messages. By returning a bounce message, you may avoid further spam from that spammer; unfortunately, many spammers falsify their return address information, and the bounce message is likely to be sent to the wrong place.

- *Bounce the message with a permanent error.* With this approach, your MTA informs the sending site during the SMTP transaction that the message is rejected and should not be resent. The sender usually receives a notification that her message was rejected. This is the most common response to spam blocked by the MTA and the most effective: it conserves your resources and provides immediate feedback to the spammer that he can't deliver to your address.

- *Bounce the message with a temporary error.* With this approach, your MTA informs the sending site that the message couldn't be delivered due to a temporary problem. The sending site will usually continue to attempt delivery regularly for some period (often, every four hours for five days). If your site has sufficient resources to handle the additional load of spammers connecting to try to redeliver their messages, this option has the useful property of tying up the *spammer's* MTA by forcing it to continue to try delivering the message. On the other hand, it ties up your system, as well.

Which option you choose is a matter of taste, based on your system's resources and your own preferences. As you'll see later, it's often useful to mix these options. There are also other, less common possibilities: you could hold suspected spam for later review or deliver it with a special header that indicates it may be spam, allowing your users to filter based on that header.

Block unresolvable hosts

Spammers often forge their "SMTP From:" addresses in order to prevent complaints from getting back to them or to their providers. Some spammers use forged addresses with invalid domains, like *someone@noreply.com.* Because legitimate email should always include a valid sender email address, you can block many unwanted messages by refusing to accept email that comes from a domain that's not registered in the Domain Name Service. *sendmail* 8.9 blocks unresolvable hosts by default.

Blocking messages from domains that you can't look up in the DNS presents a problem—the domain may be a real one, yet unresolvable due to a DNS failure.* Accordingly, many administrators prefer to return a temporary error to the sender, rather than a permanent one.

Block known spammers

If you had a list of sites and users who were known to send spam, you could reject any email from those sources. Most MTAs provide a way to check the address on incoming mail against a "rogue list" and reject mail from rogue users or domains.

Where can you find a rogue list? Some of the best known are maintained by Mind-Spring (*http://www.mindspring.com/cgi-bin/spamlist.pl*), zNet (*http://www.znet.com/spammers.txt*), WSRCC (*http://www.wsrcc.com/spam/spamlist.txt*), and E-Scrub Techologies (*http://www.e-scrub.com/cgi-bin/blacklists.cgi*). You can locate others by searching Yahoo! (*http://www.yahoo.com*) for "Junk Email." And of course, as you receive spam at your system, you can add the spammer or his site to your own rogue list.

The *getspam* Perl script, by Randal Schwartz, Scott Blachowicz, and Manoj Srivastava, can automate the process of generating your own rogue list. It downloads rogue lists from other sites on the Internet, combines them into a single list with no duplicates, and formats them into the format required for *mailagent* or the *sendmail* anti-spam rule sets. See "Getting the Scripts" in the Preface for information on downloading this script.

Instead of using the MTA's configuration to reject rogue hosts, you can prevent those hosts from connecting to your SMTP port at all by using TCP wrappers. A TCP wrapper controls whether or not a host can access a given port on your system. Whenever a host tries to connect to a port protected by a TCP wrapper, the wrapper checks the host's name or IP address against a list of allowed or disallowed hosts. Because other computers must connect to your site's SMTP port (port 25) in order to deliver email, protecting this port can block unwanted messages from known rogue sites. The same TCP wrapper can be used to restrict access to other important ports on your system.

The TCP wrapper software is available at *ftp://ftp.win.tue.nl/pub/security*. In order to use it with an MTA, the MTA must either be able to link with the wrapper library (as *sendmail* can) or must be run from *inetd* using the *inetd.conf* file (as *qmail* does).

---

* Another possibility is that the address is not a true Internet address, but a UUCP address or some other kind of network address; these are valid for replies, but may not conform to RFC 822 and won't have DNS entries.

Blocking spammers by domain is effectively defeated by spammers who use forged "From:" addresses. As more spammers resort to this practice, blocking by domain will become less useful.

Use the RealTime Blackhole List

A sophisticated variation on the rogue list is the Mail Abuse Prevention System (MAPS) RealTime Blackhole List (RBL), described by Paul Vixie at *http://maps.vix. com/rbl*. The RBL is a name server that has DNS records for sites considered to be spammers, spam relays, or spam-friendly service providers. If your MTA can make decisions about sending sites by looking them up in the DNS, you can instruct it to check the RBL DNS and block any messages from sites that have records there. On many MTAs, performing a DNS lookup can be faster than searching a rogue list; it's also possible to configure your local name server to mirror a copy of the RBL to make the lookups even faster.*

The RBL probably errs on the side of blocking too much rather than too little. For example, the RBL lists sites being used as spam relays until open relaying is turned off (or until 20–30 days pass without another relaying incident). On the other hand, the RBL is probably more up-to-date than any other rogue list, and changes to the RBL are distributed instantly and transparently thanks to its use of DNS.

Information on using the RBL with *sendmail* can be found at *http://maps.vix.com/ rbl/usage.html* or *http://www.informatik.uni-kiel.de/%7Eca/email/check.html*. The RBL page also includes links to pages that explain how to use the RBL with other MTAs; for *qmail*, for example, see *http://www.qmail.org/rbl/*.

Use other systemwide filters

Chapter 6, *A User's Guide to Usenet Spam*, discusses filters that users can apply to reduce the amount of unwanted mail they receive. Perhaps your MTA can be configured to apply filtering beyond simply weeding out rogues. For example, you could weed out messages with invalid IP addresses in a "Received:" header.

If your MTA can use *procmail* as its local delivery agent (as *sendmail* and *qmail* can), you can create a systemwide *procmail* recipe file (usually */etc/procmailrc*) that will be run on every message. Consult your MTA's documentation for information about how to use *procmail* as the local delivery agent.

---

* When the RBL changes, your local name server is notified to update its copy. If you want to mirror the entire RBL, the Mail Abuse Prevention System requires that you use the BIND 8.1 (or later) software as your name server. In addition, you must sign an indemnification agreement. For a copy of the agreement, email *rbl@maps.vix.com*.

MailShield, a commercial MTA add-on produced by the Walter Shelby Group, Ltd., offers extensive and flexible filtering and spam blocking. Among its advanced techniques are *tarpitting* (gradually slowing down the refusal rate for messages to tie up the spammer's server), verification of valid header formats and addresses, adding additional tracing information to headers, and optionally accepting junk mail but prepending some text to the "Subject:" header (e.g., "SPAM:") to simplify user-level filtering. MailShield is avaiable from *http://www.mailshield.com* for $995 per server; it runs on Windows 95/NT, Solaris, HP-UX, and Irix systems and can be set up on a separate server or on the mail server if the mail server is using one of a number of popular MTAs.

At the News Server

Maintaining a Usenet news server is resource-intensive. Your newsfeed likely constitutes a significant amount of network bandwidth and takes up considerable disk space on the news server. Spam interferes with the proper operation of your news server by taking bandwidth and disk space away from appropriate articles; as a result, you probably have to expire articles sooner than you'd like in order to avoid filling up your disks.

Accept cancel messages

Cancel messages issued by the major third-party cancelers go a long way toward reducing the amount of spam you receive, especially if your site is on the periphery of Usenet, and spam is getting canceled before the news is fed to you. The two most common news server software packages, C News and InterNet News (INN), automatically accept cancel messages in their default configuration. If you don't want to accept cancels for some reason, you can alias out the pseudo-sites that spam cancelers add to their "Path:" headers.

Use NoCeM-on-spool

You can also apply NoCeM notices to your entire news spool. This helps the many users whose news readers can't process NoCeM notices and allows you to remove articles that aren't canceled by the major spam cancelers. In addition, NoCeM notices are authenticated, so you don't have to worry about forged NoCeM notices removing articles that are appropriate. Most of the major spam and binary cancelers also issue NoCeM notices, so you can ignore their (unauthenticated) cancel messages and apply their (authenticated) NoCeM notices to your spool, instead.

On the other hand, standards for issuing NoCeM notices are more lax than those for issuing cancel messages, so you need to be choosy about which NoCeM notices you want to accept. For example, Cancelmoose issues NoCeM notices for articles with a BI >= 15, instead of the cancel message threshold of 20. The

NoCeM Registry at *http://www.xs4all.nl/~rosalind/nocemreg/nocemreg.html* can be very helpful; it lists many NoCeM issuers, along with statements of their criteria for issuing notices and recommendations of whether their notices are appropriate to apply to a news spool.

Howard Goldstein maintains a version of NoCeM-on-spool for INN news systems, at *ftp://ftp.mpcs.com/pub/newsadmin/nocem*. Olaf Titz maintains NoCeM-on-spool for C News servers at *http://sites.inka.de/~bigred/devel/c-nocem.tar.gz*.

Filter incoming articles

The INN news server can be compiled to allow filtering of news articles by filters written in either TCL* or Perl (or both). Instructions for compiling with these hooks can be found in the files *README.perl_hook* and *README.tcl_hook* in the INN source code, and sample filters are included to illustrate how they work.

If you've compiled INN to use TCL, the *filter.tcl* file contains the filtering code. You must define a function called `filter_news` that returns a string: either "accept" to accept an article, or a "reason for rejection." The function can access the article headers through the `Headers` associative array (e.g., `$Headers(Message-ID)` contains the article's Message-ID) and the article body through the `$Body` variable.

If you've compiled INN to use Perl, the *filter_innd.pl* file filters incoming articles. You must define a function called `filter_art` that returns a string: either a null string ("") to accept an article or a "reason for rejection." The function can access the article headers through the `%hdr` associative array (e.g., `$hdr{'Message-ID'}` contains the article's Message-ID), and cannot access the article body.

If you're using both TCL and Perl, the Perl filter is run first. After you update one of these filters, you must instruct INN to reload it using:

```
% ctlinnd reload filter.tcl 'comment'
```

or:

```
% ctlinnd reload filter.perl 'comment'
```

Another useful filtering tool for INN (as well as Typhoon/Cyclone and nntprelay servers) is Cleanfeed, available at *http://www.exit109.com/~jeremy/news/cleanfeed.html*. Cleanfeed includes a patch to INN to pass message bodies to the Perl filter and a filter that catches spam by:

---

* The Tool Command Language (TCL), pronounced "tickle." A good guide to TCL by its author is John Ousterhout's *TCL and the TK Toolkit* (Addison-Wesley).

- Rejecting articles it has seen too many copies of before

- Rejecting articles from spamming domains or with headers generated by spamming software

- Rejecting large binary posts

- Limiting the number of cross-posts allowed per article

Cleanfeed can filter outgoing postings by your local users, as well.

Spam Hippo offers many of the same features as Cleanfeed and also works on INN and Typhoon/Cyclone servers. It's available at *http://www.spamhippo.com*.

The Narf program for C News allows C News servers to filter articles using Cleanfeed or other Perl filters (*http://utcc.utoronto.ca/abuse/antispam-stuff/narf/*).

Sites running the Diablo news server can find a patch that allows you to use filters developed for Cyclone servers (including Cleanfeed and Spam Hippo) at *http://www.nntp.sol.net/patches/diablo*.

Alias out spamming sites

Finally, if you identify a site from which little or nothing but spam originates, you can take the ultimate step of *shunning* or *aliasing out* that site. When you alias out a site, you tell your news server to pretend that your site uses the same name as the offending site. Because your news server won't accept postings with its own name in the "Path:" header, this prevents your server from receiving any articles that have passed through the offending site. Be careful to alias out the originating site and not an intermediate Usenet site that also feeds you appropriate articles.

Only INN 1.5 or later can conveniently alias out sites. To alias out a site, edit your INN *newsfeeds* file and change the "ME" line to include a comma-separated list of sites to shun, like this:

```
ME/badsite1.com,badsite2.com\
      :*,@junk,!control*,!local*,etc\
      ::
```

There must be no whitespace around the shunned sites. After editing the *newsfeeds* file, run **ctlinnd reload newsfeeds** *'reason for reload'* to ask the server to reload the file.

If you don't run INN 1.5 or later, you can still ask your feed provider to alias out sites in the feed they provide to you. If your site is *mysite.com*, a site feeding you that runs INN can use:

```
mysite.com/badsite1.com,badsite2.com:...etc
```

to specify that they should not feed you news originating from those sites.

At the Router

MAPS's RBL, discussed earlier, can also be used to block spamming sites at a network router. In order to maintain an up-to-date map of the network around them, routers communicate routing information with one another. If your router can communicate using Border Gateway Protocol (BGP), MAPS can configure its router to tell yours about spamming sites, so that your router can route packets from spammers listed in the RBL to a "black hole" address.*

A major advantage of blocking spam at your exterior router is that the router represents a choke point for data. You can, with a single router change, keep connections from RBL hosts from being made to any system on the network. If you like the RBL concept, this saves you from having to configure every system that receives email to do an RBL DNS lookup.

MAPS requires that you sign an indemnification agreement in order to use the RBL this way. For more information, see *http://maps.vix.com/rbl/usage.html.*

Stopping Outgoing Spam

Protecting your users from incoming spam is important, but the problem of spam won't go away until the spammers themselves are stopped. At the beginning of this chapter, we discussed Acceptable Use Policies (AUPs), a critical approach to discouraging users from spamming. Here we examine some technical tactics that can keep your site from being hijacked by spammers and prevent your users from spamming.

Avoid Being Abused by Outsiders

Spammers can abuse your servers in two primary ways other than by spamming your users directly: they can relay junk email through your mail server, and they can inject news spam through your news server. Here's how to configure your servers to avoid getting hijacked by a spammer.

Don't relay email

If a spammer can use your mail server as a relay, he can send spam that is harder to trace back to him; worse, the spam is easy to trace back to your site, and you'll receive complaints about it. Running a mail server that allows anyone to relay can also get you added to the RBL (discussed earlier), which will cause many other sites to refuse email from you. A February 1998 survey by the Internet Mail Consortium (*http://www.imc.org*) found that 55% of all mail servers allowed relaying.

---

* A gravitational field so dense, even spam can't escape!

The basic approach to prevent relaying is to instruct your mail server that it should accept only email that's either sent by someone at your site or addressed to someone at your site. Clearly, if you are a service provider whose users read their mail with a POP client, the definition of "sent by someone at your site" has to be expanded to include all your users' systems, usually by designating a block of IP addresses for which you are willing to relay messages. Similarly, if you serve as the secondary mail exchanger for another site and thus receive messages for them, the definition of "addressed to someone at your site" has to be expanded to include the site you receive mail for.

The MAPS Transport Security Initiative group has an excellent web site at *http://maps.vix.com/tsi* devoted to relaying. At that site, you can test your mail server to determine whether it allows relaying and learn how to disable relaying for an extensive list of servers.

In particular, *sendmail* 8.9 comes with relaying turned off by default. Earlier versions of *sendmail* allow relaying by default. Claude Assman's anti-spam rules for *sendmail* 8.8 can be used to prevent relaying or allow selective relaying with earlier versions of *sendmail*. They're available at *http://www.informatik.uni-kiel. de/%7Eca/email/check.html*.

If you use *qmail*, you can create the file */var/qmail/control/rcpthosts* and list only hosts you will accept mail for, one per line. If you need to allow relaying from some sites, see Michael Samuel's "How to Configure qmail to be a Selective Relay" at *http://www.surfnetcity.com.au/~michael/qmail-antirelay.html*.

Don't allow open news posting

Another common spammer practice is to post news to Usenet through someone else's open NNTP server. Recall that there are two ways to transfer news to an NNTP server: the `POST` command, used by news readers, and the `IHAVE` command, used by other news servers exchanging news. You should configure your news server to accept `POST`s only from machines in your domain or subnet and to accept `IHAVE`s only from sites you have explicitly agreed to trade news with.

If you use C News with the NNTP Reference Implementation, the *nntp_access* file (usually in */usr/lib/news*) controls access to your server. Each line is formatted like this:

```
host ihave-privileges post-privileges newsgroups
```

The *host* is a hostname, network name, "*.domain.suffix," IP address, or "default." The *ihave-privileges* can be:

read

The client can read news, but cannot use `IHAVE` or `POST` commands.

xfer

> The client can only use news transfer commands, including `IHAVE`. This allows posting via the `IHAVE` command.

both

> The client can use any command but `POST`.

no The client cannot read news at all.

The *post-privileges* can be either `post` (client may use the `POST` command) or `no`. Finally, *newsgroups* is an optional, comma-separated list of newsgroups the client may read; newsgroups prefaced with an exclamation point (!) are denied to the client.

To prevent news posting from other sites, make sure the file contains the line:

```
default        read    no
```

or:

```
default        no      no
```

depending on whether you want to allow outsiders to read news from your server or not, respectively.

If you use INN, the *nnrp.access* file controls which sites can read or post news. The sample file distributed with INN contains the key line to restrict open access:*

```
*:: -no- : -no- :!*
```

This should be the first line in the file. You can allow outsiders to read news but not post news by replacing that line with:

```
*:R: -no- : -no- :*
```

INN can also allow outsiders to post if they have a username and password for logging in to the server; for information about this, see the INN documentation or Henry Spencer and David Lawrence's *Managing Usenet* (O'Reilly & Associates, Inc.).

---

* Chris Lewis notes that older INN servers have bugs that will allow spammers to spam through your server to groups that your server doesn't carry, even if you try to explicitly prevent it in *nnrp.access*. If you must permit `POST`, make sure your server is up-to-date and supplies full tracing information, including "NNTP-Posting-Host:" headers and logging. If you must permit open `IHAVE`—a very bad idea—modify your news server to insert the IP address of the connecting system into the "Path:" line.

Keeping an Eye on Your Users

Finally, here are some ways you can keep an eye on your own users to be sure they're not spamming from your site.

Keep good logs

If you're providing an online service to users, you should keep logs of your computer's activity. These logs can be important evidence if a user is spamming from your site; a mail log showing thousands of posts being relayed from your user's dial-up connection in a short time is highly suggestive.

If you allow dial-up connections, your modems, PPP daemon, or SLIP daemon should be configured to record the date and time of each dial-up connection or disconnection, the identity of the user dialing up, and the IP address assigned to the connection.

If your users connect to local shell accounts, your login daemon should similarly record the date and time of each connection and the username. On Unix systems, enable system accounting so you can review the commands your users have typed, should you need to investigate a spam complaint.

Although the format of logs from mail transport agents and news servers varies a bit from program to program, all can log the basic information critical to documenting abuse: the date and time, the user's login name (for local users) or the IP address of the connecting user's computer (for dial-up users), the number and addresses of recipients or the names of newsgroups to which the message is posted, the Message-Id of the message, and how your server disposed of the message. If your MTA or news server rejected the message, the log should indicate the reason for rejection.

Establish a log retention policy for dial-up access logs, mail server logs, and news server logs. Keep logs for at least a week—ideally, at least a month, if you have the resources to do so.

Run an IDENT server

When a client connects to a server, the server always knows the client's IP address. Under some conditions, the server can also determine the specific user at that address who initiated the connection. RFC 1413 describes the IDENT protocol, a way for servers to ask connecting clients for the name of the user running the process that controls the connection. You may have seen the effect of this protocol if your MTA does an IDENT query when it receives mail for you: the "Received:" header may say "Received: from *username@host*" instead of just "Received: from *host*."

On the one hand, the IDENT protocol doesn't seem to add much security. Because you can't be sure the other site is being honest in its responses to IDENT queries, you can't really trust the username you see.

On the other hand, IDENT becomes very useful when *you* run the IDENT server. If one of your users starts spamming, his messages may enable another system administrator to trace the message back to the user himself, not simply to your site, and to provide you with better evidence with which to confront the user.

When one of your users connects to a remote site (to send email or post news), that site can identify the port number of the connection and ask your IDENT server for the name of the user. If you're concerned about privacy, you can compile the IDENT server to return an encrypted token instead of a username; the server includes a program you can use to decrypt the token into the user's ID and the date, time, and address of the connection the user made.

You can download the *pidentd* IDENT server daemon from *ftp://ftp.lysator.liu.se/ pub/ident/servers*.

Active techniques

There are a variety of techniques you can use to actively detect and stop your users from sending spam mail. Unfortunately, there is little or no off-the-shelf software to implement these techniques. Active spam stopping is pretty much a do-it-yourself affair today.

The easiest way to actively stop spamming is to establish a limit for the number of email messages each user can send in a single day. Then you simply monitor the number of email messages each user sends, and suspend their account (or their ability to send mail) when this limit is exceeded. Here are some details:

Step #1: monitor local usage

  The first step to setting up an active system is to monitor all usage of your mail server by each user. Using Perl or a similar language, you can create a small database that keeps track of the number of email messages sent by each user.

  Now write a small program that examines your log files to detect each incoming TCP/IP connection to your outgoing mail server, determine whether the connection originated from one of your users, and then calculate the number of email messages sent. Add this number to the user's database entry. If the total number of messages sent for the user exceeds a threshold, such as 2,000, disable the user's account and log them off.

  Finally, you'll need to write a small program that clears each user's tally in the database every night.

Once in place, the scripts will prevent your users from sending more than the specified number of email messages on any given day. Unfortunately, your users will still be able to send outstanding mail using other mail servers on the Internet that permit relaying. In order to plug all of these methods, you must take additional measures, as follows.

Step #2, option #1: prevent your users from relaying

The simplest way to prevent your users from sending spam mail through mail servers on the Internet that permit relaying is to block access to those machines from your users. For dial-up users, this can easily be accomplished by using access control lists on your router or Internet gateway. Simply block all outgoing TCP/IP connections originating at the IP addresses associated with your dial-up users with a destination of port 25 for any host on the Internet.

Such an access control list will have no impact on legitimate users who send mail through your mail server. But this list will block email from customers who send mail using mail servers belonging to other organizations.

Step #2, option #2: monitor relaying attempts from your users

Instead of blocking outbound email from your users, it is possible to simply monitor these connections for abuse. One way is to use an access control list such as the one described in the previous section, but instead of using the access control list to block IP packets, simply use it to set off an alarm. Then modify your monitoring scripts to count the number of alarms for each user, adding that number to their daily quota of outgoing email messages.

Alternatively, you can monitor your users directly using a program such as *tcpdump*. The *tcpdump* program, available for many versions of Unix, monitors every TCP/IP packet sent over a local area network. If you place a computer running *tcpdump* between your dial-up users and your outgoing Internet connection, it is possible to monitor every packet your users send and receive. Using a *tcpdump* filter, you can have the program report each outgoing TCP connection that originates on your dial-ups and has a destination of port 25 on a remote host.

 You should notify your users if you engage in any monitoring to actively stop spamming. Most ISP end-user agreements allow the ISP to monitor any user for any purpose whatsoever. However, if you make it clear to your users that spamming will be actively monitored and stopped, the notice may act as a deterrent and stop spammers from obtaining accounts with your ISP in the first place.

Filter outgoing news postings

If you use INN as your news software, and you've compiled it to use Perl for filtering incoming news, you can also write Perl filters for outgoing news. This won't stop users from connecting directly to the NNTP port at a another site and transferring their article by hand, but it can keep inexperienced users from reposting "Make Money Fast" articles and other spam.

The file *filter_nnrpd.pl* controls the filtering of news from news readers before it's injected into the news system. You must define a function called `filter_post` that returns either a null string ("") if the article should be accepted for postings, or a "reason for rejection" that will be returned to the news reader. Just as with incoming filters, the headers of the article are accessible from the associative array `%hdr` (e.g., `$hdr{'Subject'}` contains the article's subject). The sample *filter_nnrpd.pl* file shows how you might prevent users from sending messages with a subject containing "make money" or with invalid "From:" addresses.

The *spamfind* program, by Jonathan Kamens and Chris Lewis, monitors news articles in an attempt to identify authors who send messages to too many newsgroups in a given time. It notifies you about these messages so that you can issue cancel messages or take other action. You can download *spamfind* from the Web at: *http://spam.abuse.net/spam/tools/cancel.txt.**

Another approach to preventing your users from spamming is to limit the rate at which they can post news to your server. Dave Hayes has developed a patch for *nnrpd* (the news server's daemon for the news reader protocol) that does "exponential backoff"—the faster the rate of postings, the slower the server is willing to accept them. After implementing this patch on EarthLink, an ISP that had problems with its customers spamming Usenet, Hayes reported a significant drop in the amount of spam. The patches are available from *http://www.jetcafe.org/~dave/usenet/backoff.html.*

---

* In fact, *spamfind* contains hooks for two functions, *despam* and *udp*, that can be used to turn it into a cancelbot.

8

Community Action

Most of the chapters in this book focus on how an individual user or system administrator can identify, avoid, and respond to spam. This chapter considers ways that groups of people can work together against spam. Although the heterogeneity of experience, attitudes, and beliefs makes it difficult to talk about an "Internet community" or even a "Usenet community," users and administrators working together in common cause against spam have achieved some notable successes. Here we discuss some ways we can help each other.

Sharing Information

When you receive an unsolicited email message, you can't tell whether it was sent in bulk to thousands of recipients. When you see an off-topic posting on Usenet, you can't always tell whether it's been posted to enough newsgroups to constitute spam. One of the key ways in which Internet users work together against spam is by sharing information about the extent and source of unwanted messages.

The Net Abuse Newsgroups

The *news.admin.net-abuse* newsgroups are devoted to reports and discussion of net abuse—abuse *of* the Net, rather than abuse *using* the Net.* Spam and unsolicited email constitute the two biggest topics of discussion. These newsgroups are an excellent resource if you need help tracking down the source of a message, or if you believe you're the first person to notice a Usenet spam. Here's the scoop on these groups.

---

* Sending a stranger an unsolicited email message is net abuse. Sending an acquaintance a threatening email message is abuse using the Net. Sending a stranger a threatening email message is both net abuse and abuse via the Net.

news.admin.net-abuse.bulletins

This moderated group is used to report actions taken against spammers. This is where ISPs post their lists of terminated accounts, spam cancelers post their recent cancelations, spam watchers post analyses of which sites cause the most spam, and so on.

Here's an example of a posting to *news.admin.net-abuse.bulletins*, reporting a set of cancel messages issued for *misc.invest.futures*:

```
Path: news.cc.uic.edu!newsfeed.acns.nwu.edu!vixen.cso.uiuc.edu!alpha.
+      math.uiuc.edu!tskirvin
From: Kirk Rafferty <kirk@rafferty.org>
Newsgroups: misc.invest.futures,news.admin.net-abuse.bulletins
Subject: misc.invest.futures cancel report for 3/1/98
Followup-To: news.admin.net-abuse.usenet
Date: 2 Mar 1998 16:21:34 GMT
Message-ID: <6dek2j$e8o$1-NANA@quasar.dimensional.com>
NNTP-Posting-Host: alpha.math.uiuc.edu
Originator: tskirvin@alpha.math.uiuc.edu
Xref: news.cc.uic.edu misc.invest.futures:66300 news.admin.net-abuse.
+      bulletins:17389

Report ID: TGIFWGASAFBIA.Mon Mar  2 08:40:25 MST 1998

** Short list this week folks, been on vacation :-) **

This report is posted weekly to misc.invest.futures and
news.admin.net-abuse.bulletins.  You can see a daily update at
http://www.rafferty.org/cancel-report.txt.

A copy of this is being posted to news.admin.net-abuse.bulletins.
Followups should be posted to news.admin.net-abuse.usenet.

The following posts to the newsgroup misc.invest.futures have been
canceled by me during this report period.  Only the headers have
been reproduced in this article.  The reason for cancelation is listed
in the summary header.

For a list of criteria used to cancel messages to this group, see
the end of this article.  For a detailed explanation of the criteria
used, go to http://www.rafferty.org/cancel-reasons.html or send email
to cancel@rafferty.org.


----------------------


Subject:    Is Day Trading For You?
From:       "Ned Gandevani" <Gandevani@worldnet.att.net>
Date:       24 Feb 1998 01:57:45 GMT
Message-ID: 6cjuuo$eni@bgtnsc02.worldnet.att.net
Newsgroups: misc.invest.futures
Summary:    EMP Spam, BI>=20
```

```
Subject:    www.finacial-futures.com
From:       "antony north" <antony@financial-futures.com>
Date:       24 Feb 1998 02:00:15 GMT
Message-ID: 01bd3e03$45aafe20$75fa82c1@default
Newsgroups: misc.invest.futures
Summary:    EMP Spam, BI>=19

Subject:    JUST CALL AND MAKE USD 30K !!!
From:       30K@moneyline.com
Date:       24 Feb 1998 02:30:17 GMT
Message-ID: 34EF438B.9E5D2196@moneyline.com
Newsgroups: misc.invest.futures
Summary:    EMP Spam, BI>=20
----------------------
```

Usenet Posts are cancelable under the following criteria:

```
   ...criteria list...
```

news.admin.net-abuse.policy

This moderated group is used to discuss policy issues related to preventing or responding to net abuse. This is where people discuss Acceptable Use Policies (AUPs), what constitutes cancelable spam or other kinds of net abuse, and so on. The group does not allow cross-posting of articles to any other newsgroup.

news.admin.net-abuse.sightings

This moderated group is used to report sightings of spam, unsolicited email, and other forms of net abuse. It's robomoderated—the moderation software allows postings that meet the following guidelines:

- The "Subject:" header should begin with a bracketed "tag" indicating the type of abuse. The most common tags are [`usenet`] for Usenet spam and [`uce`], [`ube`], or [`email`] for unsolicited email.

- The "From:" or "Reply-To:" header must contain a valid Internet address.

- The "Followup-To:" header must be set to *news.admin.net-abuse.email, news. admin.net-abuse.usenet,* or *news.admin.net-abuse.misc.*

- The message body should not contain lines longer than 78 characters.

Here's an example of a posting in *news.admin.net-abuse.sightings*:

```
Path: news.cc.uic.edu!newsfeed.acns.nwu.edu!vixen.cso.uiuc.edu!nanas
From: Joe "We are Borg" Foster <joe@bftsi0.gate.net>
Newsgroups: news.admin.net-abuse.sightings
Subject: [email] Quality Candidates Delivered To You -TAHC
Followup-To: news.admin.net-abuse.email
Date: 28 Feb 1998 06:25:52 GMT
Message-ID: <19980228062201.AA24149@bftsi0.gate.net>
```

```
NNTP-Posting-Host: alpha.math.uiuc.edu
X-Original-Organization: Barbara Foster Tax Service, Inc.
X-Submissions-To: nanas-sub@cybernothing.org
Originator: tskirvin@alpha.math.uiuc.edu
Xref: news.cc.uic.edu news.admin.net-abuse.sightings:14607

Sprint and BigFoot, you know what to do.

> From somewhere!Sat Sat Feb 28 01:14:50 1998
> Received: by bftsi0.gate.net (FlakyMail 0.2)
>         id AA24147; 28 Feb 98 01:14:49 EST (Sat)
> Received: from pima.gate.net (pima.gate.net [198.206.134.30]) by
>           inca.gate.net(8.8.6/8.6.9) with ESMTP id AAA101892 for
>           <joe@bftsi0.gate.net>; Sat, 28 Feb 1998 00:23:43 -0500
> Received: from 206.133.65.47 (sdn-ts-002gaatlaP12.dialsprint.net
>           [206.133.65.47]) by pima.gate.net (8.8.6/8.6.12)
>           with SMTP id AAA46844; Sat, 28 Feb 1998 00:20:11 -0500
> Date: Sat, 28 Feb 1998 00:20:11 -0500
> Message-Id: <199802280520.AAA46844@pima.gate.net>
> Subject:  Quality Candidates Delivered To You -TAHC
> Content-Type: text/plain; charset=ISO-8859-1
> Content-Transfer-Encoding: 7bit
>
>
> E.T.I. is proud to introduce. To selected new clients.
> Our revolutionary document database. Which is available
    ...etc...
```

As in the example, some people post copies of their complaint email to *news. admin.net-abuse.sightings*. It's a good idea to check the group before posting to be sure that no one has already posted about the message you received. If someone has, feel free to follow up her posting in the appropriate follow-up group.

news.admin.net-abuse.email

This group is the place to discuss abuses of email, including unwanted messages. Abuse *by* email (harassment by email, for example), is not an appropriate topic for this group, and reports of large-scale unsolicited email belong in *news.admin.net-abuse.sightings*.

news.admin.net-abuse.usenet

This group is the place to discuss abuses of Usenet, including spam (ECP and EMP), "Make Money Fast" chain letters, forgery, and improper cancelation. Again, abuse *by* news is not appropriate, and reports of abuse belong in *news.admin.net-abuse.sightings*.

news.admin.net-abuse.misc

This group is for discussion of net abuse that doesn't fall into the other groups.

Mailing Lists

The SPAM-L mailing list is a high-traffic mailing list devoted to discussion of spam prevention. To subscribe, send email to *LISTSERV@peach.ease.lsoft.com* with `SUB-SCRIBE SPAM-L` *Your Name* in the body of the message. The mailing list has a Frequently Asked Questions page at *http://www.bounce.to/spam-l*.

Another mailing list that serves as a source of spam information is *spam-list@hiss.han.de*. This list accepts only spam; list subscribers forward spam messages to the list with complete headers. No discussion is allowed, and a filter ensures that the same spam is distributed only once. The list is an ideal source of spam for people who are devising filters. To subscribe, send a message to *majordomo@hiss.han.de* with `subscribe spam-list` in the body of the message.

Group Action

Although there's a lot that individual administrators can do about spam sent to (or from) their users, coordinated anti-spam actions, particularly on Usenet, can be even more powerful.

Usenet Spam Traps

It's harder to cancel excessively cross-posted articles than excessively multiposted articles, because there may not be enough copies of the article to reach a Breidbart Index (BI) of 20. This is especially true when an article is cross-posted to all the groups, appropriate or inappropriate, in some newsgroup hierarchy.

A particularly clever approach to these problems is the spam trap newsgroup. A spam trap is a newsgroup chartered specifically to permit cancelation of any article posted or cross-posted to the spam trap. The trap group must have some indication of its function in its name. The group is created in a hierarchy that is beset with articles cross-posted to the entire hierarchy.

The current best example of a spam trap is the newsgroup *alt.sex.cancel*. Anything posted (or, more often, cross-posted) to *alt.sex.cancel* is fair game for a third-party cancel, and this helps eliminate many articles (usually adult advertisements) that are blindly cross-posted to all the *alt.sex* groups. When a spammer instructs his software to cross-post an ad in all *alt.sex* groups, the ad appears in *alt.sex.cancel*, and someone's cancelbot automatically issues a cancel message for the article. This removes the article not only from *alt.sex.cancel*, but from *every other newsgroup in which it was cross-posted*.

If you think a spam trap would be useful for a newsgroup hierarchy that you participate in, open a discussion of the idea on *news.admin.net-abuse.usenet*. The other readers of that group can offer opinions about whether a spam trap is a viable option and help you learn how to propose the creation of the spam trap newsgroup.

The Usenet Death Penalty

When a site has consistently proven to be a source of Usenet spam and has failed to take action against spammers when incidents are reported, Usenet news administrators may call for a Usenet Death Penalty (UDP) against the rogue site. A UDP amounts to cutting the rogue site off from Usenet until it shapes up. A UDP proceeds in one of two ways:

- A *passive UDP* involves news administrators agreeing to alias out the rogue site and accept no postings that have passed through it.* If many news administrators honor the UDP, especially administrators of major news sites that feed many other sites, the rogue site will effectively vanish from Usenet—they may continue to receive news, but nothing posted from the site will propagate elsewhere. Because many new administrators are likely to forget to stop aliasing out the site, even if it makes improvements, a passive UDP can have indefinitely lingering effects and is considered to be an extremely serious measure. For historical reasons, a passive UDP is sometimes also referred to as a *phase 1* UDP.

- An *active UDP* involves a group of news administrators issuing third-party cancel notices for every article posted from the rogue site (often with the exception of articles destined for *news.admin.net-abuse.usenet*, so the site can post evidence that it is taking steps to contravene spam). These cancel notices include the pseudo-site `udpcancel` in the Path: header as well as a pseudo-site specific to the rogue site (such as `netcomudp`). This allows news administrators who don't want to participate in the UDP to alias out the UDP cancels and continue to receive news from the rogue site. For historical reasons, an active UDP is sometimes also referred to as a *phase 2 UDP*.

Active UDPs are generally preferred because they are easier to initiate, easier to end, and provide valuable statistics on the effect of the UDP, such as the number of canceled articles. In addition, news administrators can more easily choose not to participate in an active UDP. Passive UDPs tend to be reserved for use against sites that have no legitimate users, aggressively post only spam, and are at the fringes of Usenet.

---

* Chapter 7, *Spam Stopping for Administrators and ISPs*, explains how to alias out a site.

There is no central administration for Usenet; a UDP can be suggested by anyone and takes place when enough news administrators at important news sites agree to join in. In order to give the rogue site a chance to clean up its act, however, some generally accepted UDP procedures have been established:

1. A potential UDP is discussed on *news.admin.net-abuse.usenet*; representatives from the rogue site are invited to respond and explain their plans for addressing spam. Being responsive to complaints about Usenet abuse is the primary way to avoid a UDP.

2. If a consensus builds that the rogue site has been unresponsive, a UDP warning is mailed to the rogue site and posted to *news.admin.net-abuse.usenet*, *news.admin.net-abuse.policy*, and *news.admin.announce*. The warning gives the rogue site five business days to show improvement in handling of spam and gives other news administrators time to prepare for the UDP.

3. If there has been no change in the amount of spam from the rogue site after five business days, the UDP is declared with posts to the same set of newsgroups. During the UDP, postings of spam statistics in *news.admin.net-abuse. sightings* and *news.admin.net-abuse.bulletins* are closely monitored to assess the UDP's effect.

4. Once the rogue site shows improvement—typically evidence of less spam and an action plan for dealing with future spammers (often an improved AUP and more responsive abuse staff)—the administrator who posted the UDP declaration posts a notice lifting the UDP. The action plan is more significant than the reduction in spam itself; spam nearly always drops when a UDP is declared because spammers desert the cut-off site for another spam-friendly provider.

If third-party cancel messages are controversial, UDPs are doubly so because they punish any innocent users at the targeted site as well as spammers. It's important to note, however, that participation in a UDP is totally voluntary—any site can alias out the UDP cancel messages and continue to receive postings from the rogue site. Users at the rogue site can still read and post news, but their posted articles may not be accepted by other news sites. This can pose a problem if a Usenet newsgroup is moderated by a user at a rogue site, but other news sites typically step forward to provide the moderator with an account from which to approve articles.

Moreover, the UDP works. In 1997, UDPs were pronounced on some major ISPs, including CompuServe and UUNET. In both cases, the UDP had its desired effect—within a week, each ISP had instituted better spam controls and had become more responsive to spam complaints. Because the UDP has proven so effective, even the threat of a UDP can now be sufficient to cause a provider to act; in February 1998, Netcom narrowly averted a UDP by greatly reducing the amount of spam from its customers.

If a UDP is declared, and you support the action, you can participate by running a *UDPbot*, a program that removes postings that originated at the rogue site from your own news server. This kind of bot doesn't generate cancel messages; it only affects your users and sites to which you feed news. Running a UDPbot ensures that you're not seeing articles from the rogue site; relying on the UDP cancel messages may not.* A somewhat dated UDPbot by Richard Salz is available at *http://spam.abuse.net/spam/tools/salz*. Salz's bot, written in Perl, removes articles based on the user in the "From:" header, but could be easily modified to make decisions based on the "Path:" header instead. Peter da Silva's UDPbot, written in TCL and intended for use with the INN server, removes articles based on the address in the "Message-ID:," "From:," or "Reply-To:." It's available at *http://spam. abuse.net/spam/tools/udp.txt*.

Ken Lucke's Usenet Death Penalty FAQ is at *http://www.stopspam.org/usenet/faqs/ udp.html*.

The Internet Death Penalty

In the spirit of the Usenet Death Penalty, the Internet Death Penalty (IDP) seeks to punish sites that abuse the Internet through unsolicited bulk email. In an IDP, network administrators configure their routers to block any connections from the rogue site. The site is effectively cut off from the Internet. Although IDPs are discussed in *news.admin.net-abuse.email*, they're much harder to declare. Usenet is decentralized, but administrators of backbone news sites still maintain some collective power; the Internet as a whole has no such group. Moreover, an IDP is a much more serious step than a UDP, and administrators are correspondingly more reluctant to block rogue sites at the router, rather than simply filter email.

Legal and Legislative Action

Spam is a social problem, and technical solutions, while helpful, do not address the larger societal context. Recently, considerable attention has focused on legal and legislative approaches to curbing unwanted messages.

 As this book went to press, the U.S. Attorney's office in Boston said that as a matter of policy, spamming cases would not be prosecuted pending the adoption of new legislation on the matter.

---

* Although the UDP cancel messages are injected at major news sites on the Usenet backbone, you might have the misfortune to receive news from the rogue site before you receive the cancel messages for that news, depending on how your feed is arranged.

Legal Approaches

Legal approaches come in three flavors: licensing arrangements, civil lawsuits, and criminal charges. We describe each of these in the following sections.

Licensing

Acceptable Use Policies (AUPs), discussed in Chapter 7, are the most familiar contractual agreement that can prohibit spamming and deter spammers. Another focus of licensing is the software used for sending email. Pegasus Mail is a popular free Windows email client by David Harris. Because it's free and full-featured, it's been bundled with many spamming software packages. In 1996 and 1997, Harris modified the license agreement under which Pegasus can be used. The license agreement now includes these paragraphs:

```
3: The supply or promotion of Pegasus Mail for the purpose of sending
bulk, unsolicited email is incompatible with the basic aims of the
program, which revolve around the free provision of a service that
enhances the quality of peoples' communication. Pegasus Mail may not
be included in any package designed for this purpose, whether free or
otherwise, nor may vendors of such packages use the "Pegasus Mail"
trademark or other related material in the promotion of their package.

Vendors or suppliers currently including Pegasus Mail in their bulk
email products are hereby required to remove copies of and all
references to the Pegasus Mail software from their products. Failure
to comply with this requirement will lead to legal action.

3a: Prohibited use: Pegasus Mail may not be used for the purpose of
sending Bulk Unsolicited Commercial Electronic Mail. For the purposes
of this section, this shall be construed to mean electronic mail sent
to a total of more than 50 recipients for the purpose of advertising a
commercial product or service, where the recipient has not explicitly
expressed interest in receiving such advertisements.
```

The Pegasus Mail licensing agreement prohibits unsolicited commercial email, and Harris can now sue spammers who use his software. Although this will not stop spammers from writing their own email software, the time required to write such software is substantial enough that spammers may be deterred.

If this sort of licensing spreads to other email packages, it could have a significant impact on spam. In fact, any piece of software could include a license prohibiting its use by companies that engage in spamming or other Net-abusive practices. If you develop software, consider including such a stipulation in your license.

Civil suits

If you can prove that you have been harmed by spam, you are probably entitled to relief in the form of an injunction against the spammer and/or monetary damages. This isn't easy or fun: it's difficult to prove harm from a particular spammer or company. It's not cheap to file even a small-claims lawsuit when you include the cost of serving papers to the spammer, and you can expect a lot of trouble collecting the damages if you win the lawsuit. If a spammer forges your email address (or an address at your site, if you're an ISP), you have much stronger grounds for a civil suit.

Some anti-spam activists attach a notice to their Usenet postings or their complaints about unsolicited email, offering to critique unsolicited messages for a fee and noting that receipt of further unsolicited mail constitutes acceptance of the contract. When they receive another unsolicited message from the spammer, they take the spammer to small-claims court to collect their fee. Junkbusters Corporation advocates this approach, and includes a sample contract and instructions for its use at *http://www.junkbusters.com/ht/en/spam.html#strong*.

Does it work? Greg Byshenk, in "Legal Approaches to Dealing with Junk Email" (*http://www.tezcat.com/~gbyshenk/spam.legal.html*), argues that the contract is probably not legally binding unless the spammer has received legal notification of the contract (e.g., by certified mail); the spammer has the right to disavow the contract in any case. And you'll certainly have difficulty collecting even if you get a settlement.

ISPs may have a better chance than individuals. R&D Associates has sent bills to a number of spammers for the cost of storing messages on their servers, training clients in dealing with junk email, and deleting junk email. When the spammers refused to pay, R&D turned their bills over to their collection agents and initiated some lawsuits against spamming companies. As of February 1998, one of the companies had attempted unsuccessfully to settle out of court. For further updates on their success, see R&D's web page at *http://www.kclink.com/spam*. America Online has initiated a number of trademark-infringement lawsuits against spammers who forge their return addresses to resemble AOL addresses.

A number of ISPs have won injunctions and restraining orders against spamming companies, especially the late Cyber Promotions, Inc. U.S. courts have generally found that the spammers do not have the right to distribute their messages on other companies' systems, use other systems as spam relays, or forge return addresses that appear to be from other systems.

In late 1997, Juno Online Services initiated a $5 million U.S. District Court lawsuit against spammers for sending spam with forged *juno.com* "From:" addresses, charging them with false designation of origin and false description, misappropriation of name and identity, misrepresentation, common law fraud, and unjust enrichment.

In June 1998, a federal court issued a permanent injunction against spammers who had forged *hotmail.com*'s domain name in their messages. It also ordered three companies to pay Hotmail a total of $337,500 in damages.

Information on a host of other cases is available from Professor David Sorkin's web site, *http://host1.jmls.edu/cyber/cases/spam.html*.

Criminal charges

If the unwanted messages are illegal in themselves, you might be able to get criminal charges filed against the spammer. In New York v. Lipsitz (1997), the Attorney General of New York charged a New York resident with violations of consumer fraud and false advertising statutes for email messages, with forged return addresses, that sold magazine subscriptions that subsequently failed to arrive.

Another basis for criminal charges is denial of service. If spam received is sufficient to prevent your mail or news server from functioning, the spammer may have committed an illegal attack on your system. Many countries have laws against breaking into computer systems that might be applied in this situation.

If spam from a particular organization becomes a major problem for you, have an administrator contact the spammer's organization, demand that they cease mailing your domain, and state that further mailings will be considered trespassing. This sometimes works.

If you think a spammer has broken the law, consult the police or the Attorney General's office.

Legislation

Internet law is murky; little legislation has direct bearing on email or Usenet news. Some anti-spam activists argue that the 1991 Telephone Consumer Protection Act, 47 U.S.C. 227 (TCPA) already prohibits junk email. The TCPA was written to outlaw junk faxes, but could be interpreted as outlawing junk email as well. The relevant text of the law is:

> (a) Definitions . . .
> > (2) The term "telephone facsimile machine" means equipment which has the capacity (A) to transcribe text or images, or both, from paper into an electronic signal and to transmit that signal over a regular telephone line, or (B) to transcribe text or images (or both) from an electronic signal received over a regular telephone line onto paper . . .
> (b) Restrictions on use of automated telephone equipment
> > (1) Prohibitions
> > > It shall be unlawful for any person within the United States . . .
> > > > (C) to use any telephone facsimile machine, computer, or other device to send an unsolicited advertisement to a telephone facsimile machine

The definition of a telephone facsimile machine could be construed to refer to any computer connected to both a modem and a printer or scanner. Under this construal, unsolicited commercial email is already illegal, and the act provides the right for anyone who receives it to sue the sender for at least $500 per violation. On the other hand, Mark Eckenwiler argued in the March 1996 issue of *NetGuide* that by specifically naming "computer" separately from "telephone facsimile machine" in (b)(1)(C), the act implicitly fails to provide remedy against junk email. Certainly, there is room for argument.

Federal legislation

Four bills in the U.S. Senate and House of Representatives have been proposed to clarify the legality of bulk email:

The Smith Bill (H.R. 1748)

Sponsored by New Jersey Representative Christopher Smith, the Netizens Protection Act of 1997 makes it unlawful to:

> use any computer or other electronic device to send an unsolicited advertisement to an electronic mail address of an individual with whom such person lacks a pre-existing and ongoing business or personal relationship unless said individual provides express invitation or consent/permission.

and to:

> use a computer or other electronic device to send an unsolicited advertisement to an electronic mail address unless such person clearly provides, at the beginning of such unsolicited advertisement, the date and time the message was sent, the identity of the business, other entity, or individual sending the message, and the return electronic mail address of such business, other entity, or individual.

The Smith Bill has received broad support from the Internet community. It extends the highly successful junk fax ban, allowing the recipient of the junk mail a direct remedy against the spammer, whether the spam was sent knowingly or not.

The Murkowski Bill (S. 771)

Sponsored by Alaska Senator Frank Murkowski, the Unsolicited Commercial Email Choice Act of 1997 requires that unsolicited commercial email contain the word "advertisement" in the "Subject:" header and include valid contact information for the sender, including a valid email address. It also requires ISPs to allow their customers to "opt out" of unsolicited commercial email by filtering messages with "advertisement" in the "Subject:" header.

On May 12, 1998, the Senate passed a modified version of S. 771 as an amendment to to S. 1618, the Anti-Spamming Amendments Act. The passed version requires spammers to include valid contact information in unsolicited commercial email and to allow recipients to opt out by replying with `remove` in the subject of the message. It prohibits forgery of headers and places no burden on ISPs. A companion House Resolution, H.R. 3888, has been introduced with identical language.

The Murkowski amendment allows spam to continue, albeit in a clearly marked fashion, and places the burden of spam on the shoulders of the recipient. It has not received support from anti-spam activists, because it legitimizes unsolicited commercial email.

The Torricelli Bill (S. 875)

Sponsored by New Jersey Senator Robert Torricelli, the Electronic Mailbox Protection Act of 1997 makes it unlawful to:

- Send unsolicited email with a fake return address

- Fail to remove people from mailing lists on request

- Distribute a list containing people who've asked to be removed

- Send unsolicited email to someone who's asked not to receive it

- Register a domain name for the purpose of unlawfully sending unsolicited email

- Send email to the users of an ISP when the email violates the ISP's policies

- Harvest email addresses from an ISP's server when this action violates the ISP's policies

The Torricelli Bill was drafted with the help of the Direct Marketing Association and suffers from some of the same problems as the Murkowski Bill: notably, users must opt out of spam. Similar bills, H.R. 4124 and H.R. 4176, were introduced into the House of Representatives in June 1998 by Utah Representative Merrill Coole and Massachusetts Representative Edward Markey.

The Tauzin Bill (H.R. 2368)

Sponsored by Louisiana Representative William Tauzin, the Data Privacy Act of 1997 establishes voluntary guidelines for harvesting email addresses and transmitting unsolicited commercial email. The act especially addresses obtaining information from children and suggests that consumers be allowed to opt out of the disclosure of their email address or other information. Unsolicited commercial email should identify the sender accurately and should provide a means to opt out. An industry working group will create a registration system for spammers who agree to follow the guidelines—spammers who register will be protected from charges of unfair trade practices and allowed to use binding arbitration to resolve complaints from users.

The Tauzin Bill has aroused genuine ire and concern among anti-spam activists because it legitimizes both spam and information harvesting. Not only are the guidelines voluntary, but companies that accept the guidelines and register gain some protection from lawsuits.

 Call your representative or senator to express your opinion about each of these bills; they're very interested in hearing public opinion on matters of this sort. You can find your congressperson's phone number at *http://www.access.gpo.gov/congress/*.

State legislation

Many state legislatures have also introduced bills on spam. As introduced, many of these bills would have effectively banned unsolicited commercial email. Unfortunately, the versions of the legislation that have actually been enacted have focused less on whether junk email should be permitted than on keeping spammers from disguising their addresses. For example, Nevada's Senate Bill 13, which took effect in July 1998, provides civil damages against unsolicited commercial email unless:

> (c) The advertisement is readily identifiable as promotional, or contains a statement providing that it is an advertisement, and clearly and conspicuously provides:
> (1) The legal name, complete street address and electronic mail address of the person transmitting the electronic mail; and
> (2) A notice that the recipient may decline to receive additional electronic mail that includes an advertisement from the person transmitting the electronic mail and the procedures for declining such electronic mail.

In short, spam remains legal as long as the spammer is identified and offers an opt-out option.

Similarly, Washington House Bill 2752, which took effect in June 1998, says that commercial email that:

> (a) Uses a third party's internet domain name without permission of the third party, or otherwise misrepresents any information in identifying the point of origin or the transmission path of a commercial electronic mail message; or
>
> (b) Contains false or misleading information in the subject line is a violation of Washington's Consumer Protection Act.

In July 1998, a Washingtonian received a $200 settlement from a spamming company after threatening legal action under the act.

Many other states have introduced legislation addressing spam. For an excellent list of statutes and bills related to spam, see *http://host1.jmls.edu/cyber/statutes/email/index.html*.

Informing the Public

Public opinion can be very influential in passing legislation. Spammers typically defend themselves and argue against new laws on the basis of unrestricted free speech and unrestricted commerce. Anti-spam activists need to make the public aware of the dangers posed by spam and why restrictions on spam do not constitute censorship or a restriction on legitimate commerce.

The Spam Media Tracker at *http://www-fofa.concordia.ca/spam/news.shtml* maintains a list of media mentions of spam. In addition to being a useful resource for keeping up-to-date on who's saying what and who's suing whom, the Media Tracker may alert you to articles about spam in your local media. If a local newspaper article presents only spammers' views on unsolicited email, consider writing a letter to the editor.

CAUCE, the Coalition Against Unsolicited Commercial Email, is a volunteer group of anti-spam activists that promotes H.R. 1748 and other legislative approaches that they consider to be positive steps toward resolution of the problem of spam. They've testified at government hearings and worked to direct media attention to the dangers of unsolicited commercial email. If you're interested in CAUCE, check out their home page at *http://www.cauce.org/.* Joining CAUCE and expressing support for anti-spam consumer protection laws is another way to fight spam.

A

Tools and Information

This appendix is a reference to the programs, web sites, and documents mentioned in the book.

General Resources

"Help! I've been spammed! What do I do?," originally written by Chris Lewis and now maintained by Greg Byshenk, is a good guide to spam and spam prevention for the beginner. It's posted regularly to *news.answers, news.newusers.questions* and *news.admin.net-abuse.misc* and is at *http://www.tezcat.com/~gbyshenk/ive. been.spammed.html.*

The first academic study of spam has recently been performed. See Lorrie Faith Cranor and Brian A. LaMacchia, "Spam!" in *Communications of the ACM*, Vol. 41, No. 8 (Aug. 1998), pp. 74–83, *http://www.acm.org/pubs/citations/journals/ cacm/1998-41-8/p74-cranor/.*

See also "Report to the Federal Trade Commission of the Ad-hoc Working Group on unsolicited commercial email," a comprehensive report that was organized by the Center for Democracy and Technology, *http://www.cdt.org/spam.*

The other resources listed in this section provide helpful background information.

RFCs

Internet Request For Comments (RFC) documents describe or propose standards for the Internet. You can get RFCs by FTP from *venera.isi.edu*, in the *in-notes* directory, or on the Web at *http://www.isi.edu/rfc-editor/rfc.html*, or *http://www.cis. ohio-state.edu/hypertext/information/rfc.html.*

Some notable RFCs for spam fighters include:

- RFC 821, *Simple Mail Transfer Protocol*, explains SMTP, the protocol used to transfer email from system to system.

- RFC 822, *Standard for the Format of ARPA Internet Text Messages*, is the basic document that describes the formatting of email messages.

- RFC 974, *Mail Routing and the Domain System*, clarifies the interactions between mail and the Domain Name System (DNS).

- RFC 977, *Network News Transfer Protocol*, describes NNTP, the protocol used by both Internet news servers to exchange news.

- RFC 1034, *Domain Names—Concepts and Facilities*, introduces DNS.

- RFC 1036, *Standard for Interchange of Usenet Messages*, documents the formatting of Usenet news articles.

- RFC 1855, *Netiquette Guidelines*, outlines a minimal set of rules that users should follow to be good Internet citizens. A good document to cite if a spammer claims that netiquette is a myth.

- RFC 2151, *A Primer on Internet and TCP/IP Tools and Utilities*, covers *traceroute*, *whois*, and a variety of other useful Internet tools.

Mailing Lists and Newsgroups

Two mailing lists related to spam are SPAM-L and spam-list. SPAM-L is devoted to discussions of how to fight spam; information on SPAM-L is available at *http://bounce.to/spam-l*. spam-list is a list for junk email itself—people forward copies of spam to spam-list and use the messages as a resource for learning how to successfully filter junk email. To join spam-list, send email to *majordomo@hiss.han.de* with `subscribe spam-list` in the message body.

The groups in the *news.admin.net-abuse* Usenet hierarchy are devoted to discussion and reporting of net abuse, including spam. These groups are discussed in detail in Chapter 8, *Community Action*.

Tracking Spam

This section describes resources for tracking the source of spam messages.

Documents

A list of Internet domain name registries that you can search with *whois* can be found at *http://rs.internic.net/help/other-reg.html*.

Tools

The AGNetTools IP toolkit is a free *ping/traceroute/lookup/whois* program for Mac and Windows users. It's at *http://www.aggroup.com*.

Consumer.net offers a *traceroute* tool on its web page at *http://consumer.net/trace-rt.asp*.

Blighty Design has a web page called "Sam Spade, Spam Hunter" that offers many handy lookup tools at *http://www.blighty.com/spam/spade.html*.

You can perform a *whois* lookup on the InterNIC's registry at *http://whois.internic.net/cgi-bin/whois*.

DejaNews archives Usenet articles and can help you find identical articles to document a case of spamming. It's at *http://www.dejanews.com*. AltaVista at *http://www.altavista.digital.com* offers similar features.

Avoiding Spam

This section describes resources for avoiding spam in the first place.

Documents

A list of email-to-Usenet gateways is available at *http://www.sabotage.org/~don/mail2news.html*.

Tools

You can get a free email account from Hotmail (*http://www.hotmail.com*) or Juno (*http://www.juno.com*). If you post to Usenet with these accounts, you don't have to worry about spammers harvesting your real email address. You can use these accounts to register for web-based news posting services at *http://www.dejanews.com* or *http://www.reference.com*.

The Replay anonymous remailer can provide you with anonymous email. It's at *http://www.replay.com/remailer/*.

Private Idaho by Joel McNamara is anonymous email and news posting software for Windows. It's at *http://www.eskimo.com/~joelm/pi.html*.

Mac users can try anonAIMouS by Chris Riley at *http://hyperarchive.lcs.mit.edu/HyperArchive/Archive/comm/inet/mail/* or Yet-Another-NewsWatcher by Brian Clark at *ftp://ftp.acns.nwu.edu/pub/newswatcher/*.

premail by Raph Levien is a system to simplify anonymous remailing from Unix accounts. It's at *ftp://ftp.replay.com/pub/replay/pub/remailer/premail*.

John Harvey's *makebait* Perl script at *http://linux.lan.com/spam/tools/makebait.txt* creates web pages full of phony addresses to confound harvesters. You can find variations on this idea by searching Yahoo! (*http://www.yahoo.com*) for "Bot Bait."

Blocking Spam

This section describes resources for blocking spam at your site.

Documents

The MAPS Transport Security Initiative (*http://www.vix.com/tsi*) offers comprehensive information about disabling open relaying in many Mail Transport Agents (MTAs).

If you use *sendmail* as your MTA, two excellent guides to blocking spam with *sendmail* rules are *http://www.sendmail.org/antispam.html* and *http://www.informatik.uni-kiel.de/%7Eca/email/check.html*. If you're not a *sendmail* guru, pick up Bryan Costales's *Sendmail, Second Edition* (O'Reilly & Associates, Inc.). It's the *sendmail* bible.* Another good source is Frederick Avolio and Paul Vixie's *Sendmail: Theory and Practice*, published by Digital Press.

If you use *qmail* as your MTA, spam-blocking information is available at *http://www.qmail.org/#addons*. Also check out Michael Samuel's "How to Configure qmail to be a Selective Relay" at *http://www.surfnetcity.com.au/~michael/qmail-antirelay.html*.

Four sites that maintain rogue lists are:

- MindSpring (*http://www.mindspring.com/cgi-bin/spamlist.pl*)
- zNet (*http://www.znet.com/spammers.txt*)
- WSRCC (*http://www.wsrcc.com/spam/spamlist.txt*)
- E-Scrub Techologies (*http://www.e-scrub.com/cgi-bin/blacklists.cgi*)

User Tools

Junkproof offers automatically filtered email accounts for a fee. See *http://www.junkproof.com* for details. Bigfoot offers a similar service at no charge (*http://www.bigfoot.com*).

If you prefer to do your filtering yourself, check out the suggestions by Multimedia Marketing Group at *http://www.mmgco.com/nospam*.

---

* If you *are* a *sendmail* guru, you probably already have a copy!

The most popular and powerful Unix filtering program is *procmail*. It's available at *ftp://ftp.informatik.rwth-aachen.de/pub/packages/procmail/*. A good tutoral on filtering spam with *procmail* is *http://shell3.ba.best.com/~ariel/nospam/proctut.shtml*.

Administrator Tools

The *getspam* script compiles a master spammer list from one or more of the rogue lists on the Web. You can get it from this book's web and FTP sites; see "Getting the Scripts" in the Preface.

Once you've got a list of spamming hosts, you can block their access to any TCP port on your system using TCP wrappers (*ftp://ftp.win.tue.nl/pub/security*).

Mail Abuse Prevention System's Realtime Blackhole List (MAPS RBL) is a well-maintained rogue list in the form of a name server: if you can look up a host in the RBL name server, you don't want to get mail from it. RBL can also be used by your router to route packets from rogue hosts into oblivion. For basic information, see *http://maps.vix.com/rbl* and *http://maps.vix.com/rbl/usage.html*. For details about doing an RBL lookup within *sendmail*, see *http://www.informatik.uni-kiel.de/%7Eca/email/check.html*; for *qmail*, see *http://www.qmail.org/rbl/*.

If you don't use InterNet News (INN) as your news server, maybe you should. It offers good filtering capabilities right out of the box. Get it at *http://www.isc.org/inn.html*.

If you use INN, Cleanfeed at *http://www.exit109.com/~jeremy/news/cleanfeed.html* adds even better filtering capabilities. If you use C News, consider Narf (at *http://utcc.utoronto.ca/abuse/antispam-stuff/narf/*), which manages to make Cleanfeed work on C News systems.

Running an IDENT server can help you identify problem users at your site. You can get *pidentd* at *ftp://ftp.lysator.liu.se/pub/ident/servers*.

Responding to Spam

This section provides resources for responding to spam.

Complaining

Phil Agre's article, "How to Complain About Spam, or Put a Spammer in the Slammer," available at *http://dlis.gseis.ucla.edu/people/pagre/spam.html*, gives a nice introduction to how to complain about spam.

If the message sounds like a scam, you can report it to the National Fraud Information Center (NFIC) by using its online report form at *http://www.fraud.org/info/repoform.htm*.

The U.S. Postal Inspector's final words on chain letters, suitable for inclusion in responses to them, is at *http://www.usps.gov/websites/depart/inspect/chainlet.htm*.

Handy tools for automating spam complaints include:

- Spam Bouncer (*procmail*-based): *http://www.best.com/~ariel/nospam*.

- Antispam for MS Exchange: *http://www.bsitech.com/antispam/antispam.zip*.

- Spam Hater (MS Windows): *http://www.cix.co.uk/~net-services/spam/spam_hater.htm*.

- adcomplain (Unix Perl): *http://agora.rdrop.com/users/billmc/adcomplain.html*.

- mspam (Unix Perl): John Levine's original version is at *http://www.abuse.net/mspam.txt*; Dougal Campbell's adaptation is at *http://advicom.net/~dougal/antispam/mymspam.txt*.

- jmfilter (Unix): *http://www.io.com/~johnbob/jm/jmfilter.html*.

Cancel Messages

This section provides resources related to cancel messages.

FAQs

Tim Skirvin's Cancel Messages FAQ is the basic FAQ for cancels. It's posted regularly to *news.answers* and is also at *http://www.uiuc.edu/ph/www/tskirvin/faqs/cancel.html*.

The Spam Thresholds FAQ, originally by Chris Lewis and now maintained by Tim Skirvin, explains the current consensus about what constitutes spamming. It's at *http://www.uiuc.edu/ph/www/tskirvin/faqs/spam.html*.

Shaun Davis-Gluyas' Bincancel FAQ explains the rules for canceling large binaries in nonbinary newsgroups. It's at *http://www.southcom.com.au/~geniac/binfull.txt*.

Rosalind Hengeveld's Newsgroup Care Cancel Cookbook tells you how to issue cancel messages (or NoCeMs) to enforce a newsgroup charter. *http://www.xs4all.nl/~rosalind/faq-care.html*.

Ken Lucke's Usenet Death Penalty FAQ explains the UDP. *http://www.stopspam.org/usenet/faqs/udp.html*.

Tools

The Usenet Moderator's Archive at *http://www.landfield.com/moderators/* has a collection of programs for newsgroup moderators, many of which can issue cancel messages.

Chris Lewis's *spamfind* and *artcancel* programs, at *http://spam.abuse.net/spam/tools/cancel.txt*, can help identify spam and cancel articles.

Two UDP bots are Richard Salz's (written in Perl) at *http://spam.abuse.net/spam/tools/salz* and Peter da Silva's (written in TCL) at *http://spam.abuse.net/spam/tools/udp.txt*.

NoCeM

To issue NoCeM notices, you must have a copy of PGP. See *http://www.pgp.com* (USA only) or *http://www.pgpi.com* (international) for information.

Cancelmoose's web site, *http://www.cm.org*, is the basic source for all NoCeM information.

The *news.lists.filters* is where NoCeM notices should be posted. This group is also a good place to look if you want to learn what properly formatted notices look like.

The NoCeM Registry lists a number of NoCeM issuers, their policy for issuing notices, and whether their notices are appropriate to apply "on-spool." It's at *http://www.xs4all.nl/~rosalind/nocemreg/nocemreg.html*.

Alan Schwartz's *mknocem* Perl script issues NoCeM notices for an article or a group of articles saved in an mbox-style file. It's available from this book's web and FTP sites; see "Getting the Scripts" in the Preface.

If you want to apply NoCeM notices to your entire news spool, check out NoCeM-on-spool. The INN version is at *ftp://ftp.mpcs.com/pub/newsadmin/nocem*; the C News version is at *http://sites.inka.de/~bigred/devel/c-nocem.tar.gz*.

Outlawing Spam

Most ISPs will have Acceptable Use Policies (AUPs) that you can use as a basis for your own. Some good examples of AUPs are Netcom (*http://www.netcom.com/netcom/aug.html*), Demon Internet, Ltd. (*http://www.demon.net/connect/aup/*), Sprintlink (*http://www.sprint.net/acceptableuse.htm*), and America Online (*ftp://ftp.aol.com/pub/usenet/aol-usenet-aup.txt*).

Junkbusters offers a number of ideas for legal approaches to fighting spam at *http://www.junkbusters.com/ht/en/spam.html#strong*. For another, more skeptical view, see Greg Byshenk's "Legal Approaches to Dealing with Junk Email" (*http://www.tezcat.com/~gbyshenk/spam.legal.html*).

R&D Associates has been suing spammers for the resources they use when they spam R&D users. Follow the fights at *http://www.kclink.com/spam*.

Law Professor David Sorkin tracks spam-related cases (*http://host1.jmls.edu/cyber/cases/spam.html*) and statutes (*http://host1.jmls.edu/cyber/statutes/email/index.html*). These sites are excellent resources for people interested in the legal aspects of junk mail. Tigerden (*http://www.tigerden.com*) also has pages that track cases and legislation.

The Spam Media Tracker lists media mentions of Net abuse at *http://www-fofa.concordia.ca/spam/news.shtml*.

CAUCE, the Coalition Against Unsolicited Commercial Email, is a major lobbying body for legislation against spam. You can read about their actions and join them at *http://www.cauce.org/*.

B

Cyber Promotions Timeline

The information in this appendix is gathered here to illustrate the rise and fall of one of the most notorious spammers, Cyber Promotions, Inc. By focusing on this company as a case history, we can see that spamming, while apparently profitable at first, is ultimately not a sustainable business endeavor.

1994

Sanford Wallace, a 25-year-old restaurant promoter in Philadelphia, starts a mass-email business called Promo Enterprises.

1995

Renaming his company Cyber Promotions, Wallace amasses a customer base and a list with the email addresses of more than 1 million AOL subscribers. By the end of the year, he is sending AOL's 6 million subscribers more than 900,000 email messages each day.

1996

September 3

AOL blocks email from five sites—three belonging to Cyber Promotions, one belonging to a company distributing bulk email software, and one for a company that sends advertisements for Internet video pornography. Arguing that its block abridges the First Amendment right to free speech, Cyber Promotions immediately files suit against the company and asks for a restraining order against AOL.

September 6

U.S. District Judge Charles Weiner orders AOL to stop blocking email to its customers from Cyber Promotions, pending a November trial date.

September 20

The Third U.S. Circuit Court of Appeals overturns the preliminary injunction against AOL and allows AOL to resume blocking email sent by Cyber Promotions. It notes that the First Amendment, designed to protect free speech from government infringement, does not apply to AOL, a private company.

October 2

Concentric Networks sues Cyber Promotions, arguing that Cyber Promotions' use of *concentric.net* return addresses on spam sent from other sites violates federal law and harms Concentric.

October 18

Sprint disconnects Cyber Promotions' high-speed Internet connection. Cyber Promotions sues Sprint for termination without notice.

On the same day, Prodigy files suit against Cyber Promotions, arguing that Cyber Promotions' use of Prodigy return addresses constitutes trademark violations.

October 24

CompuServe wins a restraining order prohibiting Cyber Promotions from sending junk email to the online service.

October 29

Sprint agrees to an out-of-court settlement in which Cyber Promotions is allowed to use Sprint's service until November 15, at which time Cyber Promotions must find a new ISP. Cyber Promotions also agrees to use only domain names registered to it "and to promptly remove from its mailing lists any addressee who so requests."

November 4

Federal Judge Charles Weiner declares that Cyber Promotions "does not have a right under the First Amendment ... to send unsolicited email advertisements over the Internet to members of America Online." It is the first ruling of its kind.

On the same day, the Federal Court for the Northern District of California issues a permanent injunction against Cyber Promotions, prohibiting the company from subscribing to Concentric, sending email to its subscribers, trafficking in addresses of Concentric subscribers, or forging messages to appear to be from Concentric sites. The court also awards $5,000 in damages to Concentric.

November 7

> Cyber Promotions files a new motion against AOL, saying that the company is violating federal antitrust laws by limiting Cyber Promotions' access to nearly 7 million Internet users, while AOL continues to send those same customers its own advertisements.

December 5

> CompuServe argues before U.S. District Judge James Graham in Ohio that Cyber Promotions should be barred from sending any unsolicited email to CompuServe customers, even though CompuServe has not implemented technical measures to keep out spam mail.

December 13

> Cyber Promotions settles with Prodigy, promising to stop using Prodigy email addresses as return addresses for Cyber Promotions spam mail. Cyber Promotions also agrees to make a cash settlement rumored to be around $10,000.

1997

February 4

> Cyber Promotions and AOL reach a settlement that allows AOL to continue to offer blocking services and allows Cyber Promotions to continue sending unsolicited email to AOL's users.

February 23

> Sanford Wallace registers the domain *spamford.com*, officially adopting what has been a personal slur as his moniker.

March 10

> Hackers attack and shut down one of Cyber Promotions' web sites for six hours. Wallace laughs, saying that the hackers got the wrong computer, "not the one that sends mail, sorry to say."

March 21

> Hackers break into Cyber Promotions' web site twice more in two days, altering web pages and stealing the password file.

April 15

> Cyber Promotions announces that it has signed a three-year contract with WorldCom for a net connection that can spam the world.

April 25

> Apex Global Information Services (AGIS), a Michigan Internet backbone provider, announces that it will create an Internet E-Mail Marketing Council (IEMMC) to legitimize bulk email. A key part of AGIS's plan is to create a

master list of all people who do not wish to receive unsolicited commercial email. The company is criticized for hosting bulk email providers and for attempting to legitimize spamming.

April 28

Email to more than 5,000 Netcom customers is delayed for a day or more because of a massive spam sent to the company's mail server.

May   Cyber Promotions moves to its new headquarters in Dresher, PA. The company now has more than seven employees.

May 6

Cyber Promotions agrees to stop sending messages to CompuServe customers and to pay $65,000 in legal fees, provided that CompuServe allows its members to choose to be on junk email lists and provide Cyber Promotions with $30,000 in advertising space on the CompuServe system.

May 6

EarthLink obtains a temporary injunction against Cyber Promotions to prevent the company from spamming EarthLink customers and to stop using EarthLink email addresses in its spam messages.

June 5

ATX Telecommunications Services, Cyber Promotions' Internet provider, terminates the company's connection, saying that it was forced to do so by its upstream provider, IDCI. The upstream company said that other ISPs had blocked access to IDCI's network because of ATX's connection to Cyber Promotions.

June 6

Web Systems, a web development company, wins a temporary restraining order against Cyber Promotions after the company uses the email address *business@webs.com* in a widely circulated spam message.

June 24

WorldCom cancels Cyber Promotions' contract before Cyber Promotions even goes online; Cyber Promotions files suit in response.

June 26

Hormel Foods Corporation sends Cyber Promotions a cease-and-desist letter to stop using the word "SPAM," a trademark of the company.

August

Wallace claims that Cyber Promotions now has 11,000 customers.

August 12

Hackers break into Cyber Promotions' web site again, erasing web pages, internal files, and email. A customer list is stolen. Wallace says that some customers are terrorized by late-night threatening phone calls.

September 19

AGIS disconnects Cyber Promotions after the AGIS network is subject to a *ping*-flood denial-of-service attack (see Chapter 7 for information about the Unix *ping* command). Cyber Promotions files suit against AGIS.

September 30

U.S. District Judge Anita Brody in Philadelphia orders AGIS to reconnect Cyber Promotions until October 16, since the company's contract specified that AGIS would give Cyber Promotions 30 days' notice of any disconnection.

September 30

Wallace announces that he will pool funds with other spammers to purchase an Internet backbone provider or start his own.

October 6

Bigfoot files suit against Cyber Promotions, seeking $1 million in damages and an order prohibiting Cyber Promotions from using Bigfoot's name or computers to send junk email.

October 16

AGIS terminates Cyber Promotions' connection for the second time. Wallace says that his company has lost its web site but can still send spam messages through its "bandwidth partners"—companies that Cyber Promotions is paying $1,000 per month for use of their Internet connections. But the threat appears to be empty.

November 20

Sanford Wallace and Walt Rines, another notorious spammer, announce that they have teamed up with an unnamed company to form their own Internet backbone, Global Technology Marketing, Inc. (GTMI), which will allow spam and other forms of commercial email. The network's ground rules stipulate no pornographic spamming and no hijacking of mail servers belonging to other organizations.

November 21

Anti-spammers attack Dr. Robert Elliot, chief technology officer of Global Telemedia International, Inc. (GTII) with 4:00 a.m. phone calls and threats. The vigilantes had mistaken GTII for Wallace's new company and Dr. Elliot for another Robert Elliot named in Wallace's press release.

1998

January 12

Sanford Wallace and Walt Rines obtain a web site for GTMI from Galaxy.Net for $30 per month.

January 16

Anti-spammers discover the GTMI web site and begin a campaign of harassment against Galaxy. Hours later, the GTMI site is taken down.

February 20

GTMI announces the availability of Internet connections for spamming. T1s are priced at $5,900 a year, while T3s are $73,500 per month. Customers must agree to GTMI's ground rules, designed to legitimize spam email.

March 5

AOL publishes "AOL's Ten Most Wanted Spammer List." Wallace's name is notably absent.

March 10

Bigfoot wins a permanent injunction prohibiting Sanford Wallace and Cyber Promotions from sending unsolicited email to Bigfoot's customers or to the customers of Bigfoot's partners.

March 12

Cyber Promotions and EarthLink reach a settlement in which Cyber Promotions will pay EarthLink $2 million and refrain from sending junk email into its network. Wallace says that he plans to return to his career of promoting restaurants.

March 30

Settlement with EarthLink is finalized.

April 8

Sanford Wallace and Walt Rines announce that they have signed a $10 million contract with GetNet in which GetNet will be paid to receive spam mail and pass it on to its customers, who presumably will get a lower cost of service in return.

April 13

Sanford Wallace announces that he is retiring from spam.

May

Sanford Wallace announces that he is now providing expert-witness services in several anti-spamming cases.

Index

About the Authors

Alan Schwartz is an assistant professor of clinical decision making in the Department of Medical Education at the University of Illinois at Chicago. In his spare time, he develops and maintains the PennMUSH MUD server and brews beer and mead with his wife. He is the author of *Managing Mailing Lists* (O'Reilly & Associates, 1998). Alan runs multiple mailing lists for the Society for Judgment and Decision Making and for PennMUSH users and developers; he has been managing mailing lists for at least five years now. Turn-ons for Alan include sailing, programming in Perl, playing duplicate bridge, and drinking Anchor Porter. Turn-offs include subscription requests sent to list addresses and watery American lagers.

Simson Garfinkel is a computer consultant, science writer, and columnist for both *The Boston Globe* and *HotWired, Wired Magazine*'s online service. He is the author of *PGP: Pretty Good Privacy* (O'Reilly & Associates, 1994) and the coauthor of *Practical UNIX & Internet Security* (O'Reilly & Associates, 1996) and *Web Security and Commerce* (O'Reilly & Associates, 1997). Mr. Garfinkel writes frequently about science and technology, as well as their social impacts.

Colophon

The animal featured on the cover of *Stopping Spam* is a pig, a cloven-hoofed mammal of the family *Suidae*. There are nine living species of pig and hogs. The domesticated pig is believed to be descended from the European wild boar. From its Eurasian origins, the pig has been introduced all over the world by humans. Christopher Columbus introduced the first pigs to the New World. Pigs are not found in regions such as the Middle East, where Judaism and Islam are the predominant religions, because they are considered to be unclean animals in these religions.

Pigs have a keen sense of smell and excellent hearing, but poor vision. They have unusually versatile voices—they can grunt, squeak, squeal, and snort, as circumstances dictate. Their highly mobile snouts enable them to root in the ground for food. Their reputation for being dirty presumably comes from the fact that they wallow in mud. They do so in order to protect themselves from the sun and heat and from parasitic insects. Despite this reputation, pigs are very clean animals. That, combined with their intelligence, adaptability, and trainability, has led to their increasing popularity as household pets. The small Vietnamese potbellied pig is the current frontrunner in the race for most popular pet pig.

Nancy Kotary was the production editor for *Stopping Spam*. Sheryl Avruch was the production manager; Debby English was the copy editor; Claire Cloutier LeBlanc provided quality control; Kimo Carter provided production assistance. Robert Romano created the illustrations. Lenny Muellner provided tools support. Ruth Rautenberg wrote the index.

Edie Freedman designed the cover of this book (and Hanna Dyer designed the CD label) using a 19th-century engraving from the Dover Pictorial Archive. The cover layout was produced with QuarkXPress 3.3 using the ITC Garamond font. Whenever possible, our books use RepKover™, a durable and flexible lay-flat binding. If the page count exceeds RepKover's limit, perfect binding is used.

The inside layout was designed by Nancy Priest and implemented in troff by Lenny Muellner. The text and heading fonts are ITC Garamond Light and Garamond Book. The illustrations that appear in the book were created in Macromedia Freehand 7.0 and screen shots were created in Adobe Photoshop 4.0 by Robert Romano. This colophon was written by Clairemarie Fisher O'Leary.

 # More Titles from O'Reilly

All the Facts. Not the Frills.

Internet in a Nutshell

By Valerie Quercia
1st Edition October 1997
450 pages, ISBN 1-56592-323-5

Internet in a Nutshell is a quick-moving
guide that goes beyond the "hype" and right
to the heart of the matter: how to get the
Internet to work for you. This is a second-
generation Internet book for readers who
have already taken a spin around the Net
and now want to learn the shortcuts.

The Whole Internet: The Next Generation

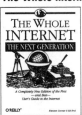

By Kiersten Conner & Ed Krol
3rd Edition January 1999 (est.)
480 pages (est.), ISBN 1-56592-428-2

Once *The Whole Internet* showed you
how to work with the Internet. Now
The Whole Internet: The Next Generation
shows you how to make the Net work for
you. It covers how to minimize junk email,
master your mailing lists and customize
your mailer, play virtually any online game, buy and sell on the
Net, and protect your privacy. It also covers some of the newest
Internet applications, such as "push" technologies, conferencing
tools, and tools for receiving audio and video broadcasts that
turn your computer into a telephone, television, or movie screen.

NetResearch: Finding Information Online

By Daniel J. Barrett
1st Edition February 1997
200 pages, ISBN 1-56592-245-X

NetResearch teaches you how to locate the
information you need in the constantly
changing online world. You'll learn
effective search techniques that work
with any Internet search programs,
present or future, and will build intuition
on how to succeed when searches fail. Covers America Online,
CompuServe, Microsoft Network and Prodigy, as well as direct
and dial-up Internet connections.

AOL in a Nutshell

By Curt Degenhart & Jen Muehlbauer
1st Edition June 1998
536 pages, ISBN 1-56592-424-X

This definitive reference breaks through the
hype and shows advanced AOL users and
sophisticated beginners how to get the most
out of AOL 4.0's tools and features. You'll
learn how to customize AOL to meet your
needs, work around annoying idiosyncrasies,
avoid unwanted email and Instant Messages, actually understand
Parental Controls, and turn off intrusive advertisements. It's an
indispensable guide for users who aren't dummies.

Windows 95 in a Nutshell

By Tim O'Reilly & Troy Mott
1st Edition June 1998
528 pages, ISBN 1-56592-316-2

A comprehensive, compact reference that
systematically unveils what serious users of
Windows 95 will find interesting and useful,
capturing little known details of the operating
system in a consistent reference format.

Windows 98 in a Nutshell

By Tim O'Reilly & Troy Mott
1st Edition December 1998 (est.)
600 pages (est.), ISBN: 1-56592-486-X

From the authors of the bestselling *Windows
95 in a Nutshell* comes this easy-to-use
quick reference for all serious users of
Windows 98. It summarizes differences
between Windows 95 and Windows 98,
covers almost every Windows 98 command
and utility available, gives advice for using the Registry, includes
short-hand instructions on many important Win98 tasks, and
much more.

O'REILLY™

TO ORDER: **800-998-9938** • **order@oreilly.com** • **http://www.oreilly.com/**
OUR PRODUCTS ARE AVAILABLE AT A BOOKSTORE OR SOFTWARE STORE NEAR YOU.
FOR INFORMATION: **800-998-9938** • **707-829-0515** • **info@oreilly.com**

Annoyances

Windows Annoyances

By David A. Karp
1st Edition June 1997
300 pages, ISBN 1-56592-266-2

A comprehensive, detailed resource for all intermediate to advanced users of Windows 95 and NT version 4.0. This book shows step-by-step how to customize the Win95/NT operating systems through an extensive collection of tips, tricks, and workarounds. Covers **Registry**, **Plug and Play**, networking, security, multiple-user settings, and third-party software.

Word 97 Annoyances

By Woody Leonhard, Lee Hudspeth & T.J. Lee
1st Edition August 1997
356 pages, ISBN 1-56592-308-1

Word 97 contains hundreds of annoying idiosyncrasies that can be either eliminated or worked around. This informative book takes an in-depth look at what makes Word 97 tick and shows you how to transform this software into a powerful, customized tool.

Outlook Annoyances

By Woody Leonhard,
Lee Hudspeth & T. J. Lee
1st Edition June 1998
400 pages, ISBN 1-56592-384-7

Like the other Microsoft Office-related titles in the Annoyances series, this book points out and conquers the annoying features of Microsoft Outlook, the personal information management software included with Office. It is the definitive guide for those who want to take full advantage of Outlook and transform it into the useful tool that it was intended to be.

Excel 97 Annoyances

By Woody Leonhard, Lee Hudspeth & T.J. Lee
1st Edition September 1997
336 pages, ISBN 1-56592-309-X

This book uncovers Excel 97's hard-to-find features and tells how to eliminate the annoyances of data analysis. It shows how to easily retrieve data from the Web, details step-by-step construction of a perfect toolbar, includes tips for working around the most annoying gotchas of auditing, and shows how to use VBA to control Excel in powerful ways.

Office 97 Annoyances

By Woody Leonhard, Lee Hudspeth & T.J. Lee
1st Edition October 1997
396 pages, ISBN 1-56592-310-3

This book illustrates step-by-step how to get control over the chaotic settings of Office 97 and shows how to turn the vast array of applications into a simplified list of customized tools. It focuses on the major components of Office 97, examines their integration or lack of it, and shows how to use this new Office suite in the most efficient way.

Windows 98 Annoyances

By David A. Karp
1st Edition October 1998 (est.)
448 pages (est.), ISBN 1-56592-417-7

Based on the author's extremely popular Windows Annoyances Web site (http://www.annoyances.org), this book provides an authoritative collection of techniques for customizing Windows 98. It allows you to quickly identify a particular annoyance and immediately offers one or more solutions, making it the definitive resource for customizing Windows 98.

O'REILLY™

TO ORDER: **800-998-9938** • **order@oreilly.com** • **http://www.oreilly.com/**
OUR PRODUCTS ARE AVAILABLE AT A BOOKSTORE OR SOFTWARE STORE NEAR YOU.
FOR INFORMATION: **800-998-9938** • **707-829-0515** • **info@oreilly.com**